WITHDRAWN

Amy Lowell, American Modern

Amy Lowell, American Modern

EDITED BY ADRIENNE MUNICH
AND MELISSA BRADSHAW

Rutgers University Press
New Brunswick, New Jersey, and London

Library of Congress Cataloging-in-Publication Data

Amy Lowell, American modern / edited by Adrienne Munich and Melissa Bradshaw.
  p. cm.
  ISBN 0–8135-3355-4 (alk. paper)—ISBN 0–8135-3356-2 (pbk. : alk. paper)
  1. Lowell, Amy, 1874–1925. 2. Women and literature—United States—History—20th
century. 3. Poets, American—20th century—Biography. 4. Imagist poetry—History and
criticism 5. Modernism (Literature)—United States. I. Munich, Adrienne. II. Bradshaw,
Melissa, 1969–
  PS3523.O88Z54 2004
  811'.52—dc21

                                                                                2003005859

British Cataloging-in-Publication information is available from the British Library.

Manufactured in the United States of America

For Rachel Jacoff and Cecilia Konchar Farr

CONTENTS

Acknowledgments *ix*

Introduction *xi*
ADRIENNE MUNICH AND MELISSA BRADSHAW

Chronology *xxvii*

Amy Lowell and Cultural Borders   *1*
PAUL LAUTER

*Family Matters: Genealogies and Intertexts
in Amy Lowell's "The Sisters"*   *9*
ADRIENNE MUNICH

*Amy Lowell and the Unknown Ladies:
The Caryatides Talk Back*   *27*
ELIZABETH J. DONALDSON

A Transatlantic Affair: Amy Lowell and Bryher   *43*
JEAN RADFORD

*"Which, Being Interpreted, Is as May Be,
or Otherwise": Ada Dwyer Russell in
Amy Lowell's Life and Work*   *59*
LILLIAN FADERMAN

Lesbian Chivalry in Amy Lowell's Sword Blades
and Poppy Seed   *77*
JAIME HOVEY

*Amy Lowell, John Keats, and the "Shielded Scutcheon"
of Imagist Art*   *90*
MARGARET HOMANS

Unrelated Beauty: Amy Lowell, Polyphonic Prose, and the Imagist City   *104*
ANDREW THACKER

Putting on the Voice of the Orient: Gender and Sexuality in Amy Lowell's "Asian" Poetry
MARI YOSHIHARA   *120*

Amy Lowell's Letters in the Network of Modernism   *136*
BONNIE KIME SCOTT

Amy Lowell, Some Imagist Poets, *and the Context of the New Poetry*   *154*
JAYNE E. MAREK

Remembering Amy Lowell: Embodiment, Obesity, and the Construction of a Persona   *167*
MELISSA BRADSHAW

Afterword: Amy Lowell: Body and Sou-ell   *186*
JANE MARCUS

Notes on Contributors   *199*

General Index   *203*

Index of Lowell's Works   *206*

ACKNOWLEDGMENTS

It gives us great pleasure to acknowledge the Trustees under the Will of Amy Lowell and the Houghton Library, Harvard University, who generously have granted permission to use Lowell materials in this collection. Grateful acknowledgement is given to the University of Georgia Press for permission to reprint Paul Lauter's essay. Our thanks also go to colleagues, friends, and family for their insights, advice, and enthusiasm: Christine Froula, Carlos Garay, Jaime Harker, Richard Munich, Rachel Poulsen, Ce Rosenow, and Frank Yeomans. Special thanks go to Jane Marcus, whose energetic and passionate belief in the worth of Amy Lowell as both a poet and a modernist gave us hope from the earliest stages of this project, and who suggested the anthology's title. Warm thanks to our editor, Leslie Mitchner, for her unflagging support. We're particularly grateful to our contributors, many of whom generously took time from their current research to write for us. Their outstanding scholarship has made this volume possible. It has been a pleasure to watch their essays develop, to see them engage Lowell's words with critical vigor and sophistication. Melissa Bradshaw wishes to thank Cecilia Konchar Farr for her courageous example and abiding commitment to feminist scholarship. Adrienne Munich thanks Rachel Jacoff, who from "The Late Bloomers" to this moment has given the best kind of affirming, constant, and life-clarifying friendship.

INTRODUCTION

ADRIENNE MUNICH AND MELISSA BRADSHAW

"Amy Lowell Again Assails Tradition" reads the headline of William Stanley Braithwaite's review of Lowell's third volume of poetry, *Men, Women and Ghosts,* in the October 21, 1916 edition of the *Boston Evening Transcript*.[1] Braithwaite applauds the poet's courageous use of new poetical forms, her comprehension that in "bringing a new force into the world," she must "begin by killing, or at least wounding a tradition, even if that tradition once had all the virtues." The accompanying photograph of the poet, her head cocked slightly to the side under a jaunty, feathered hat, staring straight into the camera with expressive, even mischievous eyes, her mouth set in a firm line with a trace of a smile at the corners, shows a woman secure in her role as one of the most powerful and popular poets of the day, confident of her ability to lure readers away from the safety of conventional verse and into the experimental forms, unrhymed lines, and uneven meters of modern poetry. Her look is defiant and self-assured, a challenge to those who would question her right to assail tradition and a promise of reward to those willing to risk their own deeply ingrained ideas of what poetry should be.

The Amy Lowell whose unflinching gaze stares out from the middle of Braithwaite's review was at the top of her game. Her second volume of poetry, *Sword Blades and Poppy Seed* (1914), had established her as one of America's premier poetic innovators; the following year, with the critical and popular success of her first volume of literary criticism, *Six French Poets* (1915), she earned a reputation as a literary critic. *Men, Women, and Ghosts* (1916) would establish her as a popular poet, almost selling out before it was published. That same year saw the publication of the second of three imagist anthologies edited by Lowell. The next few years would prove just as productive: in addition to a steady stream of reviews and critical essays, Lowell published five more volumes of poetry, another volume of literary criticism, *Tendencies in Modern American Poetry* (1917), and a two-volume biography of John Keats before her sudden death from a stroke at the age of fifty-one in 1925. She left behind enough material for three more volumes of poetry, the first of which, *What's O'Clock*, won the 1926 Pulitzer Prize for poetry.

The many memorial tributes at Lowell's death unanimously sounded a note of grief and surprise, not only for the loss of a woman many called friend, but for the loss of a vital presence in American letters. In their shock and disbelief Lowell's peers, many of whom had long-standing feuds with the poet, expressed their confidence that the legacy of Lowell's brief but intensely productive career—her unwavering belief in a poetics both modern and inimitably American, her conviction that anyone "with a spark of poetry in them, be they blacksmiths or millionaires" could find pleasure in poetry—would leave a lasting mark on twentieth-century literary history.[2]

They were apparently, if temporarily, mistaken. In the intervening years Amy Lowell has been reduced to a footnote, sometimes a derisory one, in the history of modern poetry. There is no single explanation for the neglect of Lowell in current debates and discussions about American poetry and modernism. Literary historians agree that her contribution to the consciousness of both the self-described New Poetry movement in American letters and to international modernism was central to ways of defining and understanding the period.[3] For poetry readers from 1912 through the 1920s, Lowell's imposing presence dominated the scene. It would not be overstatement to claim that Lowell *was* modern poetry to the majority of readers: her opinions about other poets, her views about literary history, her popular and well-attended lectures reading her own poems and those of her contemporaries definitively reshaped conceptions of the literary scene.

Today Amy Lowell is best remembered as the self-appointed leader of the imagist poets. The imagists, writing in vers libre, strove to capture the sounds, colors, and textures of the sensory world. They aimed for conciseness of image, not the evocation of sentiment or the imputation of morality. As Lowell explained, "the modern poet has a passionate desire for truth, and a dispassionate attitude towards whatever his search for truth may bring him. He records; he does not moralize. He holds no brief for or against, he merely portrays."[4] But what the poet attempts to portray—the hard, clear image of an instant's perception—is at once objective and subjective. That is to say, the poem strives for the objective presentation of the artist's subjectivity, as in Ezra Pound's 1913 "In a Station of a Metro" ("The apparition of these faces in the crowd; / Petals on a wet, black bough."), which uses only fourteen words to convey Pound's experience of stepping out of a subway car into a pressing crowd of people. The poem's energy comes from a flash of recognition as the reader, however briefly, shares the poet's visualization. For this reason, Michael Levenson has described imagism as a "radical literary individualism."[5]

Few poems in the imagist canon so purely illustrate the tenets of imagism as Pound's haiku. Amy Lowell imitated many such haiku, such as "Nuance" (1919; "Even the iris bends / When a butterfly lights upon it"). More typical of

Lowell's short lyrics is her 1922 "Vespers," with its subtle interplay of sound and image:

Last night, at sunset,
The foxgloves were like tall altar candles.
Could I have lifted you to the roof of the greenhouse, my Dear
I should have understood their burning.

In a manner characteristic of Lowell, the poem moves from images to powerful personal emotion, the cadences set up by a gathering of the rhymes "could," "should," and "understood" that deftly brings together other echoing vowels. Many of Lowell's longer poems aim for a direct impression of the sensory world, imitating musical sounds, loading the poem with color images, trying to force language beyond conventional boundaries. The issues swirling around the concept of modernism are not so much about these matters; they have more to do with egos than with images.

Lowell's well-known schism with Pound over the use of the term *imagism* and leadership of the movement is the stuff of modernist legend. Whether she is remembered as the interloper who used money and family connections to wrest the term away from Pound, water it down, and sell it to the masses; or whether she is remembered as pivotal in introducing modern poetics to American audiences through her clever deployment and marketing of the term depends on who is telling the story.[6] Certainly, the drama of her dispute with Pound, and her subsequent, infamously vociferous promotion of imagist poetry obscures Lowell's other accomplishments, but the feud is worth briefly revisiting here inasmuch as it underscores where Lowell and Pound's aesthetic principles differed, and where their aims diverged.

Initially, Lowell and Pound enjoyed a cordial relationship. When she traveled to England in the summer of 1913 to meet the enigmatic *Imagiste* poets whose poems and critical writings had appeared in several issues of Harriet Monroe's *Poetry* magazine, Pound arranged her introductions, read her work, and offered editorial suggestions, and included her poem "In a Garden" in his anthology *Des Imagistes* (1914). Their brief alliance quickly collapsed when Lowell announced plans to publish a yearly imagist anthology, to be brought out by a major U.S. publishing house, with each poet receiving an equal allotment of poems and sharing editorial responsibilities. Pound argued that such a project would dilute the concept of imagism, conflating it with any poem written in vers libre. Having nominally acceded to Pound's wishes by dropping the final *e* in *imagiste*, Lowell went on to edit three anthologies of *Some Imagist Poets* (1915, 1916, and 1917).

In addition to the struggle for dominance between two immense egos, the battle between Lowell and Pound centered on the very concept of an avant-garde. Whereas they both agreed that modern poetry should "make it new" and strip the line of any Victorian excess, Pound imagined poetry as an elite enterprise and accused Lowell of trying to turn imagism into "an uncritical democracy with you as intermediary between it and the printers."[7] Three years later, he was still hectoring her. "My dear Amy," he wrote, "You tried to stampede me into accepting as my artistic equals various people whom it would have been rank hypocrisy for me to accept in any such manner. There is no democracy in the arts."[8] Amy would agree about standards, but not about elites. Aiming for a far-sighted and inclusive canon in poetry, Lowell wanted to admit as much quality of as varied a kind as possible, and, unlike Pound, she was interested in repre-senting the immense energies of American voices. Although certainly not free of the ethnic and racial prejudices of her time and class, she espoused a democ-racy of letters, celebrating a wide range of poets, wildly different from herself. In a lecture introducing such poets to an audience avid for enlightenment, Lowell encouraged literary patriotism and the development of a uniquely American brand of modern letters: "the New Poetry is blazing a trail toward Nationality far more subtle and intense than any settlement houses and waving the American flag in schools can ever achieve."[9] Pound disparaged Lowell for encouraging a wide audience and betrayed to Margaret Anderson, editor of the *Little Review*, a fear of spawning inferior American women poets in a literary democracy of equal suffrage: "Do you honestly think that a serious writer OUGHT to be reminded of the United States?? . . . Ought one to be distracted, ought one to be asked to address that perpetual mother's meeting, that chaste Chitaqua [*sic*]; that cradle of on-coming Amys???"[10] Pound resisted an imaginary army of hugely menac-ing Lowells, as if their sheer numbers (or her single threat) would squelch, si-lence, overpower him. His disparagement of Lowell can be understood in part as a defense against her.

The battle over the packaging and promotion of imagist poetry, however, only scratches the surface of Pound and Lowell's ideological differences. With the beginning of Pound's friendship and poetic alliance with T. S. Eliot in the autumn of 1914 came a dramatic reversal in his methods and a return to the classical models and forms he had studied and practiced earlier in his career; Lowell's aesthetic, meanwhile, remained closely tied to the early modernism of T. E. Hulme, Ford Madox Ford, and Pound himself, focusing on freedom of form, revolt from tradition, and above all, the presentation of "an intellectual and emotional complex in an instant of time."[11] This divergence is telling on a number of levels. A primarily self-educated woman, Lowell had a sturdy knowl-edge of traditional poetic forms and of classical literature (albeit through trans-lations), but she approached them as a common reader. A life-long, voracious student, first in her father's library, later in the Boston Athenaeum, she enthusi-astically but haphazardly studied those authors and topics that most excited her, without a set curriculum, and without a sense of obligation to tradition. This has to do, in part, with the restrictions of gender: as a woman raised in the nine-teenth century she was not allowed the education in Greek and Latin that would have granted her access to this kind of elite knowledge. But it has to do as well with Lowell's background as a New Englander—and as a Boston Brahmin—raised in a post-Emersonian age: hers was a confident relationship to her American cultural inheritance that goes back to the flowering of the American Renaissance. The questions and anxieties that inform later modernism were not hers.

Lowell's continued adherence to early modernist principles reflects her belief that poetry can be both innovative and accessible. She took from her time with Pound a commitment to conciseness, to vividness of image, to the clear presentation of the poet's subjectivity, and, ultimately, to the poem as performative. Her biographer, S. Foster Damon, explains that "she believed poetry was a spoken art—was communicative and not merely self-expressive—that no poem was complete until it had functioned in the mind of its audience."[12] But it is precisely in this regard for audience, in this assumption that her words will reach a seemingly boundless readership, that Lowell deviates from high modernism as we understand it today. In developing a popular modern poetics Lowell should be seen not, as Pound termed her, "Amy-just-selling-the-goods," but as a serious artist making formal choices that allow her to make a connection with audiences.[13] "Great poetry," she explained to Richard Aldington, "is and must be universal, above the customs and cliques of the initiated."[14]

One of the greatest challenges in evaluating Amy Lowell's poetic work as a whole, then as well as now, is that her forms, her voices, her prosody are so varied that the work defies neat categories. She is known for skillful individual poems, such as "Patterns" (1915), and, increasingly, her powerful love lyrics, but those works by no means define her poetic talent. Some of her most popular poems were dramatic monologues and long narrative poems, genres not touched on in this collection or included in our volume, *The Selected Poems of Amy Lowell*, with the exception of "Patterns." As we explain below, many of these poems are potentially important to understanding a more complete range of Lowell's representation of gender. The narratives might show that "Patterns" is only the most famous of her representations of the constraints women suffer in a patriarchal world. Perhaps the concept of "middlebrow poetry" would place these poems in a genre comparable to the romances devoured by women readers today.[15] When we can learn to situate such poems, we will gain another perspective on Lowell's place as a self-consciously woman poet.

In addition, we did not include any New England narratives in our volume of selected poems because they are written in what she terms the "Yankee" dialect and, as such, are difficult for contemporary readers unfamiliar with the New England accent of almost a century ago. Writing in 1917 of Robert Frost's poems written in a similar dialect, Lowell notes, "It is commonly said that an author adds many decades to his literary life, and widens his appeal at the time of writing, if he does not use dialect. I would amend that dictum by suggesting that it depends upon the author."[16] Although Lowell offered Robert Burns and J. M. Synge as authors whose use of dialect has not impeded their continued popularity, she most likely hoped readers would count her as a member of that group as well: only a year earlier she had written a series of poems using a similar dialect in *Men, Women, and Ghosts*.[17] Apparently, she felt that she, unlike Frost, had managed to approximate a rural New England accent in a way that would stand the test of time. This is unfortunate, because these difficult, dated, and consequently neglected, poems, grouped under the heading "The Overgrown Pasture" (1916) contain some of Lowell's most powerful analyses of gender roles and the strictures placed on women's lives, as her narrators, four women of rural New England, tell stories of oppression, isolation and helplessness. In "Number 3 on the Docket," for example, a poem that eerily echoes Susan Glaspell's play *Trifles*, produced that same year, a lonely woman on trial for the murder of her brooding, silent husband explains her actions as a result of "th' silence. / The long, long silence."[18] Had she written these poems in more accessible, straightforward language, with the same commitment to clarity and simplicity evidenced in so many of her lyrics, they might have remained in circulation and served as important texts in early feminist revisions of the literary canon.

Many of Lowell's long, narrative poems similarly present an important gender critique, but do so in a context of excessive melodrama, and at times even gratuitous violence and bloodshed, that strains credulity and obfuscates her message. Lowell considered such poems as "The Basket" (1914), in which a woman eats handfuls of eyeballs from a basket against the background of a moon dripping blood as she watches her lover's home burn, and "Pickthorne Manor" (1916), in which a jealous husband drowns himself and his wife, to be some of her finest poems, written in what she called the "dramatico-lyric," but letters to and from her collaborators in the *Some Imagist Poets* anthologies, as well as her correspondence with Harriet Monroe, suggest that her colleagues strongly favored her shorter lyrics over her narratives.[19] And yet these were some of her most-requested poems during readings, an indication both of the power of Lowell's performances and a shift in taste.

Lowell's popularity was buoyed by her own forceful exuberance, a kind of life aura. Perhaps because of her charisma many of her detractors, and even some admirers, found that her poetry deflated and faded after she was no longer around to read it. At any rate, Lowell's popularity began to wane soon after her death. Ad hominem attacks worked to undermine her critical reputation. The first to appear was a truculent 1926 biography by Clement Wood, a critic and poet with whom Lowell shared a mutual dislike. Winfield T. Scott's 1935 essay "Amy Lowell after Ten Years" asserts that she "was not a poet at all."[20] This allegation was echoed by Horace Gregory and Marya Zaturenska's judgment-laden questions in *A History of American Poetry* (1942): "Was she a great poet? Was Amy Lowell a poet at all?" Gregory's 1958 biography of Lowell closed by claiming her continued importance would not be as a poet or even as a critic, but merely as the recipient of letters written to her by D. H. Lawrence. Even when her *Complete Poetical Works* were published in 1955, a moment that might have yielded a renaissance in Lowell studies, a lukewarm introduction by Louis Untermeyer lamenting the lack of vitality in the poems without Lowell's voice to read them may have assured their continued neglect, warning away any would-be champions.[21]

One could equally well charge Lowell with too much vitality as too little, with a crushing prolific imagism gone reckless, even to seed. In *A Critical Fable* (1922), her anonymously published satire of her contemporaries, she includes a self-caricature that anticipates negative evaluations of her anomalous poetic voice:

> And you'll guess by this time, without farther allusion,
> That the lady's unique and surprising profusion
> Creates in some minds an unhappy confusion.[22]

As the poet herself recognizes here, reading Amy Lowell can cause disruption and confusion in readers who desire predictability. One wants to satisfy one's expectations when picking up a new volume of a favorite poet, and Lowell rarely presents the reader with more of the same. In "La Vie de Boheme" (1919) she acknowledges a prodigality in her writing, an insistence on interpreting the world in lavish colors, explaining how she takes "the keen / Unwrinkled sky" and first polishes, then damascenes it; how, through her eyes "twined bands of roadways, liquid in the sheen / of street lamps and the ruby shine of cabs, / Glisten for my delight." She describes her soul as "fretted full of gleams and darks, / Pulsing and still." But because the world resents this expression of individual vision, this celebration of difficult beauty, she must struggle to maintain her artistic perspective:

> My soul is blunted against dullard wits,
> Seared with sick juices,
> Nicked impotent for other than low uses.
> Its arabesques and sparkling subtleties
> Crusted to grey, and all its changing surfaces
> Spread with unpalpitant monotonies

Lowell resists, bouncing back from discouragement to find, once again, the patterns, "like buried proofs / Of old, lost empires bursting on the eye," and declares herself "prodigal once more, a reckless spender/ of disregarded beauty, a defender/ Of undesired faiths."[23]

As Harriet Monroe notes, "One detects a certain scientific rapture in many of Miss Lowell's interesting experiments in technique. She delights in the rush and clatter of sounds, in the kaleidoscopic glitter of colors. . . . In a few poems . . . one's ears and eyes feel fairly battered."[24] F. Cudworth Flint puts it more bluntly: "Miss Lowell's command of cadence and color, and her ability to sustain animation, are amazing. But to be amazed so prolongedly results at last in exhausted stupification."[25] Lowell might have fallen out of favor, therefore, because she tired some readers with endless experiments, with a refusal to repeat herself. Other readers, however, might admire these same exuberant qualities were they given access to a wide range of Lowell's poetry.

With her poetry and criticism out of print for the last half of the twentieth century and Lowell the historical figure confined to cameo appearances in critical evaluations of modernism and American poetry, contemporary readers have not had the opportunity to seriously evaluate her poetry. As a companion to our recently published *Selected Poems of Amy Lowell,* the goal of this essay collection is to begin in earnest a critical reevaluation of Amy Lowell, to build a solid critical basis for evaluating her poetry, her criticism, her politics, her influences, and her influence.

The authors in this volume of essays explore the varied contributions of Lowell as a woman poet, as a modernist, and as a significant formulator of literary debates about poetry and poetics in the early twentieth century. The volume demonstrates how Lowell's writings—poems, essays, reviews, and lectures—contribute to the formation of early modernist aesthetics and reinstates her at the center of early-twentieth-century literary culture. In addition to placing Lowell in her proper historical context, these essays demonstrate Lowell's centrality to current critical and theoretical discussions: feminist, gay and lesbian, post-colonial, disability studies, American studies, and cultural studies. The variety of critical approaches represented here demonstrates the many ways that a full-blown critical appraisal of Lowell's work and career in all its multiple dimensions might proceed. The essays in this collection open up a critical conversation and establish a foundation for future assessments.

The collection begins with Paul Lauter's meditation on the intensity of the seemingly gratuitous emotions that fueled the attacks on Lowell. He wonders about cultural authority in relation to these attacks and suggests that a significant reason for Lowell's eclipse is not about the quality or importance of her contribution to modern American poetry but is rather about the threat she posed. Lauter troubles Gregory and Zaturenska's questions, exploring their attitudes and assumptions. He argues that it is precisely her boundary-dissolving contradictions that pose an intolerable threat and lead to this disproportionate hostility. Lowell's sexuality, her size, her privilege—laid out in contradictory verse with ambiguous speakers and yet with flamboyant passion—trespassed on too much forbidden territory. Lauter historically situates Lowell's threat to boundary maintenance and suggests that our being more tolerant of such disruptions has better prepared us for a more balanced assessment of Lowell's work—as recent critical interest, including his own, indicates.

The uncertain boundaries of gender take up the attention of the next few essays. Adrienne Munich gives an intertextual reading to "The Sisters" (1922), a poem that is required Lowell reading because it partakes of features of an ars poetica, albeit a negative one—how three women poets, Lowell's "sisters," have not provided adequate models for Lowell's kind of poetry. Munich points out that the autobiographical persona in "The Sisters" uncharacteristically places herself among women poets because she desires models for writing about female eroticism. Attending to the implications of Lowell's choice of Sappho, Elizabeth Barrett Browning, and Emily Dickinson as her literary ancestors, Munich shows the eccentric and necessarily exclusive path Amy Lowell walks. The poet eventually arrives at an aesthetic that proclaims the necessity for an enforced and lonely inventiveness; only then might Lowell herself discover a poetics that could anatomize female sensuality. To arrive at this conclusion, Lowell made her "sisters" into an overly feminized, reticent sorority, constrained by social prohibition and exclusion. Lowell's fanciful genealogy also selects according to restrictions of race and class, so that she constructs a proper Yankee genetic tree. However, haunting that tree are the specters of other women poets (some her contemporaries), and the presence of Robert Browning, who refuses to be locked out of her consciousness. Reading this poem illuminates how Lowell herself, in resisting her own self-contextualization, unwittingly also marginalizes her place in literary history.

Sometimes in dialogue, sometimes in debate with Munich's essay, particularly about the issue of women's writings, Elizabeth Donaldson examines how one might discover a feminist sympathy and alliance in Lowell's poems. In her close attention to strictures of literary convention, Donaldson shows how Lowell was a "formidable public advocate" not only for American poetry but more covertly for women poets. What emerges from Lowell's poetry and criticism is a consciousness of how the sexual economy of the poetic voice shapes women writers. Through an interpretation of Lowell's anonymously published humorous verse essay on her contemporary poets, *A Critical Fable*, adroitly read in the context of "The Sisters" and "To Two Unknown Ladies" (1927), Donaldson shows how discussions of Greek statuary often refer approvingly to women's writing. The prevalence of marble statuary in Lowell's poetry in general enables Donaldson to consider this one poem as exemplary of a symbolic system in Lowell's oeuvre. By considering the identities of the two unknown ladies—that is, by making them known as Edith Somerville and Violet Martin, writing together as Somerville and Ross—the essay brings to the surface the question of women's physical and literary intimacy. At the same time, Donaldson demonstrates Lowell's acknowledgment that for women writing is inextricably tied up with "issues of embodiment and the regulation of sexual energy."

The next essay extends the consideration of the relationship between women writers and women's writing to important literary friendships in Lowell's life and in the way one friend represented her. In delineating the encounter between Lowell and Annie Winifred Ellerman, the British heiress writing under the penname of Bryher, Jean Radford begins with an image from Lowell's "The Sisters" to argue that Lowell had already experienced the encounter she imagines in that poem between a younger writer seeking mentorship and herself as a would-be mentor. Radford uses the psychoanalytic concept of identification to analyze some of Bryher's fictionalized portrayals of Lowell. On her part, Bryher wrote an adulatory recognition of Lowell, while Lowell wrote a generous preface to Bryher's first autobiographical fiction, *Development* (1920). Bryher's fictionalized account of Lowell appeared in her third novel, *West* (1925). Radford takes Bryher out of the shadow of H.D., who eventually was her life partner, the two brought together by Lowell. Radford shows how a juxtaposed reading of Lowell and Bryher can reveal Lowell's encoded erotic "coming out" and, further, how such a reading generates a fuller taxonomy of emotional states. In multiple literary encounters with Lowell, Bryher found a worthy antecedent in whom she could be disappointed yet from whom she could also learn.

While it would not be accurate to characterize Lowell's literary lesbian relationships as being quite as supportive as those Shari Benstock delineates in *Women of the Left Bank*, there are telling overlaps between the Left Bank women and those who interacted with Lowell; a more thorough study is yet to be made.[26] Thus far, as suggested in Lillian Faderman's essay, such a history awaits a more judicious consideration of what is most valuable in Lowell's poetry. This evaluation would convince us that Lowell deserves a place in the history of literary associations and relationships and would initiate a rewriting of modernism with Lowell as more than a curiosity. Accounting for Lowell's eclipse, Faderman asserts that the poet's best verse got lost amid her overproduction. Finding Lowell's unique, accomplished poetry in the lyrics (particularly the love lyrics), Faderman cites the example of Clement Wood's biography of the poet to buttress her claim that homophobia factored into Lowell's erasure. Faderman argues that one can read the poems from *Sword Blades and Poppy Seed* as a chronicle of the early relationship of the poet with Ada Dwyer Russell. Then in the "Two Speak Together" section of the later volume *Pictures of the Floating World* (1919), Lowell achieves an erotic lesbian verse incomparable to anything until Adrienne Rich's 1974–76 sequence, "Twenty-one Poems." Combining biography with literary criticism, Faderman reads the poems documenting the course of the Lowell-Russell relationship as a collaborative venture, and assesses the great positive impact Russell exercised on Lowell's career. Although Lowell acutely felt the burdens of having to mask her lesbian lyrics, Faderman shows how the poet found a way—through personae and religious imagery—to write gloriously erotic lesbian verse, despite the censorious eye of the "Watch and Ward Society."

Augmenting Faderman's argument with an analysis of Lowell's poetic personae, Jaime Hovey argues that the theme of unrequited desire is often overlooked in Lowell's poems. Hovey embarks on a close consideration of the volume *Sword Blades and Poppy Seed*, showing that the figuration of courtly love and the assumption of the persona of the courtly lover enable Lowell to express an unrequited lesbian or queer desire that is often also the subject of her amorous lyrics. Drawing attention to contemporary views of Sappho's love lyrics as expressing unrequited lesbian desire, Hovey derives a notion of "lesbian chivalry" and shows how this position and the desire from which it emanates does not fit into the Freudian notions of either sublimation or fetishism but rather "reworks cultural notions of sublimation that erase homosexuality." Hovey discovers that Lowell can rework cultural concepts of chivalry and a homophobic denial of lesbian desire, thus enabling her to offer a route to overcoming impotence and sterility in her lesbian lyrics.

Reading Margaret Homans's essay in the context of Hovey's essay suggests a way that the lesbian American modernist transformed the romantic medievalism of John Keats to derive a dominant persona. With its focus on the most profound conscious influence on Amy Lowell's concept of the poet as Keats, Homans's essay explores the meaning of Lowell's claim that she learned "more about writing poetry from a careful study of Keats's manuscripts than anything else in the world." Examining the interplay between Lowell's two volume biography of Keats and her own poetic practices, Homans argues that in the course of her Keats study, Lowell remade Keats as an imagist poet. That is to say that Lowell's Keats serves as an authorizing tradition for her own poetic practice. Lowell identified with Keats as a collector of allusions, of beauties for their own sake—in other words, of *images*, in the modernist understanding of that term. By using Keats as a model, Homans argues, Lowell was demonstrating her own worthiness by acknowledging her indebtedness. Yet by ignoring Keats's own interest in allegory and by making a superficially beautiful phrase of Keats's observation that "a man's life is a continual allegory, and very few eyes can see the mystery of his life," Lowell confidently reads Keats's life as if she knew it and writes herself as an indispensable guide to his imagism and his life.

Whereas Lowell considered through the prism of Keats yields a complex notion of the seeds of her brand of imagism, those seeds yielded a unique fruit too little considered in Lowell's publications. Although we noted earlier that Lowell's narrative vernacular poems—and, we would add, her retelling of legends in the volume *Legends* (1921)—deserve new interpretations yet to be tackled, we confidently assert that Andrew Thacker's essay constitutes an important contribution at this early stage of creating an Amy Lowell canon. Thacker's essay is the first contemporary critical essay about Lowell's polyphonic prose. He sees the form as exemplifying an aesthetic of modernity, attending to "the links among the crowd, the metropolis, and the notion of polyphonic voices." Thacker suggests that Lowell's polyphonic prose is an undervalued form of modernist revolution, independent from Ezra Pound's version of modernism. Thacker compares Lowell's polyphonic practice and Mikhail Bakhtin's notion of polyphony in the revolutionary aesthetics of Russian novelists while drawing upon modernist synesthesia to show how it forms an aesthetic of music and painting in Lowell's prose poetry. Polyphonic prose uses musical analogy but also musical techniques, while visual experiences shape images. Thacker's nuanced reading of the quotidian in Lowell's polyphonic poems places them in the context of James Joyce's evocation of the everyday life of cities. Finally, Thacker shows how Lowell's polyphonic range opens even more in the history poems, where polyphonic techniques enable Lowell to bring a greater complexity to the theme of warfare.

The next essay, by Mari Yoshihara, begins to assess Lowell's Eastern influences. Like many of those who influenced her—James McNeill Whistler and Ezra Pound, for instance—Lowell was inspired by Eastern art, something that came to her not only through literary and visual culture but through New England commerce and politics. Lowell had family connections with the East, her brother Percival spending many years in Japan and Korea and writing several books about the experience. Yoshihara examines the considerable Asian influence on Lowell's poems, showing how the imperialist attitudes derided by Lowell on the one hand nonetheless emerge in the sexual stereotyping on the other. Yoshihara defines Lowell's brand of orientalism as part of the modernist project in translating Asian texts into English. While Lowell threw herself into a collaboration with her friend Florence Ayscough, she alone influenced the sexual stereotyping when she turned Ayscough's prose translations into verse. She also participated in the gendering of the Orient as female, while at the same time she ignored suggestions to include Chinese women poets in the "Englished" canon she was endorsing. Yoshihara demonstrates how Lowell emphasizes the feminine exoticism of female servitude, playing on existing stereotypes. In "going native," Yoshihara argues, Lowell enabled a certain kind of imaginative liberation. In the poem "Guns as Keys: And the Great Gate Swings" (1917) for example, Lowell portrays a pre-industrial Japan as an elegant yet backward woman being penetrated by brash, crude, and devastating American machismo.

That high modernism itself has been shaped by male writers and a sometimes blatant misogyny is a generally acknowledged fact of literary history. Perhaps because Lowell entered the modernist scene in her first encounter with Ezra Pound in 1913, she had already set herself up as a challenger to male hegemony, though she presented herself with great panache, aided by her considerable fortune, as an apprentice. As soon as she read H.D.'s poems and Pound's description of imagism, she recognized an affinity and sailed for England to learn more. She quickly became an imagist entrepreneur, and it is not an overstatement to claim that the demeaning comments about the now devalued imagism as "Amygism" reflect a competitive and somewhat adolescent reaction of male modernists.

Such feminist scholars as Shari Benstock and Bonnie Kime Scott have greatly contributed to understanding how this history of male modernist art worked against such women writers as Lowell, and they have done much to counter this bias with a rewriting of modernism. Scott's essay in this volume closely examines the dynamic and revealing correspondence between D. H. Lawrence and Lowell to demonstrate how the cordial and supportive relationship between these two volcanic personalities fit into a modernist network. Scott includes many other correspondences in this network: with Florence Ayscough, Lowell's collaborator on Chinese translations; with Margaret Anderson and Harriet Monroe, editors of the *Little Review* and *Poetry*; with the influential critic Louis Untermeyer; and with H.D., Richard Aldington, and Bryher. Scott thus reweaves Amy Lowell into modernism's essential fabric.

Considering Amy Lowell's editorial work and magazine publications in the context of the American New Poetry, Jayne Marek discusses how Lowell's career as an editor established "a context in which modern poetry could find popular acceptance as well as a place in the literary canon." Marek focuses her attention on the genesis, dissemination, and importance of the three imagist anthologies that Lowell edited. Without Lowell's continuing the idea of an imagist anthology, unsuccessfully begun by Pound's *Des Imagistes*, the imagist movement might have sputtered. Lowell's energetic promotion of the volumes and her various efforts to explain their principles of composition, on the other hand, brought the movement to the public's attention, even as they spurred great controversy. In carefully documenting the serial publication of the imagist anthologies, Marek opens the way for a more accurate understanding of imagism's place in the New Poetry, a more nuanced view of the relationship between Pound and Lowell, and a greater appreciation of Lowell as a critic and promoter of poetry.

Viewing the enigma, the problem of Lowell's reputation and the difficulty of evaluating her poetry out of the context of her very substantial self, Melissa Bradshaw's essay demonstrates how a fearless consideration of the body itself— Amy Lowell's privileged lesbian body—affected and still interferes with a more impartial consideration of her contribution to poetry and to literary criticism. It is her corpulence and her love of cigars (and not her considerable literary contributions) that have kept Amy Lowell in literary memory, according to Bradshaw's examination of descriptions of Lowell's body. Her essay investigates the implications of this cultural memory, demonstrating not merely that such characterizations add to a misogynistic, homophobic view that denigrates unconventional body size, unseemly wealth, and unapproved bodily pleasures, both gustatory and sexual, but also enables literary history to ignore the poet's considerable ability and essential contributions. Amy Lowell's adroit performances and controversial aesthetic theories fade with her death, while the specter of her body draws the outline of an Amazonian queen who flouted great social constrictions to produce, define, and then promote an American literary scene. The delineation of New Poetry in Lowell's lectures and essays remain uncredited to her, producing a history that is impoverished and more inaccurate because of her exclusion. Bradshaw's attention to changing meanings of corpulence, all of which arouse revulsion, reveals that her body fat rather than her body of poetry has been the wildly irrational measure of Lowell's career. This cultural irrationality has distorted both the history of modernism and the history of American poetry.

As a grand finale to this volume, Jane Marcus's memoir about the place of Amy Lowell in her own New England heritage crosses the borders of ethnicity and class as it symbolically uses her own crossing of the Charles River from Boston's Irish and black neighborhoods to Cambridge's Radcliffe College and Harvard University. By insistently joining the female body—hers, Lowell's, and ultimately, those of feminist writers— to the feminist soul, Marcus demonstrates how Lowell's work and her imposing presence inspired emulation and ambition, while the sheer volume of both body and work blurred boundaries between genders and classes. Marcus's personal essay contributes to solving the mystery of Lowell's effacement from the official, academic, literary canon. When Marcus crossed the Charles to enter Radcliffe she was carefully tutored to leave her reverence for Lowell on the other bank. Professors elevated T. S. Eliot and Ezra Pound as exemplary modernists while demeaning Lowell's democratic American

branding of modern poetry. Thanks to the mysteries of character, Marcus re-
belled against total assimilation, treasuring Lowell's way of being in the world
as well as her way of writing herself out of the Boston Brahmin box. Lowell
has become a part of her, and Marcus's essay invites readers to take in Lowell
"body and sou-ell."

When Harriet Monroe omitted Lowell's name from a 1917 editorial on
leading British and American poets, justifying her decision by explaining that
"it doesn't seem necessary to mention you in a casual aside—those less con-
spicuous need it more," Lowell's infuriated response indicated that she was well
aware of the instability and impermanence of literary fame. She argued that for
Monroe to be casual about her role as an arbiter of literary taste was as danger-
ous as a physician "being casual about measuring out medicine" and that while
she perhaps did not *need* the attention at the moment, she deserved it: "I want
the serious recognition of thinking people, and I want you to accord me the place
which I have won for myself as well as to have others accord it to me."[27] The
editors and the authors of this volume are aware that Lowell has not been ac-
corded the "serious recognition of thinking people," and that the essays herein
constitute the most sustained examination of Lowell to date. Many of these es-
says arose from the editors' vigorous persuasion; it is safe to assert that as a
result, over the course of one summer more people were writing scholarly criti-
cism about Amy Lowell than at any other moment in recent history. This vol-
ume offers itself as a starting point for putting Amy Lowell back into a
conversation, into a literary history, where she belongs.

Notes

1. William Stanley Braithwaite, "Amy Lowell Again Assails Tradition," *Boston Evening Transcript*, October 21, 1916.
2. Amy Lowell, quoted in S. Foster Damon, *Amy Lowell: A Chronicle with Extracts from Her Correspondence* (Boston: Houghton Mifflin, 1935), 486.
3. According to David Perkins, "Amy Lowell did more than anyone else to win from the general public an understanding reception for the new poetry," because she of-
fered "the clearest, the most comprehensive [account of modern poetic theories] then available." See Perkins, *A History of Modern Poetry: From the 1890s to the High Modernist Mode* (Cambridge, Mass.: Belknap Press of Harvard University Press, 1976), 328.
4. Amy Lowell, quoted in Damon, *Amy Lowell: A Chronicle,* 339.
5. Michael H. Levenson, *A Genealogy of Modernism: A Study of English Literary Doc-
trine 1908–1922* (Cambridge: Cambridge University Press, 1984), 46.
6. Hugh Kenner's characterization of Lowell as overeager pupil turned robber baron has been unfortunately influential. Bonnie Kime Scott's essay in this volume quotes some of his more vicious comments about her. One of the most recent examples of this continued, unexamined hostility toward Lowell appears in Timothy Materer's "Make it Sell! Ezra Pound Advertises Modernism," in *Marketing Modernisms: Self-*

Promotion, Canonization, and Rereading, ed. Kevin J. H. Dettmar and Stephen Watt (Ann Arbor: University of Michigan Press, 1997).

7. Ezra Pound to Amy Lowell, 19 October 1914, in *The Letters of Ezra Pound 1907–1941,* edited by D. D. Paige (New York: Harcourt Brace and World, 1950), 44.

8. Ezra Pound to Amy Lowell, 30 August 1917, in Paige, ed., *Letters,* 122.

9. Amy Lowell, quoted in Damon, *Amy Lowell: A Chronicle,* 341.

10. Ezra Pound to Margaret Anderson, 22 April 1921, in *Pound/The Little Review: The Letters of Ezra Pound to Margaret Anderson: The Little Review Correspondence,* ed. Thomas L. Scott and Melvin J. Friedman with Jackson R. Bryer (New York: New Directions, 1988), 267.

11. Ezra Pound, "A Few Don'ts by an Imagiste," *Poetry,* March 1913, 200–206.

12. Damon, *Amy Lowell: A Chronicle,* 254.

13. Ezra Pound to Alice Corbin Henderson, 5 May 1916 in *The Letters of Ezra Pound to Alice Corbin Henderson,* ed. Ira B. Nadel (Austin: University of Texas Press, 1993), 137.

14. Amy Lowell, quoted in Damon, *Amy Lowell: A Chronicle,* 449.

15. Middlebrow culture has been an increasing topic of study in the last fifteen years, first receiving attention in Joan Shelley Rubin's *The Making of Middlebrow Culture* (Chapel Hill: University of North Carolina Press, 1992) and Janice Radway's *A Feeling for Books* (Chapel Hill: University of North Carolina Press, 1997). While middlebrow authorship is an expanding field of inquiry, particularly in the essay collection *Middlebrow Moderns: Popular American Women Writers of the 1920s,* edited by Meredith Goldsmith and Lisa Botshon (Boston: Northeastern University Press, 2003), and Jaime Harker's dissertation "America the Middlebrow" (Temple University, 1998), to date this work has focused primarily on middlebrow fiction, with no studies exploring the middlebrow in American poetry.

16. Amy Lowell, *Tendencies in Modern American Poetry* (New York: Macmillan Company, 1917), 126.

17. Lowell again used a New England dialect in *East Wind* (1926) which, though published posthumously, was prepared before her death.

18. Amy Lowell, "Number 3 on the Docket," in *The Complete Poetical Works of Amy Lowell* (Boston: Houghton Mifflin, 1955), 136.

19. Amy Lowell to Harriet Monroe, 29 January 1916, bMS Lowell 19.1 (909). Publication by permission of the Houghton Library, Harvard University; unpublished letters by Amy Lowell are printed and made available by permission of the Trustees under the Will of Amy Lowell.

20. Winfield Townley Scott, "Amy Lowell after Ten Years," in *Exiles and Fabrications* (New York: Doubleday, 1961).

21. Horace Gregory and Marya Zaturenska, *A History of American Poetry 1900–1940* (New York: Harcourt, Brace, 1942) 183; Horace Gregory, *Amy Lowell: Portrait of the Poet in Her Time* (New York: Thomas Nelson and Sons, 1958); Louis Untermeyer, Introduction to *The Complete Poetical Works of Amy Lowell* (Boston: Houghton Mifflin, 1955).

22. A Poker of Fun [pseud. of Amy Lowell], *A Critical Fable* (Boston: Houghton Mifflin, 1922), 47.

23. Amy Lowell, "La Vie de Boheme," in *Complete Poetical Works,* 226.

24. Harriet Monroe, *Poets and Their Art* (New York: Macmillan, 1926), 81.

25. F. Cudworth Flint, *Amy Lowell* (Minneapolis: University of Minnesota Press, 1969), 30.
26. Shari Benstock, *Women of the Left Bank: Paris, 1900–1940* (Austin: University of Texas Press, 1986).
27. Amy Lowell, letter to Harriet Monroe, 4 May 1917, Houghton Library, Harvard University, bMS Lowell 19.1 (909).

CHRONOLOGY

1874	February 9, born in Brookline, Massachusetts, youngest child of Augustus Lowell and Katherine Bigelow Lawrence Lowell.
1887	*Dream Drops, or Stories From Fairyland*, coauthored with her mother and her sister Elizabeth Lowell; is privately printed and sold at a Faneuil Hall Fair, Boston, Massachusetts, with profits donated to the Perkins Institution and Massachusetts School for the Blind.
1890–91	Final year of the poet's formal education; sometime during this year she finds Leigh Hunt's *Imagination and Fancy* on her father's bookshelf, which introduces her to the poetry of John Keats.
1895	Her mother dies.
1897–98	Spends winter traveling down the Nile in a small boat with two friends and a retinue of servants. The intense Egyptian heat and a strict diet of asparagus and tomatoes were intended as a weight-loss regimen.
1899	Lives in relative seclusion in San Diego County, California, recovering from the effects of the trip—possibly from amoebic dysentery and the disastrous effects of the diet.
1900	Her father dies.
	Purchases family estate Sevenels from siblings and settles permanently in Brookline.
1902	Performance by Italian actress Eleonora Duse inspires her to decide on poetry as her vocation; begins rigorous self-education in poetry and poetics.
1909	March 25, a fire destroys the poet's stables and all its horses; anonymous letters over the next several days suggest arson, and that the Lowells had been targeted because of their suppression of union activity in their mills and factories; the poet purchases a revolver, which she keeps on her desk as she writes at night.

Her brother, Abbot Lawrence Lowell, becomes president of Harvard University.

1910   Publishes first poem, the sonnet "A Fixed Idea," in *The Atlantic Monthly*.

1912   *A Dome of Many-Coloured Glass*.

March 12, meets actress Ada Dwyer Russell as she passes through Boston, touring with the play *The Deep Purple*.

1913   Travels to London; meets Ezra Pound, H.D., Richard Aldington, John Gould Fletcher, D. H. Lawrence, and Henry James.

The poet's love of cigars becomes news when she is observed smoking during her return trip across the Atlantic; arrives in Boston to outraged nationwide newspaper reports that the sister of President Lowell of Harvard smokes cigars.

1914   *Sword Blades and Poppy Seeds*.

"In a Garden" included in Pound's *Des Imagistes* anthology. June, Ada Dwyer Russell accepts poet's invitation to live with her at Sevenels.

Returns to England, where she meets Thomas Hardy.

Stranded in England during the first months of World War I.

Convinces Houghton Mifflin to issue a New Poetry series that will publish eighteen volumes over the next three years, including her imagist anthologies.

December 17, gives first public reading at Steinert Hall in Boston.

1915   *Six French Poets*.

Some Imagist Poets (editor).

February, performance of two French operettas, *Pierrot Qui Pleure et Pierrot Qui Rit* and *La Latière de Trianon*, translated and produced by the poet for the Boston Women's Municipal League, accompanied by the Boston Opera Orchestra.

March 31, first public battle over the New Poetry when she promotes *Some Imagist Poets* at the annual meeting of the Poetry Society of America. The poet's comments so enrage audience members that they charge the podium when she finishes speaking.

1916   *Men, Women and Ghosts*.

Some Imagist Poets II (editor).

Travels to New York and Chicago for her first lecture tour. Summer, tears stomach muscles in a carriage accident.

October, overwork leads to neuralgia, gastritis, and jaundice; spends a month bedridden and sedated with morphine, too sick to be told of sudden death of older brother Percival Lowell on November 13.

1917   *Tendencies in Modern American Poetry* and *Some Imagist Poets III*, of which she is the editor, are published.

Two lecture tours, much more extensive than the previous year, stopping in Brooklyn; Princeton, New Jersey; St. Louis; Chicago; Cincinnati; and Buffalo.

1918 *Can Grande's Castle.*

Reinjures stomach muscles, resulting in an umbilical hernia. September, the first of four operations over the next two years attempting to repair the hernia.

1919 *Pictures of the Floating World.*

The poet's last public fight over the New Poetry, at the Contemporary Club of Philadelphia's celebration of the Walt Whitman Centenary.

1920 Honorary doctorate in literature, Baylor University, Waco, Texas.

1921 *Legends.*

Fir-Flower Tablets (Florence Ayscough).

1922 *A Critical Fable* published anonymously by "A Poker of Fun."

1925 *John Keats.*

May 12, the poet recognizes her imminent death from a stroke when she sees the right side of her face drop while looking in a mirror; she dies a half hour later, at home in Brookline.

May 15, her ashes are placed in Lowell family plot, Mount Auburn Cemetery, Boston.

1925 *What's O'Clock.*

1926 May 3, awarded Pulitzer Prize for *What's O'Clock.*

East Wind.

1927 *Ballads for Sale.*

1930 *Poetry and Poets* (previously unpublished essays and lectures).

Amy Lowell, American Modern

Amy Lowell and
Cultural Borders

PAUL LAUTER

I began thinking about Amy Lowell in connection with a book I have been writing on the construction of cultural authority, and particularly academic cultural authority, in the 1920s and thereafter. The hegemony of New Critical and Cold War cultural paradigms in which I had been trained in the 1950s at Indiana and Yale had long troubled me, even as I had to acknowledge their continuing power. Work on the book led me to ask what alternatives had been in the field when Eliot, Pound, and their academic successors developed the literary canon I had initially learned and shaped accounts of literary history and poetic value so determinative of later pedagogical and critical practice. Since history, including cultural history, is, if not written by the winners, certainly written about them, it is easy to forget the conflicted nature of social and cultural change. Yet any historical moment, looked at closely, will display a contest for authority, among differing—and generally antagonistic—parties. The problem is to unearth those accounted as "losers" from the cultural debris heaped upon them by their opponents.

I followed Cary Nelson's proposal that, to know the real character of a culture, one should look most closely at what it scorns.[1] Apart from the working-class writers in whom I had long been interested, I was quickly drawn to writers of the New Negro Renaissance, marginalized in ways even a political activist like me found remarkable, and, odd choice at first glance, to Amy Lowell. What was striking to me as I read about her (to the extent that there was anything useful to read) was the degree to which she had been and continued to be marginalized, even in the midst of a feminist revival.[2] And, she was, moreover, the subject of a degree of vituperative comment that made some of the attacks on Kate Millett's *Sexual Politics* seem mild.

To fill out the first point with a few statistics: in the last twenty-five years, according to the MLA *Bibliography,* about 28 books and articles devoted to Lowell have been published. By way of comparison, 33 have been devoted to Nella Larsen, 44 each to Louise Bogan and Edna St. Vincent Millay, 112 to Djuna

Barnes, 202 to Zora Neale Hurston, 318 each to H.D. and Marianne Moore. The champion, with a score of 426, is Gertrude Stein. Champion among the women, to be sure. Eliot's total of books and articles is 522—with many more in earlier decades—and the indefatigable Pound's an amazing 2,063. The figures register what we are mostly familiar with: that interest in Lowell declined sharply after her death in 1925 and that writers like Pound and Eliot, and even Stein and H.D., preoccupy the academics most likely to produce books and articles on literary subjects.

Indeed, the figures alone really do not tell us much that we did not know. The character of the writing about Lowell is much more indicative. By *writing*, I mean not only chapters, articles, or substantial units devoted to her work, but brief comments as well, a sentence or phrase here, a nasty crack there. For Lowell often provides an object of derision against which the virtues of other writers, especially male modernists like Pound, are constructed. In fact, I began to find it puzzling that critics should devote all the energy it takes to write a book to a person many of them seemed altogether to despise. Immediately after Lowell's death, for example, Clement Wood prepared a volume on her which attacks her poetry as, in its nature, an expression of her perverse desires.[3]

More characteristically, perhaps, Horace Gregory in 1958 published a two-hundred-page volume that concludes that Lowell was an "archetypical American clubwoman," a circus barker for poetry, a Leigh Hunt of her time. But, he writes, "one should not conclude that the 'barker' because of his activity is a poet."[4] Similarly, a decade later Cudworth Flint concludes his Minnesota pamphlet with, "She cannot be left out of any history of American poetry of her time" any more than the stage manager of a new company could be absent from its performance of *Hamlet*.[5] The operative tone of much of the writing on Lowell between her death and the last few years is represented by the questions posed in Horace Gregory and Marya Zaturenska: "Was she a great poet? Was Amy Lowell a poet at all?"[6] They go on to answer their questions, in the negative, by quoting Winfield Townley Scott: "Her poems are the work of a woman who would have shown as extraordinary in any career; they are, even at their most expert, remarkable in the very light of their weakness, for Amy Lowell was not a poet at all."[7]

More and more it came to seem to me that Lowell was peculiarly threatening to many of her critics, less personally engaged with her than the vituperative Pound had been. I wondered what it was in Lowell that so menaced, even at distances of a quarter century and more. I will return to this question shortly.

To be sure, there was much about Lowell's background and manner to antagonize opponents. From one of New England's most prominent and wealthy families, she lived much of her life in the family's Brookline mansion, Sevenels. Shy, overweight, and preferring the avocations of boys, she disliked schools, spending as little time as she could trapped in them. With her father's death in 1900, she came into possession of Sevenels, a prominent social position, and more money, but little sense of vocation. Sometime during the first decade of the century, however, she began to chart out a course for herself as a literary figure, and toward that goal she applied her talents, prodigious energy, and funds. She wrote poetry extensively (eleven books in fifteen years), including her funny and controversial take on her peers, *A Critical Fable* (1922). She also collected volumes and manuscripts of Keats; she was ultimately to publish an impressive two-volume study of the poet. She sought out the young movers and shakers of the new renaissance in American poetry and organized a number of them into imagist collections and other poetic ventures, read widely to great response (favorable and otherwise) at poetry societies and colleges across the country, and entered into well-publicized cultural brawls with poetry traditionalists as well as with figures like Pound. In 1914, she also persuaded Ada Dwyer Russell to share her life at Sevenels, where they were able to build a certain sanctuary within a life of activity and contest. In ill health, to which her obesity contributed, through much of the last eight years of her life, Lowell died just after the Keats book was published in 1925, at age fifty-one.

In reading Lowell and her adversaries I was struck by the discrepancy between the considerable body of her critical writing and the virtual absence of discussion of it, even by commentators willing to examine her poetry. Gay Wilson Allen (later to be known as the biographer of Whitman) devoted considerable space to Lowell (and none to Pound, incidentally) in his 1935 book on *American Prosody,* but few have followed his lead and, so far as I know, none of Lowell's prose works has been in print for over thirty years.[8] I was reminded of the question: "What counts as theory?" For Lowell's critical work provides an interesting contrast to that of Eliot and Pound. Pound, it has seemed to me, is filled with negative prescriptions, poetic "don'ts," which is what he entitled a brief manifesto of the imagist period. While he was obviously a significant force in encouraging and teaching some younger poets, and in editing Eliot, he somehow always evokes for me Blake's line from "The Garden of Love" about "binding with briars my joys & desires." He is concerned to differentiate the modern from the Victorian, the hard-edged from the "sentimental," the discipline of rhyme from the "prose kinema"—in short, to establish and ardently to police borders. Eliot, too, takes on such roles. His canon-establishing essay "The Metaphysical Poets" is primarily concerned to trace the trite "main current" of English poetry, from the Elizabethan dramatists, through the Metaphysical poets, and, by way of certain French *symbolistes*, to the high modernism of . . . well, himself. And thus to distinguish the legitimate line of succession from the false alternatives of Milton and Dryden and, more particularly, from the dissipating ruminations of his Romantic predecessors. Eliot's project, after all, was not simply to validate tradition over against the lure of personal expressiveness, but to establish a *particular* tradition as central to what is nowadays talked about as "western civilization."

By contrast, Lowell's theoretical work, including the "Manifesto" she and Richard Aldington prepared for the first imagist collection she gathered, is more eclectic, inclusive, perhaps unsystematic.[9] Some have seen it as theoretically sloppy, even contradictory. Certainly Lowell's practice, as Flint, among others, points out, seems full of contradictions. While, for example, she proclaimed herself an Imagist, beginning with objects and suggesting significance for them, she as often practiced a form of symbolism, beginning with subjective states or "a significance" and finding images to express them.[10]

This kind of contradictory practice suggested to me that maybe it was precisely Lowell's boundary-dissolving qualities that have been the source of her threat, personal and poetic. She represents a sharp departure from late Victorian and Pre-Raphaelite models, as the poetry societies of her time recognized. Yet neither did she fall into the high modernist camp, at least as its boundaries were constructed by Pound and Eliot, and walled higher by academic New Critics. She was a poet and a promoter of poetry (a "demon saleswoman" of poetry, Eliot called her), but she clearly saw these roles as integrated, not discontinuous, much less contradictory, as critics like Gregory supposed. In particular she did not see opening venues for women to write poetry and writing it herself as separable enterprises. Similarly, she was unwilling to separate poetry as an object of study from poetry as a performed text. Indeed, she insisted—a point to which I will return—that "Imagism is presentation, not representation."[11] She was a woman, but—as many of her biographers have insisted on describing it— "masculine" in her demeanor, in her enterprise, as well as in the public persona she constructed with an acute, sometimes campy mix of humor and seriousness.

It is worth quoting at length Alfred Kreymborg's 1929 comment to get a sense of how contradictorily, and indignantly, she was often viewed:

> Her own role was not the role of an artist, so much as a mummer's—an actress in male attire. One thought of her as a buccaneer scuttling the craft of conservatives and even going so far as to strip radical vessels of their best prizes. But the masculine Miss Lowell was more than a pirate. The one time I dined at the Brookline estate, I felt as if I were in audience with a late Roman emperor—possibly Nero fiddling among the flames. And yet, I learned to know her a little more closely, perhaps more accurately. In unguarded moments, she seemed an intensely feminine person, not without innocence and wistfulness, and I decided— if one can ever decide anything—that her abnormal ambition and industry had obscured her true character. The role she played for the world was masculine, valiant, combative—and the inner being, private, lonely susceptible to human fragility.[12]

And this, I need to emphasize, was a relatively sympathetic portrait.

Finally, as every male and many female writers about Lowell make it impossible to forget, she is insistently embodied: she read poetry about throwing off clothes, asserting in a culture increasingly mad for feminine thinness her corporeal self (about which, at the same time, she was intensely embarrassed—and very possibly proud, too). It was not, then, only her poetry that she conceived, and delivered, as "presentational," but her self.

It came to seem to me, then, that Lowell's boundary-challenging qualities were distinctively threatening, especially in times, like the 1920s and 1950s. A hysteria over boundary maintenance, indeed, in times when maintaining the borders became matters literally of life and death. One thinks of texts from Nella Larsen's *Passing* to Adolf Schicklgruber's *Mein Kampf,* in which the boundaries between black and white, Jew and Aryan take on lethal dimensions. For myself, I came to contemplate particularly the cold-war culture in which I was trained as a New Critic in the 1950s. One might view that time as a culminating moment of boundary hysteria, when the search for duplicitous Reds, hiding as democrats, obsessed even supposed political liberals, let alone traditionalists; when drawing and policing boundaries—the 38th Parallel, the Berlin Wall, the divide between the Vietnams—became a central goal of national elites, on both sides of the Iron Curtain.[13] It was a time, too, of often savage efforts to reinscribe gender boundaries, loosened by the movement and urban concentration brought on by World War II.[14] Rosie was to learn to be content at home, and Johnnie could learn to be cured of "homosexual tendencies" in the therapist's office. One turns to Ginsberg's "America"—"Go fuck yourself with your atom bomb / . . . I'm putting my queer shoulder to the wheel"—with a profound breath of relief.

I feel confirmed in this view of Lowell's threat by the recent turn toward serious interest in her. It comes precisely at the moment in which the dissolution of borders, the stance of liminality, is embraced by many cultural workers, even in the face of right-wing attacks on lesbian and gay studies in colleges, on the rights of homosexuals in the military, and on their bodies in the streets of American cities.[15] Suddenly Lowell seems to be emerging as a striking transitional figure in the work of Lillian Faderman, Cheryl Walker, and Betsy Erkkila, to name three of the most prominent critics. Faderman poses Lowell's grouping "Two Speak Together," a series of effective love poems front the 1919 volume *Pictures of the Floating World,* as the most fully articulated sequence of lesbian poetry between Sappho and the 1960s, so successfully coded that critics even within the past decade miss its point.[16] Walker presents Lowell as an archetype of the androgynous, desiring "to melt her categories, male and female." Walker takes her up precisely because her "contradictions are instructive"[17] Erkkila's brilliant reading of "The Sisters," one of Lowell's most important poems, opens the poet's altogether conflicted relationships both with the women writers she claims as her predecessors and those others Lowell herself ambivalently marginalizes.[18]

Lowell thus becomes interesting in our conflicted and tense cultural moment because she was not in any sense "free" either to express her sexuality or to police it. She could not have the confidence—or perhaps bravado—of overseas 1920s lesbian communities, or even of the more modest bohemianism of the Village. On the contrary, at the center of many of her most interesting poems, like "Venus Transiens," are painfully contradictory impulses toward revelation, display, or even a certain form of "flaunting," and hiding, a poetics of the closet, as I have suggested elsewhere.[19] A much less familiar, but excellent, poem may serve to focus this point, entitled "The On-Looker":

Suppose I plant you
Like wide-eyed Helen
On the battlements
Of weary Troy,
Clutching the parapet with desperate hands.
She, too, gazes at a battle-field
Where bright vermilion plumes and metal whiteness
Shock and sparkle and go down with groans.
Her glances strike the rocking battle,
Again—again—
Recoiling from it
Like baffled spear-heads fallen from a brazen shield.
The ancients at her elbow counsel patience and contingencies;
Such to a woman stretched upon a bed of battle,
Who bargained for this only in the whispering arras
Enclosed about a midnight of enchantment.[20]

Like many of Lowell's best poems, this one presents a speaker ambiguously gendered, a distinctly female "you," and a woman from history or myth (like Botticelli's Venus in "Venus Transiens"). Unlike the lesbian sequence in *Pictures of the Floating World*, however, this poem is filled with combat, weariness, even desperation derived from a secretive "midnight of enchantment": the enclosed closet of passion has become a painfully public "bed of battle." Both the person addressed and Helen look down at "a battle-field," a too-brightly etched male domain of metal and contention, in which the weapons of the on-lookers' gaze are ineffectual. Nor do traditional pieties offer comfort; on the contrary, the language of convention sounds insulting to the ear of such an embattled woman. All this the speaker knows. Yet is she warning, inviting, or perhaps both? The poem remains elusive at that level: on one hand, the speaker clearly wishes to connect the desperation of Helen and potentially the woman addressed with two familiar arenas of female literary experience: The enraptured bed and the on-looking parapet. On the other hand, did not Helen, does not the person addressed, "bargain" the consequences of a perhaps sado-masochistic and certainly closeted passion? Read in an orthodox way, hypothesizing a male speaker, this poem can be connected to Lowell's similar "Patterns" and other poems of war-abandoned women. But read from within the framework of knowledge that the speaker, the addressed, and Helen seem to share—a woman's knowledge—the poet proposes a less literal set of events, a symbolic and direct engagement *in* battle rather than a reaction of isolation *from* it. One could, indeed, argue that battle is here posed both as the consequence of and the alternative to the closet of passion, the story of which is concealed and, it may be, simultaneously "whispered" abroad by Lowell's verbal tapestry.

Such different readings depend critically upon the construction of the speaker's gender, a matter, I would argue, decisive to far more of Lowell's better poems than has usually been accounted. One of Lowell's accomplishments, as Lillian Faderman has shown at length, was her clearly calculated strategy of fusing the conventions of amorous male poetry, to encode lesbian desire. Not surprisingly, as I have tried briefly to suggest here, the reevaluation of Lowell derives in some measure from such an ambiguously gendered borderland, where traditional narratives of women as observers are converted into metaphors that construct and dismantle the closet.

Which suggests one further basis of the renewed interest in Lowell: her insistence, about which I commented briefly above, on "presentation" or performance as central to constructing poetry as well as identity. In poetry as in life, I think, Lowell struggled precisely with the contradictions between experienced and constructed sexual identities that preoccupy Queer theory today.[21] "The On-Looker" begins with "Suppose," an invitation to pretend, to don the mask of Helen, "stretched upon a bed of battle." Here a fourth participant, the reader, enters the poem's action: toward what midnight masque are we being invited? In whose production are we being asked to join? Paris, of course, is nowhere to be found, only a conflicted writer invoking beauty and anguish, the bedroom and the battlefield, to create her possible identities. I would not wish to argue that Lowell anticipates the complex arguments of today's essentialists and social constructionists, only that her work embodies the lived experience of one who found herself "stretched upon a bed" of equivalent battle.

During and after her life, Amy Lowell was often the butt of male humor. Indeed, the more she rushed into literary combat, the more she was derided. Whether she ever sufficiently turned the joke while she lived we will probably never know. But there is a fine and pleasing irony in the fact that now, seventy-some years later, her work can become part of a cultural movement bringing into question the borders her antagonists struggled so hard to erect and maintain.

Notes

1. "We also need to reevaluate precisely those texts we habitually mark as mediocre. A second axiom, then, can be stated baldly: we should always read what people assure us is no good. Finally, we need to rediscover poets whose work is no longer even mentioned in most literary histories" (*Repression and Recovery: Modern American Poetry and the Politics of Cultural Memory, 1910–1945* [Madison: University of Wisconsin Press, 1989], 51).
2. Useful information, including a selected and annotated bibliography, is contained in Richard Benvenuto, *Amy Lowell* (Boston: Twayne, 1985). Jean Gould, *Amy: The World of Amy Lowell and the Imagist Movement* (New York: Dodd, Mead, 1975) is probably the most useful biography.
3. Clement Wood, *Amy Lowell* (New York: Harold Vinal, 1926). Ironically, perhaps the publisher is the same fellow derided in e. e. cummings's "Poem, or Beauty Hurts, Mr. Vinal."

4. Horace Gregory, *Amy Lowell* (New York: Thomas Nelson and Sons, 1958), 208, 206.
5. F. Cudworth Flint, *Amy Lowell* (Minneapolis: University of Minnesota Press, 1969), 44.
6. Horace Gregory and Mary Zaturenska, *A History of American Poetry, 1900–1940* (New York: Harcourt, Brace. 1942), 183.
7. The Scott quotation is from his "Amy Lowell after Ten Years," *New England Quarterly* 8 (September 1935).
8. Gay Wilson Allen, *American Prosody* (New York: American Book Company, 1935).
9. Amy Lowell and Richard Aldington, eds., *Some Imagist Poets (With a Preface on Imagism* (Boston: Houghton Mifflin, 1915). Lowell reproduces and comments interestingly on these tenets in "H.D. and John Gould Fletcher," *Tendencies in Modern American Poetry* (Boston: Houghton Mifflin, 1917), 239–247.
10. Flint, *Amy Lowell*, 25.
11. *Tendencies in Modern American Poetry*, 245.
12. Alfred Kreymborg, *Our Singing Strength* (New York: Coward-McCann, 1929), 354.
13. See, for example, William Epstein, "Counter-Intelligence: Cold-War Criticism and Eighteenth-Century Studies," *ELH* 57 (1990): 63–99.
14. See, for example, John D'Emilio, "Capitalism and Gay Identity," in *The Lesbian and Gay Studies Reader,* ed. Henry Abelove, Michèle Aina Barale, and David Halperin (New York: Routledge, 1993), 467–476; and Robert J. Corber, *In the Name of National Security: Hitchcock, Homophobia, and the Political Construction of Gender in Postwar America* (Durham: Duke University Press, 1993).
15. The widespread interest in Gloria Anzaldúa's *Borderlands/ La Frontera* (San Francisco: Spinsters/Aunt Lute, 1987) reflects such concerns.
16. Lillian Faderman, "'Which, Being Interpreted. Is As May Be, Or Otherwise': The Lesbian Poetry of Amy Lowell," ms. from forthcoming book on lesbian encoding. Cf. Faderman's earlier groundbreaking essay "Warding Off the Watch and Ward Society: Amy Lowell's Treatment of the Lesbian Theme," *Gay Books Bulletin* 1 (Summer 1979): 23–27.
17. Cheryl Walker, *Masks Outrageous and Austere* (Bloomington: Indiana University Press, 1991), 17, 43, and more generally, 16–33.
18. Betsy Erkkila, "Rethinking Women's Literary History," *The Wicked Sisters* (New York: Oxford, 1992), 8–14.
19. Paul Lauter, "Little White Sheep; or, How I Learned to Dress Blue," *Yale Journal of Criticism* 8 (1995): 103–129, especially 113–120.
20. Amy Lowell, *What's O'Clock* (Boston: Houghton Mifflin, 1925*),* 66–67. The volume contains some of Lowell's best work, including "The Sisters," "Lilacs," "Purple Grackles," and "Which, Being Interpreted, Is as May Be, or Otherwise."
21. A useful summary of some of the arguments by, among others, Judith Butler, Sue-Ellen Case, and Mary Ann Doane is provided by Ruth D. Johnston in "Academic Voguing, or the Politics of Appropriation," *Concerns* 23 (Fall 1993): 17–24. On the issue of "performance" see, among other works, Sue-Ellen Case, ed., *Performing Feminisms: Feminist Critical Theory and Theater* (Baltimore: Johns Hopkins University Press, 1990); Lynda Hart, ed., *Making a Spectacle* (Ann Arbor: University of Michigan Press, 1989); and Alisa Solomon, "Not Just a Passing Fancy: Notes on Butch," *Theater* 24 (1993): 35–46.

Family Matters

GENEALOGIES AND INTERTEXTS IN AMY LOWELL'S "THE SISTERS"

ADRIENNE MUNICH

But as she often says one is always naturally antagonistic to one's parents and sympathetic to one's grandparents. The parents are too close, they hamper you, one must be alone.
—Gertrude Stein, *The Autobiography of Alice B. Toklas*

Lies will flow from my lips, but there may perhaps be some truth mixed up with them; it is for you to seek out this truth and to decide whether any part of it is worth keeping.
—Virginia Woolf, *A Room of One's Own*

In "The Sisters," a not-quite-feminist Amy Lowell dreads the fate of women poets yet seeks mentorship in a sorority. On the face of it, this desire is strange: Lowell learned most of what she knew about writing poetry from male poets, beginning with Leigh Hunt and John Keats, through Samuel Taylor Coleridge and Robert Browning, and from Edgar Allan Poe to Ezra Pound.[1] Because older sisters can seem more equal, allowing more latitude for bossing them around and more possibilities for competition, the sister metaphor might serve better to level the playing field than a brother one; or a mother one. This is a matter of power. Then too, all the sisters Lowell mentions in this slippery monologue were safely dead when she adopted them as siblings. In chronology, even the closest of her sisters, Emily Dickinson, would count as a grandsister, the next closest, Elizabeth Barrett Browning, as a great-grandsister, while Sappho, the oldest, defies generational calculations. Still, a determined but apparently unnecessary gender choice for a poetical genealogy remains a question, with consequences probed in this essay.

Other critics have pointed out the ambivalence of Lowell's relationship to the very notion of sisterhood.[2] Though true, it is in the very texture of those mixed feelings that one discovers what is at stake not only in the general issue of gendered choices but more particularly in the choices one makes among the group. What kind of sisters are these, and what does Lowell imply by choosing them? To consider the particular texts Lowell engages, and even more tellingly, how she engages her sisters, how she characterizes them, what she seeks, and why she dismisses them provides literary historians with a detailed family tree. But even more, it offers an insight about the nature of Lowell's own way of writing herself into literary history.

First published in *The North American Review* (1922), then in the posthumous, Pulitzer Prize–winning *What's O'Clock* (1925), "The Sisters" takes place in Lowell's baronial study. It is nighttime, over the course of three hours. In the scene of writing, from her desire for a sympathetic group that might allay her sense of singularity, the poet conjures the spirits of three women poets, characterizing their poetry and their differences from her. Then, sighing affectionately, their time up, their limitations examined, she sends them off. Alone once more, she understands that she must write her womanhood differently.

So strong and rhetorically convincing is the poet's charming, bossy voice that it masks the poem's blatant exaggerations. Lowell creates a myth about the woman poet's rarity and of her social deviance, a crabbed peculiarity. The poem's opening begins to build a fable that verges on being simply a lie:

> Taking us by and large, we're a queer lot
> We women who write poetry. And when you think
> How few of us there've been, it's queerer still.[3]

Here, colloquial sincerity draws the reader into complicity, as if the speaker were confessing a dark truth—that women poets constitute a different species from other humans—as if in fact women poets weren't a dime a dozen.[4] Lowell disingenuously introduces three illustrious sisters as the whole of a meager genealogical tree, whereas her literary family actually possesses more leaves and branches. First of all, there's that grandbrother, Robert Browning, whose hard branch refuses Lowell's axe, even in the poem. The poem also hides the phantom limbs of relevant excluded sisters and brothers, ghosts that spook her mythopoetic fantasy. "Troops of shadows"—Browning's fine phrase for poetic haunting and narcissistic overreaching—haunt Lowell's myth of lonely self-creation.[5] Rather than reporting on a survey, the exaggeration conveys a psychological truth about women writers' isolation from each other and their sense of transgression when they attempt to write openly. Nonetheless, one also notes a self-serving aspect to Lowell's loneliness. In this, by the way, she resembles the male Romantic poets from whom she learned.

It is true, however, that gender and family added to a sense of isolation. The Lowell household respected the prohibition against women professionals. Augustus Lowell believed that artistic daughters, such as the fledgling writer Amy and her older sister Bessie, a would-be painter and eventually an author, could only enjoy renown as gifted amateurs, a status the sisters retained by their activities in exclusive literary, theatrical, and musical societies until both parents were dead. Outside the confines of Sevenels (the family citadel named for the parents and five Lowell children) and the upper-class educated New England world it reflected and reproduced, the female tradition was neither as queer nor as small as Lowell asserts.[6]

Many early poets would have been inaccessible to Lowell's generation, but Lowell herself was certainly aware of some impressive nineteenth-century women poets and some fine poets of her moment, even if she refused to tally the huge sentimental school of New England women poets. Her poems, in fact, suggest that she had read the fierce Victorian lyricist Christina Rossetti, whose collected poems had been available, printed in Boston as early as 1909. She did not seek out black sister poets—not her fellow Bostonian, the well-known ex-slave Phillis Wheatley, whose publications rested in the Boston Athenaeum, an institution supported by Lowell herself, [7] nor Anne Spencer, some of whose poems resemble Lowell's, nor the powerful Georgia Douglas Johnson.[8] But she had read the poems of the beautiful, accomplished, but eventually crabby Alice Meynell, and was personally acquainted with H.D., Edna St.Vincent Millay, and Sara Teasdale.[9]

If one counted only those American women poets who were part of the New Poetry movement—of which Lowell was a well-publicized member—the lot would seem quite populous but possibly almost as queer. The editors of *Poetry*, Harriet Monroe and Alice Corbin Henderson, whom Lowell knew well, included in their 1917 selection for *The New Poetry: An Anthology* poems by Zoë Atkins, Mary Aldis, Nancy Campbell, Willa Sibert Cather, Grace Hazard Conklin, Alice Corbin, Adelaide Crapsey, H.D., Mary Carolyn Davies, Fannie Stearns Davis, Louise Driscoll, Dorothy Dudley, Helen Dudley, Moireen Fox, Florence Kiper Frank, Helen Hoyt, Iris Scharmel, Agnes Lee, Amy Lowell, Alice Meynell, Edna St. Vincent Millay, Harriet Monroe, Grace Fallow Norton, Josephine Preston Peabody, Clara Chanafelt, Frances Shaw, Constance Lindsay Skinner, Sara Teasdale, Eunice Tietjens, Margaret Widdemer, Florence Wilkinson, Marguerite Wilkinson, and Edith Wyatt. Lowell owned this volume.[10] Her exclusionary criteria reveals that it is not only poetics that governs Lowell's sisterhood. Not only the Irish need not apply.

Adding to racial and class exclusions, the valences for later generations of the repeated word *queer* causes current readers to awaken to the way the poem points to gender strangeness. From Emily Dickinson's time to Lowell's Boston crowd, *queer*, at least in New England, meant "peculiar."[11] But as critics argue, the poem encodes struggles for sexual identities, including a queer one, sexuality made peculiar by shifting object choices and by challenges to any stable gender system.[12] Is Lowell looking for queer poets? It is true that by her reckoning whatever their sexual orientation, her three sisters live in queer closets.

A construction of a lesbian Sappho had been conventional by 1922, though Lowell's "Sapho" is not openly so. Her Mrs. Browning, on her couch reading Sappho in Greek, is plagued with hermaphroditism, having a female body and a male head. And although queer readings of Emily Dickinson are a phenomenon of the late twentieth century, Lowell read Dickinson's passionate letters to her sister-in-law Sue and may have connected them to her own stormy professions of love in her adolescent diary, where, among other crushes, male and female, she dwells on her love for her cousin Lotta Lowell.[13] Indications from her journal support the queerness of Lowell's self-definition as an identity restless for a bodily home and throw light on her later quest for a linguistic tradition that would admit this New Poet to its female, but insistently not feminine, lineage.

The poem eventually intimates that the perceived lack in women's poetic tradition does not depend on a census. Lowell despairs of finding a woman poet independent enough to defy social conventions to write about physical love. Even to write about love as they do, women poets must possess "the strength of forty thousand Atlases," yet they are unable openly to write about intimately female eroticism. In an age still masking the female body and still enforcing linguistic proprieties, Lowell finds plenty of women's love poetry but no poetry unconstrained in its sensuous range—poetry that sings a woman's "body electric." In a 1917 letter to Margaret Anderson, Lowell referred to an earlier conversation "on the difference between love and lust," writing that "love on the purely mental side is apt to be as dry and brittle as a withered leaf; but love on the purely physical side is as unpleasant as raw beef steak. It is the combination of the two which is perfection. . . . I have tried to do it myself in my own work, but a poet can do so little."[14] Should a woman poet manage to find adequate language to write fully about female sexuality she would risk censure, shaming, and erasure. In forming a mythopoetics for the woman poet, Lowell fashions a monster, a freak forged from having to choose between a body life and a mind life, ending up with terror either way. The ghosts of passionate women poets past, passing, and to come haunt Lowell's poem.

Sapho, plus Hilda, Sara, Edna, and . . .

> *In dealing with love in its aspect as a bodily passion, a poetess, even*
> *if she be Sappho, starts at some disadvantage. She has to overcome*
> *not only the conventional reticence expected of her sex, but the asso-*
> *ciations of language which have grown up in the poetry produced by*
> *men.*
> —J. W. Mackail, *Lectures on Greek Poetry,* 1910

When Lowell reprinted "The Sisters" in *What's O'Clock* she changed the spelling of the poet of Lesbos by removing one *p* from her name. The name in Greek has a *pi* and a *phi*, and Lowell, who despite not reading Greek, could still have found this out quite easily. It is not classical accuracy impelling her. Just what Sappho might Lowell have been signaling with the one *p*?

Most obviously, Lowell differentiated herself from the other poets, both men and women, who evoked Sappho as the muse of their poetry. From the nineteenth century, the name virtually signaled the origin of the lyric voice, as Yopie Prins demonstrates, for such poets as Felicia Hemans, Letitia Landon, Algernon

Charles Swinburne, Christina Rossetti, and Michael Field in England and hordes of women poets in America. Prins shows that to include Sappho was almost mandatory for a lyric poet, yet Lowell's modernist poetics would exclude most of them. Susan Gubar proposes that Sappho, while offering a kind of release from womanly constraints, serves as a problematic muse for modern writers. With earlier woman poets sentimentalizing love and celebrating Sappho's eroticized womanly suicide for love of a man, the strong woman who wants to write about female eroticism and live a fulfilling life finds herself in a bind. Lowell creates a paradoxical situation for her genealogy. Because all poetesses began to be identified as Sappho, Lowell's inclusion of this poet is foregone both as an announcement and a rejection of herself as a common poetess. She wants to slough off associations with a certain kind of womanly voice, associated with ideal womanhood and suicidal self-sacrifice.[15]

Lowell blackballed other modernist women poets, her peers, from her sorority, while they form shadowy Sapphic relationships to her. She knew H.D. and Sara Teasdale and regarded them with some intimacy, affection, and respect. Teasdale, whom she entertained at actual dinner parties and with whom she carried on a literary correspondence, wrote a long Swinburnean poem, "Sappho" (1911) in accomplished blank verse. In *A Critical Fable*, Lowell calls Teasdale "Our love-poet *par excellence*" and places her in a poetic family as "a great niece of Sapho," and also a relative of another of Lowell's sisters: "She is also a cousin, a few times removed, / Of dear Mrs. Browning."[16] Lowell bestowed this pedigree on Teasdale's love poetry the same year that she published "The Sisters." Amy knew how close a sister she had in the ten-years-younger Sara, whose sonnets on Eleonora Duse (1907) came out three years before Lowell's first poem, a sonnet, appeared in the *Atlantic Monthly*. Not only was Duse what inspired Lowell to her vocation as a poet, but Teasdale's sonnets taught Lowell a thing or two, a fact she acknowledges in a 1924 letter accompanying Lowell's Duse sonnets, sent to Teasdale for criticism: "I do not think that they are half as good as your sonnets which I read at intervals and cut myself upon."[17] Clearly sister Sara hovers somewhere in her poem, writing "the dainty erotic,"[18] which is not at all the Lowell manner, but close enough for family, even genetically close in New England descent and pure English colonial stock.[19] Nevertheless, to be merely Sappho's niece would not suffice for Lowell.

Lowell crossed the Atlantic to seek out H.D., a modernist Sappho. Reading H.D. Lowell saw that she herself was also an imagist poet. Hilda Doolittle, born in 1885, one year after Teasdale, wrote Sapphic fragments in a modernist (imagist) reimagining of Sappho. Appearing together in the first imagist anthology, she and Lowell remained in close contact through their poetry and lives. Lowell lectured widely on H.D. as an imagist, included a consideration of her place in literary tradition in *Tendencies in Modern American Poetry* and in an extended study of H.D.'s cadenced verse. With the "scientific" assistance of Dr. William H. Patterson, a Columbia University English professor, Lowell went so far as to measure cadences in H.D.'s "Oread."[20] As Jean Radford indicates,[21]

Lowell was cordial to H.D. and Bryher when they returned together to the United States to set up household. H.D. forms part of Lowell's apparitional Sapphic sisterhood, but she is haunted by Ezra Pound's naming and carries with her for Lowell a difficult mentorship and struggle for power with Pound, who denigrated Lowell's imagist success by labeling the poets "Amygists" and taking his marbles to play with a new group, the vorticists. If Lowell were to admit H.D. as a sister, would Ezra become her brother?

Although Edna St. Vincent Millay did not earn the same respect from Lowell as Teasdale and H.D., like Lowell she was a New England poet, though of a lower class. Her varied sexual practices made her notorious, and she was about to earn a Pulitzer Prize in 1923. Glancing at Millay in *A Critical Fable*, Lowell evaluates her as scandalous but slight—her "most charming scenery" being one of her strengths.[22] Millay's poem "Evening on Lesbos" imagines a Sappho jealous of "two shingled heads adorable / Side by side, the onyx and the gold." In a later poem, "Sappho Crosses the Dark River into Hades," Sappho, the suicide, flees Phaon's rejection and spares herself hearing "his voice go by / In scraps of talk with boys and girls."[23] The vision of Phaon's glorious body invoked in earlier lines ("that supple back, the strong brown arm / That curving mouth, the sunburned curls") marks the last line of the poem as doubly erotic, since Phaon and Sappho would talk to both boys or girls .

Lowell also displayed a dusting of erudition when she deleted the one *p* from Sappho's name. In the year before her death, when she was putting together *What's O'Clock*, David M. Robinson published *Sappho and Her Influence* in Boston. From Robinson, Lowell could find out that the name appeared on vases and papyri with one *p*. Robinson, who chivalrously defended Sappho's sexual purity, revered any trace of her shadowy presence, even her "soft Aeolic dialect, in which the ancient poet herself spelled her name,"'psapha.'"[24] Lowell could also recognize Sappho as the counterpart on Lesbos of Boston high society in Robinson's characterization of her as "president of the first women's club."[25]

Lowell exhibited her cosmopolitan fluency in French, where Sappho was spelled in just this way. By removing a *p* Lowell exhibited a French Sapho whose morals were no better—and a good deal worse—than they had to be. Robinson worked overtime to burnish Sappho's image as a sublime, if not sublimated, sweet passion devoid of eroticism because French nineteenth-century writers such as Alphonse Daudet and Pierre Louys had "done most to degrade her good character." Robinson referenced Daudet's novel *Sapho* (1888), in which the name had "degenerated from the name of a goddess to that of a malady."[26] With a barely disguised leer, Daudet dedicated his novel, subtitled *Moeurs parisienne,* to his sons when they reach the hormonally prime age of twenty ("Pour mes fils quand ils auront vingt ans").[27] In removing one *p*, Lowell simultaneously honored Sappho's reputation as part of her own heritage and imported a Parisian Sapho whose sexual practices suggest another, more borderline and risky apparition haunting her text.[28] Lowell's French Sapho can be a lesbian, a prostitute, and an erotic poet.

Lowell did some poking around in Sappho scholarship. As a poet known in fragments and through phantasmic reconstruction, a scholar's Sappho had come to Lowell by way of the Boston Athenaeum, whose building she had fought to save from demolition. In 1918 Lowell borrowed a book on Greek poetry by J. W. Mackail, an Oxford don.[29] With the private library stamping its imprimatur on Mackail's volume, Lowell could imagine that Sappho's aristocratic background resembled her own. As Mackail noted, "That [Sappho] belonged by birth to the Lesbian aristocracy; that she was the center of a society of highly cultivated women who practiced the arts of music and poetry in the island . . . may be taken as fairly certain."[30] Mackail portrayed a life on Lesbos that corresponded with the dramatic societies, literary clubs, and other cultural institutions supported by Lowell's Boston society; Sappho's was "a society of high culture, of refined taste, of that ease of intercourse and freedom of manners which within its own narrow circle is the privilege and the grace of the aristocracy."[31] Because Sappho had become the requisite tenth muse for women poets, Lowell includes her in her queer band of sisters, but, as Joan De Jean, Gubar, Prins, and others point out, this complicated the matter for women poets eager to break out of the constraints of women's poetry as a genre. Lowell's strong desire to find a sisterhood in a socially comparable sample leads her to adapt Sappho to fit into her WASP sisterhood, but not without serious complications.

As this section's epigraph points out, Mackail portrayed Sappho as a gender-bound poet, as much hampered by her aristocratic heritage as liberated by it. In addition to the encoded hope for a lesbian poet, Lowell describes in "The Sisters" a passionate but constrained Sapho of Lesbos:

> There's Sapho, now I wonder what was Sapho.
> I know a single slender thing about her:
> That loving, she was like a burning birch-tree
> All tall and glittering fire, and that she wrote
> Like the same fire caught up to Heaven and held there,
> A frozen blaze before it broke and fell.

In addition to playing with a contradictory fire in the paradox of the frozen blaze and its driving a burnt poet to suicide, Lowell alludes to the well-known erotic metaphors in which Sappho is the "burning Sappho," as Lord Byron calls her in *Don Juan*. Despite widely differing translations, all use Sappho's fire metaphor to describe passionate lust. However burning, that incendiary birch tree, not part of the flora on Lesbos, exposes Lowell's Sappho as a New Englander. The burning birch links Sappho's love metaphor to Robert Frost's poem "Birches," in which the poet, using a similar blank verse practice as in this first section of "The Sisters," declares in a measured tone, "Earth's the right place for love: / I don't know where it's likely to go better."[32] This is Yankee laconic poetry; it hides how such earthly love thrums in the blood to make the breast heave, the tongue savor. This buried allusion to Frost exposes Lowell's poetic encounters with Frost's poetry, where she could not find a way to write her eros, but where she attempted without notable success to write vernacular narrative verse in the manner of Frost.[33]

Lowell's appropriated birch tree locates her Sappho in a New England woods, or even a garden, bound by inhibitions of gender similar to those that Mackail gave his Greek Sappho. The slander of traditional stories—that Sappho was a prostitute and/or a lover of women—Mackail attributes to her openness in writing of the "bodily passion." Mackail sympathizes with Sappho's limitation, explaining, "She has to overcome not only the conventional reticence expected of her sex, but the associations of language which have grown up in the poetry produced by men. There is a tendency for her language to swerve into the customary forms: there is a very marked tendency to more or less unconscious impersonation."[34] In Mackail's construction of the codes of True Womanhood, Lowell could discern outlines of her own poetic practice, of her own impersonations.[35] Further, she could also identify with Sappho's repressed ladylike behavior as quite nineteenth-century Boston, and in "The Sisters," she wryly imagines herself in a striptease with Sappho:

> Ah, me! I wish I could have talked to Sapho,
> Surprised her reticences by flinging mine
> Into the wind. This tossing off of garments
> Which cloud the soul is none too easy doing
> With us today.

In a witty reversal, Lowell became a mentor to her older sister while admitting that her poetry's exposures had come at a great price. In poems such as "Aubade" (1914), "Venus Transiens" (1915) and many others, particularly in the "Two Speak Together" section of *Pictures of the Floating World*, she managed to write lesbian love poetry that was not too shocking because its lesbian context was not publicly acknowledged. In "The Letter" (1914), for instance, one perhaps notes a glance at Sapho in metaphor as well as an allusion to Sapphic meters, alternating long and short lines:

> I am tired, Beloved, of chafing my heart against
> The want of you;
> Of squeezing it into little inkdrops,
> And posting it.
> And I scald alone, here, under the fire
> Of the great moon.[36]

Invoking ancient ephemeral female genius as neither "Miss or Mrs." enables Lowell at once to imagine other constructions of family and another, freer "loveliness of words," a poetic language to articulate women's desire. How can her Sappho teach Lowell to burn but not to kill herself? How can she separate passionate poetry from its fate?

Ba/Miss Barrett/Mrs. Browning/ Queen Victoria

I know too well that you are not likely to approve of me in any way as much or nearly as much as you did last year. Indeed I have my own private fears as to being approved of at all.
—Elizabeth Barrett Browning to Mary Russell Mitford, 11 July 1839

And I did see Miss Garrow three times during the summer. She is full of talent & enthusiasm—but I confess myself disappointed in her poetry. It is feeling & graceful—IS IT MORE?
—Elizabeth Barrett Browning to John Kenyon, 7 March 1840

In her initial invocation to Elizabeth Barrett Browning, Lowell begins to build on a conventional view of the imprisoned poet of Wimpole Street for her own sense of her sister's limitations. She conjures the poet of popular mythology, the repressed daughter of a tyrannical, seductive, and pious father, rescued by the poet Robert Browning and whisked off to marriage and motherhood in warm Italy. Despite liberation through elopement to become "Mrs. Browning," in Lowell's myth the liberated poet remains queer, eternally tied to her sofa, reading Greek and only writing her great *Sonnets from the Portuguese* when "fertilized" by her genius husband. While claiming to long for close familial ties, Lowell refuses that intimacy by projecting a cold formality onto Mrs. Browning. Perhaps an embrace with her would also encompass severe Protestantism and the Victorian queen:

> But Mrs Browning—who would ever think
> Of such presumption as to call her "Ba."
> Which draws the perfect line between sea-cliffs
> And a close-shuttered room in Wimpole Street.

What is wrong with this picture? Having read the two volumes of Browning's letters, edited by Frederick Kenyon and published in 1897, Lowell knew about the poet's relatively uninhibited childhood with ten brothers and sisters at the estate Hope End, the later retreat to Torquay to recover health, the passage beyond Dover's white cliffs to France and Italy with Robert Browning. She could learn that as a determined feminist, Miss Barrett had objected to her father's tyrannical and ultimately murderous patriarchal rule.[37] Lowell chose to exaggerate Browning's social conventionality. In the 1899 edition of Browning's letters, she would have read the postscript of Miss Barrett's 1836 letter to Mrs. Martin: "Oh that you would call me Ba!"[38] In another postscript the next year, the Victorian poet expressed her gratitude for the familiarity that Mrs. Martin showed in calling her Ba in a letter to Elizabeth's sister, Henrietta: "Thank you for the 'Ba' in Henrietta's letter. If you knew how many people, whom I have known only within this year or two, whether I like them or not, say 'Ba, Ba,' quite naturally and pastorally, you would not come to me with the detestable 'Miss B.'"[39]

Lowell rejects the intimacy that Ba herself might have extended. Whereas Sappho and Lowell could play bacchantes, tossing their garments to the winds, Miss Lowell and Mrs. Browning must lace themselves in the corsets of "strict convention" their conversation limited to talk about meter, whether in Wimpole Street in London or Casa Guidi in Florence. Lowell ignores sister Browning's powerful political poems—including but not limited to those of social protest, such as "Cry of the Children," against child labor, and "The Runaway Slave at Pilgrim's Point," an antislavery poem addressing the masters' rape of slaves. Both poems exceed the conventional protests written by intensely committed feminine poets on either side of the Atlantic. *Casa Guidi Windows* seriously addresses current Italian politics, but Lowell dismisses the topic (for which Italians still revere Browning) by coupling it with Browning's dabbling in spiritualism: "Roman revolutions and mesmerism." In Browning's pioneering verse novel, *Aurora Leigh*, which Lowell also possessed, the clear-eyed feminist poet does not flinch at portraying prostitution, illegitimacy, the stench of the masses, and the opportunistic, narcissistic liberalism of the aristocracy. Moreover, she creates a heroine who supports a household with her income from writing.

It is clearly not the range of subject matter that guides Lowell's mythmaking but the way Browning wrote—or didn't write—about woman's sexual body. Invoking the most stereotyped version of what the modernists rebelled against in their ancestors, Lowell blames Browning's shortcomings on that "bat-eyed, narrow-minded" Queen Victoria, who "[s]et prudishness to keep the keys of impulse." Lowell exaggerates the conventional Queen Victoria, whose preference for Adelaide Anne Procter and Alfred, Lord Tennyson was well-known but whose affection for off-color jokes, a sip or two of whiskey, and overbearing male servants with great legs had also been caricatured on both sides of the Atlantic. It is true, however, that Browning's influential and best-selling love sonnets, though powerful, tremble with redemptive love and not with lust or insatiable desire, certainly not celebratory love divorced from respectability and Martin Luther.

Lowell's misreading of Browning seems most perverse when she worries that their conversation would not extend "[b]eyond the movement of pentameters." A close look at the meter in "The Sisters" reveals that such a conversation taught the younger poet a great deal. Lowell has been writing up to this point in blank verse that resembles in many points Browning's own metrical practices in *Aurora Leigh*. Thus, "The Sisters" could be considered homage to her older sister. When Lowell remarks, in heavily stressed feet, "I cán | not wríte | like yóu," she deflects attention from the manner in which her iambic pentameters echo yet modernize Browning's pentameter lines. To stigmatize the poetic exchange as "Tea-time talks" about meter ignores her own metrical performance in "The Sisters," as if Lowell's criticism of Browning as "not so curious a technician" inspired her to vary the blank-verse line in order to line up with those of her contemporaries Robert Frost, Edwin Arlington Robinson, Wallace Stevens, and Sara Teasdale. Whereas the first section of the poem shows Lowell writing a fairly conventional blank verse, it is in the section about Browning that the blank verse innovates, cramming syllables into a line. This would seem to qualify Browning as a fine antecedent and a perfect sister.

Vexing Lowell's family construction is an uneasy suspicion that she had in fact learned how to take metrical chances not in contrast to Elizabeth Barrett Browning but rather in emulation of Robert Browning. An almost farcical parlor scene shows Miss Lowell visiting Mrs. Browning at Casa Guidi (not the detestable Miss B. in her dusty, close Wimpole Street bedroom) when an uninvited, unruly Robert bounds into the parlor, upsetting the tea talk and upending the verse. Miss Lowell tries to keep the conversation focused on her more decorous sister, but the brother, too powerful an influence, refuses to silence his genius. It presses upon the poem. "I do not like the turn this poem is taking," Miss Lowell disarmingly protests as she seemingly loses control over her meter and her subject—to the vivacious enhancement of her poem. Without the brother, the poem's meter implies, these sisters would march forward in a more conventional fashion.

That Lowell is aware of her manipulation of her meter is clear, for when she finally banishes Robert from the poem the meter returns to a more regular, though still technically interesting, form. In an analysis of the meter in "The Sisters," Natalie Gerber argues for the conscious manipulation of meter in which conventional blank-verse practice frames some more daring metrical variations, as if in homage to Robert Browning's practices. As she bids her sisters goodbye, the meter returns to the earlier rhythms, indicating that Lowell has only momentarily inherited Robert's daring.[40]

Even when Lowell is cursing Queen Victoria's legacy on women, she imitates a rough Robert Browning line, perhaps mediated by Ezra Pound, her shadowy contemporary brother: "Confounded Victoria, and the slimy inhibitions / She loosed on all of us Anglo-Saxon creatures." The first line takes the liberties that Robert might have taken, with something approaching triple feet. The initial feet of the first line also recalls Pound's "Hang it all, Robert Browning" in his "Canto II."[41] The irony, of course, is that the poem's return at the end to the three sisters and more regular verse suggests that the more feminine sisters, repressed in their different ways by their culture's confinement of women, restrict the very rhythms of their verse and squeeze out more unrestrained, harsh liberties of the male poet's versification. Lowell's meter demonstrates what her poem argues: choosing to identify with sister poets risks repeating their repressions.

The metrical sophistication of the poem suggests that Lowell portrayed with some irony this scene of writing and its unhappiness with the failure of the sisters. The ending, where Lowell has entertained her three older sisters as if at one of her famous dinner parties, putting them into "the motor" and calling after them "Good night! Good night!" echoes Robert Browning's Andrea del Sarto, who bids farewell to his unfaithful wife ("Go, my love"), who refuses to act as his muse, and whom he blames for his failure to become a great artist. By this slight allusion, Lowell acknowledges that artists who want to be greater than they are often blame their failure on their muses' or sisters' limitations.

Emily, a Hummingbird among Nasturtiums

> *She did not belong to the life in which she found herself. . . . The times*
> *were out of joint for Emily Dickinson. Her circle loved her, but ut-*
> *terly failed to comprehend.*
> —Amy Lowell, "Emily Dickinson"

Lowell clearly feels the most affinity with her third sister. She is her di-
rect descendant in poetry as well as in ethnic background. A New Englander of
a family as old if not as rich as the Lowells, Emily Dickinson resisted the same
Anglo-Saxon American repressive religion that was part of Lowell's heritage.
Rather than meeting her in a formal parlor after sending in her card, Amy wishes
to hop over a fence to catch Emily in her garden. She imagines the poet en-
grossed in the doings of a hummingbird among nasturtiums, and the focus on
the wonders of creatures enables the two New England misses to achieve an in-
timacy mediated by deflected attention. With what pleasure she imagines a con-
versation with the poet who made the way for her own kind of poetry! In her
essay "Emily Dickinson," Lowell hailed the poet as the founder of authentically
modern American poetry:

> In the very first year of the decade [1890s] appeared a little posthu-
> mous volume of verse, issued to preserve the memory of one Miss Emily
> Dickinson of Amherst. Nobody had heard of her; the surprise was com-
> plete; the delighted public devoured edition after edition, regardless of
> some critics who were disturbed by the free rhythms and false rhymes.
> Two more volumes of selections were published, as well as her letters;
> they also went into later editions very soon. A new American poet was
> discovered and established. And with the name of Emily Dickinson, a
> history of modern American verse may well begin, for she, a belated
> daughter of the Transcendentalists, was also the great precursor of the
> Imagists.[42]

"The exact word, the perfect image, that is what makes these short poems so
telling," lectured Lowell, the literary critic. "There is one other way in which
Emily Dickinson was a precursor of the imagists. She, first of all in English I
believe, made use of what I have called elsewhere the 'unrelated' method. This
is, the describing of a thing by its appearance only, without regard to its entity
in any other way."[43]

An imagist poet before her time, Dickinson was misunderstood even as
she was loved. According to Lowell's reconstruction, such misunderstanding
drove Dickinson to a physical isolation that reflected her psychological queer-
ness. This most captivating sister heartens Lowell no more than the two others;
all three suffered mutilations because of their sex. Whereas Sappho seems to
have been either sublimed or chopped into fragments, her eloquence lost to her

sisters, her name (meaning "lapis lazuli") only a place marker, a "leaping fire we call so for convenience." And poor Mrs. Browning, earnestly reading Greek and restraining her pentameters, could write the great love sonnets only through bourgeois sex with Mr. Browning; Lowell diagnoses her sickness as an "over-topping [read: masculine] brain" that overrode her womb until Robert Browning juiced up her body and her poetry. Those two sisters could not write about real sex, although they had "had" sex—unlike the sister Lowell imagines as virginal.

Lowell reserves her most poignant regret for Dickinson's sacrifice to her poetry. Whereas Sappho had a daughter but eventually paid for passion with her life and Browning had a son but paid with her maladies, Dickinson wrote astonishing poetry but sacrificed a vital connection of her sensual body with another's, "only giving / Herself to hard cold paper." Whereas Sappho, though fragmented and a suicide, promises a possibility of uninhibited woman's sensuous poetry, Dickinson's poetic body overflows with unmediated, imagistic intensity, while her physical body remained evacuated, alienated, desexed:

> She hung her womanhood upon a bough
> And played ball with the stars—too long—too long—
> The garment of herself hung on a tree
> Until at last she lost even the desire
> To take it down.

Lowell rather crudely suggests a kind of sublimation as total alienation, as a complete mind/body split. The total energy of "this one brave, fearful, and unflinching woman" was devoted to crafting an utterly new poetry. "In a sense, she had no life except that of the imagination," Lowell thought of her sister poet. "She could not take up her life again because there was no life to take."[44] Lowell presumes to mythologize Dickinson as a tragic figure, all head and no sensual body, a construction that ignores the intensity of the poet's life and the blessedness of having at least her sister-in-law Sue, who profoundly understood Dickinson's poetry. Here too is Lowell minimizing the life of the imagination. Dickinson's response to the world was so totally absorbing that she could barely tolerate the pleasure of her own senses. Lowell's lecture on Dickinson rehearses "heart-rending" tales of an increasingly suffocating life outside her room: "Conceive of Blake sending the 'Songs of Experience' to the 'Springfield Republican!'"[45] To write poetry in such surroundings, stifled by loving family and repressive social rituals, required a strength of forty thousand Atlases. How painful yet magical to have such an exquisitely tortured sister, one who clearly could not know about sex!

Lowell has chosen sisters that in her eyes were great poets. She cannot write like them, yet she finds them "sobering," "[f]rightfully near and rather terrifying"—a good description of family. Her terror sees herself in them, and that genetic mirror makes them wonderful, awful sisters. They are not "strange" because

Lowell knows herself in them and knows them in herself. At last Lowell acknowl-
edges the mythical nature of her exaggerations, those that she requires for her
poetry and for her concept of a queer lot. She underscores her exaggeration in a
radical line break:

How

We lie, we poets!

Rather disingenuously, as Virginia Woolf intimates about her own writing
in the epigraph that begins this essay, Lowell asserts a prerogative of creative
writers: to tell, yet to hide a larger truth. Lowell looks into the lives of her adopted
sisters to see mutilation inflicted by social oppression.[46] Immense courage makes
them queer; oppression alienates their language, separates them from each other,
causes them to mask truths with lies. This separation presses on Lowell, prob-
ably unknowingly, for her lies serve her self-aggrandizing self-portrait equally
as they serve a larger truth about women. Sisterly conditions that seem to call
for some lies in a brotherly world would constitute a feminist message in the
poem, but also would reveal a more disquieting subterfuge. The smallness of
this poet's queer lot ultimately resolves itself into a group of one—Lowell, her-
self—who resists a full engagement even with the poetry of her foresisters, set-
tling instead for repression and politesse.

As a poetic monologue, "The Sisters" combines generic features of the
Victorian dramatic monologue—which builds linguistic repression into its very
form—and the romantic autobiographical conversation poem such as Coleridge's
"Frost at Midnight" (1798). In Coleridge's great blank-verse meditation on his
past and his dedication to the future, embodied by his sleeping son, the poet
imagines his legacy to his son to be an unmediated "eternal language" that will
sweeten all days and all seasons and will bring a natural eloquence to him.[47] In
a manner similar to Lowell's, Coleridge allows himself the only voice, for the
infant son to whom he speaks could not understand him even were he awake.
Lowell's poem not only concerns itself with a family legacy in language, but
also of stunted female poetic eloquence, not eternal but mired in history. At the
end of the poem, Lowell allows a vague hope for a tenuous tradition when she
foresees a possible visit from a younger sister poet:

I only hope that possibly some day
Some other woman with an itch for writing
May turn to me as I have turned to you
And chat with me a brief few minutes.

The other woman "with an itch for writing" (an echo of Robert Browning's "an
itch I had, a sting to write, a tang"[48]) visits alone, knocks at the poet's door,

chats briefly, then goes her own way. Lowell's tepid hope of a woman poet acting as a mentor to some other woman seems compromised in this dim night of
the soul by doubts about what she might transmit or perhaps acquire. Family
matters too much for Lowell to join a sisterhood where she might not be sister
number one.

Notes

1. When John Gould Fletcher delineated a genealogy for her, Lowell responded, "Your
   tracing the parentage of my work back to Keats and Poe is very interesting, and it is
   one which I should make myself, substituting Poe, however, for Poe's master,
   Coleridge, and adding another ancestor in the shape of the French *Symbolistes . . .*
   certainly Browning—although I have consciously studied him less than any of the
   other poets—has a very marked cousinship with some of my poems." Amy Lowell,
   quoted in S. Foster Damon, *Amy Lowell: A Chronicle with Extracts from Her Correspondence* (Boston: Houghton Mifflin, 1935), 360.
2. For explorations of vexed relations of modern women writers, see Sandra M. Gilbert and Susan Gubar, *No Man's Land: the Place of the Woman Writer in the Twentieth Century,* 2 vols. (New Haven: Yale University Press, 1998–94); Betsy Erkkila,
   The Wicked Sisters: Women Poets, Literary History, and Discord (New York: Oxford
   University Press, 1992); Helena Michie, *Sororophobia: Differences among Women
   in Literature and Culture* (New York: Oxford University Press, 1992) and Jane
   Dowson, *Women, Modernism, and British Poetry, 1910–1939* (Burlington, Vt.:
   Ashgate, 2002).
3. "The Sisters," in Lowell's collection *What's O'Clock* (Boston: Houghton Mifflin,
   1925), 127–137. Although the poem first appeared in the *North American Review* in
   1922, I have used the 1925 version because it is in this that Lowell edited one *p* out
   of Sappho's name.
4. In her tracing of the problematic of sisterhood, Erkkila gives a brief reading of
   Lowell's poem to pinpoint struggles within it to define the gender of the woman poet,
   neither "man-wise" nor already a mother creature; see *The Wicked Sisters,* 9.
5. The phrase comes from *Pauline* (1833), Robert Browning's first and anonymously
   published poem, a rare volume of which Lowell owned.
6. Erkkila points out that "the poet begins with an act of historical (mis)interpretation
   that immediately consigns to invisibility the large numbers of women poets who had
   been writing since at least the end of the eighteenth century, and who were particularly visible in the literary landscape" the year the poem was written; see *The Wicked
   Sisters,* 9.
7. The Boston Athenaeum owned editions by Wheatley dating 1770, 1784, 1802, 1838,
   and 1834, the last of which was a memoir with poems. In 1915 the library acquired
   a volume of poems and letters and six broadsides relating to Wheatley, along with a
   portrait and a sample of her handwriting.
8. Lowell owned James Weldon Johnson's *The Book of Negro Poetry, Chosen and Edited with an Essay on the Negro's Creative Genius* (New York: Harcourt, Brace, 1922),
   which mentions Wheatley, and though the book was published after her poem was
   written, its presence in her library may indicate that she was interested in the New
   Negro Poetry and that she at least knew about Wheatley.

9. For a devastating portrait of the aged Meynell, see Richard Aldington, *Life for Life's Sake* (New York: Viking, 1941), 131–132.

10. Harriet Monroe and Alice Corbin Henderson, *The New Poetry: An Anthology* (New York: Macmillan, 1917).

11. See, for example, Martha Dickinson Bianchi, *The Life and Letters of Emily Dickinson* (Boston: Houghton Mifflin, 1924): "Nothing could have been more alien to any of the Dickinsons than a desire to be peculiar—'queer' they would have called it—or to do what the later generation calls pose" (3). Lowell owned this volume, which was published after "The Sisters" was written.

12. Paul Lauter, "Amy Lowell and Cultural Borders," in this volume and in *Speaking of the Other Self,* ed. Jeanne Campbell Reesman (Athens: University of Georgia Press, 1997), 294.

13. In a journal entry from 3 June 1889, Lowell wrote "Dear, dear Lotta. I love her more and more. I am awfully afraid she doesn't care one strand for me. But I am not worthy of her love. A great, rough, masculine strong thing like me, even Polly [Cabot] doesn't care so much for me." On 11 August 1889 she followed this with, "*Oh, how I love her!!!!!!!!!*" Amy Lowell, Daily Journals, 1889–90; Houghton Library, Harvard University bMS Lowell 10 6.25. Publication by permission of the Houghton Library, Harvard University. Unpublished journal entries by Amy Lowell are printed and made available by permission of the Trustees under the Will of Amy Lowell.

14. Amy Lowell to Margaret Anderson, 10 April 1917, quoted in Damon, *Amy Lowell: A Chronicle*, 348.

15. The most extensive study of the traditions and meanings of invoking Sappho is Yopie Prins's *Victorian Sappho* (Princeton, N.J.: Princeton University Press, 1999).

16. A Poker of Fun [pseud. of Amy Lowell], *A Critical Fable* (Boston: Houghton Mifflin, 1922), 67.

17. Amy Lowell to Sara Teasdale, 22 January 1924, quoted in Damon, *Amy Lowell: A Chronicle,* 648.

18. [Lowell], *A Critical Fable,* 67.

19. I am indebted to many studies of the uses of Sappho in the Western literary tradition. Among them are Prins, *Victorian Sappho*; Joan de Jean, *Fictions of Sappho* (Chicago: University of Chicago Press, 1989); Susan Gubar, "Sapphistries," in *Rereading Sappho: Reception and Transmission,* ed. Ellen Greene (Berkeley and Los Angeles: University of California Press, 1996), 199–217; and Margaret Williamson, *Sappho's Immortal Daughters* (Cambridge, Mass.: Harvard University Press, 1995).

20. On Lowell's analysis of H.D.'s cadences, see *Tendencies in Modern American Poetry* (New York: Macmillan, 1917), 262–264. For information about Patterson, see Damon, *Amy Lowell: A Chronicle*, 397.

21. Jean Radford, "A Transatlantic Affair: Amy Lowell and Bryher," in this volume.

22. [Lowell], *A Critical Fable,* 97.

23. Edna St. Vincent Millay, "Evening on Lesbos," 239, and "Sappho Crosses the Dark River into Hades," 293, in *Collected Poems of Edna St. Vincent Millay* (New York: Harper and Row, 1949).

24. David M. Robinson, *Sappho and Her Influence* (Boston: Marshall Jones, 1924), 21.

25. Ibid., 29.

26. Ibid, 4.

27. Alphonse Daudet, *Sapho: Moeurs Parisienne* (Paris: C. Marpon et E. Flammarion, 1888), 1.

28. In using the word *apparition* I indicate my debt to Terry Castle, whose book *The Apparitional Lesbian* (New York: Columbia University Press, 1993) instructed readers how to discover lesbian subtext.

29. For information about Lowell's borrowing the volume, see Robert Self, "The Correspondence of Amy Lowell and Barrett Wendell," *New England Quarterly* 47 (1974): 64–85.

30. J. W. Mackail, *Lectures on Greek Poetry* (New York: Longmans, Green, 1910), 96.

31. Ibid., 97.

32. Robert Frost, "Birches," in *Complete Poems of Robert Frost* (New York: Henry Holt, 1949), 152.

33. Lowell published a long poem, *The Overgrown Pasture,* consisting of thirteen monodramas about decadent New Englanders, and then prepared for publication *East Wind* (1926), a posthumously published volume of poems about the Yankee character that Lowell encountered at her country home in Dover, New Hampshire. In these Lowell links herself with Frost's view of New Englanders but indicates that Frost's view is much more sympathetic to them, believing herself that New England stock deteriorated due to out-migration and war. In a 1925 letter she admits her separation from the native: "I pity them," she admits, "but . . . I am a complete alien, . . . and I can only regard my knowledge of his language and his psychology as atavistic"; Amy Lowell to Albert Feuillerat, quoted in Damon, *Amy Lowell: A Chronicle,* 710. In addition to the illuminating comparisons between herself and Frost, the letter indicates that Lowell believed in a blood connection between herself and those of the same stock. She thinks, as I have suggested, in racial terms.

34. Mackail, *Lectures on Greek Poetry,* 95.

35. For analyses of some of those impersonations, see the essays by Melissa Bradshaw, Jaime Hovey, and Mari Yoshihara in this collection.

36. Amy Lowell, "The Letter," in *Pictures of the Floating World* (New York: Macmillan, 1919), 40–41.

37. When Elizabeth Barrett's father ignored a doctor's advice to send her out of London, she wrote resignedly to her Greek teacher, "I do not leave England, my dear friend. It is decided that I remain on in my prison." Elizabeth Barrett to Hugh Boyd, 25 October 1845, in *The Letters of Elizabeth Barrett Browning,* ed. Frederick Kenyon (London: Smith, Elder, 1898), 1:270.

38. Elizabeth Barrett to Mrs. Martin, 7 December 1836, in *Letters,* 1:44.

39. Elizabeth Barrett to Mrs. Martin, 23 January 1837, in *Letters,* 1:50.

40. I am grateful to Natalie Gerber's immense generosity in scanning "The Sisters" for me and then analyzing the implications of her scansion, not only to the interpretation of the poem but to the links between Lowell and other modern poets, such as Frost and Stevens.

41. Ezra Pound, "Canto II," in *Selected Poems of Ezra Pound* (New York: New Directions, 1957), 98.

42. Amy Lowell, "Emily Dickinson," in *Poetry and Poets* (Boston: Houghton Mifflin, 1930), 175.

43. Ibid., 102–103, 107.

44. Ibid., 89.

45. Ibid., 91.

46. Gilbert and Gubar, in *No Man's Land,* point out that this ambivalent tribute to one's literary foremothers "almost became an initiatory ritual gesture . . . defining the

blessings and curses conferred on them by aesthetic ancestresses and peers" (1:211).

47. Samuel Taylor Coleridge, "Frost at Midnight," In *Complete Poetical Works,* ed. Ernest Hartley Coleridge (Oxford: Clarendon Press, 1912), 1: 240–242.

48. Robert Browning, "An Epistle Containing the Strange Medical Experience of Karshish, an Arab physician," in *The Poems* (New Haven: Yale University Press, 1981), 567.

Amy Lowell and the Unknown Ladies

THE CARYATIDES TALK BACK

ELIZABETH J. DONALDSON

In the poem "To Two Unknown Ladies" (1927) Amy Lowell describes her uneasy attraction to two women writers and their seemingly dull, yet strangely compelling creations. Likened to models for caryatides, architectural columns sculpted in the shape of women, these two women writers evoke the vexed position of the female artist working in a male tradition. As supporting elements of a Greek temple, caryatides are simultaneously necessary and decorative, a combination of the serviceable and the aesthetic, crafted by men but representing women. These would-be models for caryatides, however, speak themselves and, more important, speak meaningfully to Lowell about her own need, a "kind of thirst" for a female literary tradition.[1]

In general Lowell is not known for a commitment to feminist politics or for speaking out on women's issues even though today she is recognized as a lesbian poet whose lyrics speak frankly of female same-sex desire.[2] On the contrary, she is well known for keeping her domestic and personal affairs relatively closeted: her letters to D. H. Lawrence, in which she advises him to censor himself, are sometimes cited as examples of her conservative public mask.[3] Lowell warns Lawrence, "you do not want to stress your sexual side to a public incapable of understanding it."[4] According to Lowell, publicly confronting biased attitudes toward sex and sexuality in one's work is a losing proposition: "when one is surrounded by prejudice and blindness, it seems to me that the only thing to do is to get over in spite of it and not constantly run foul of these same prejudices which, after all, hurts oneself and the spreading of one's work, and does not do a thing to right the prejudice."[5]

Yet, at the same time, Lowell was no shrinking violet. Her confrontation with Ezra Pound over the leadership of the imagist poets is famous, and it is important to remember that not only did Lowell have the strength to stand up to

Pound, but she also had the savvy to succeed in publicizing and popularizing imagist poetry. And, as several critics have already noted, Lowell's struggle with Pound was as much a struggle against a well-established tradition of misogynist attitudes toward women and women writers.[6]

Lowell was a formidable public advocate for American poetry, and also for women poets, though her advocacy might take covert forms. Although she dressed the part of a Victorian lady and was often associated in readers' minds with the stiffly corseted speaker of her famous poem "Patterns" (1916) in her role as the "spokesman [*sic*] for American poetry" Lowell also seems "the embodiment of the new liberated woman."[7] This apparent paradox arises from the necessarily conflicted position Lowell inhabited as a woman poet speaking in a poetic tradition that is gendered male. She was, furthermore, a lesbian speaking in a lyric tradition structured by male heterosexual desire. As both a poet and a critic, Lowell could not fail to realize the difficulties of inhabiting such a space. Lowell never wrote a manifesto on the subject, but even so her thinking about the exigencies of women's writing may be extrapolated from a careful reading of her critical comments about other women poets and her poems that explicitly deal with literary criticism or women's writing.[8] What emerges from these texts is Lowell's consciousness of how the sexual economy of the poetic voice shapes women writers. Lowell is keenly aware of the ways poetic conventions refract women's desire and of the ways women writers must circulate as queerly animated caryatides within this system of sexual and textual reproduction.

One example of Lowell's covert public commentary on the position of the woman writer is her pseudonymously published *A Critical Fable* (1922).[9] Patterned after her ancestor James Russell Lowell's *A Fable for Critics* (1848), Lowell's new satire was an imaginary conversation between two gentlemen: a present-day American critic and the elder Lowell. The younger critic showcases the best of the modern poets, including a number of women writers. During their conversation, Lowell's modern speaker, a "gallant gentleman" (*CF* 73), also praises two women writers from the historic Lowell's day. The elder Lowell naturally protests: Emily Dickinson is dismissed as "that prim and perverse little person" (*CF* 7), and mention of Margaret Fuller elicits "My God, how I hated her!" (*CF* 45). The elder Lowell makes it clear that he has little respect for women writers in general:

> I am human,
> And can hardly bear to allow that a woman
> Is ever quite equal to man in the arts;
> The two sexes cannot be ranked counterparts. (*CF* 44–45)

In the face of such criticism, Lowell's anonymous contemporary speaker holds a politically expedient position:

> the fish I must fry
> Required considerable diplomacy

To keep in the pan and not drop in the fire.
Twas an expert affair, and might shortly require
I knew not what effort to induce him to grant
That whatever we are is worth more than we aren't. (*CF* 10–11)

Thus the new Lowell critic decides not to alienate his/her elder and shifts the discussion whenever disagreements over the value of women writers threaten to stall their exchange. Amy Lowell's decision to write in the persona of a "gallant gentleman" is yet another strategic capitulation to male dominated literary criticism: one must adopt a male voice in order to be a legitimate part of this conversation. In the last line quoted above—"whatever we are is worth more than we aren't"—the *we* is also strategically slippery, referring at once to "we" moderns and "we" women poets. In keeping with the dynamic of identification and disavowal within the poem, the anonymous publication of *A Critical Fable* presented Lowell with another opportunity to destabilize the gender politics of authorship. After the book's publication, Lowell temporarily avoided being identified as the author by attributing the poem to college professor Leonard Bacon. According to her biographer, S. Foster Damon, by associating the poem with Bacon, "a Yale man," Lowell hoped to gain a more favorable reception from the good old boy network of Yale University trained literary journalists.[10] Lowell's choice of Bacon as surrogate author/father is also, therefore, a literary drag show acknowledging and parodying the power of male privilege.

Issues of gender and writing, I would argue, comprise a significant subtext in *A Critical Fable:* the peculiar obstacles that women writers face and the sexist attitudes of male poets and critics emerge as recurring themes. For example, when the spirit of Conrad Aiken rudely interrupts her praises of H.D., the new Lowell responds:

"Young Man," I replied with some heat, "you mistake
My preoccupation. If you wish to make
Your entrance at once with the ladies, I'll see to it,
But I should have supposed you'd immediately veto it."
This was rather a staggerer, to be grouped with the women
Would tax the endurance of any male human. (*CF* 55)

Here Amy Lowell's persona playfully deploys sexist attitudes in order to create a space for female writers. Her jibes at the male ego are even more pronounced in her exceptionally quotable depictions of T. S. Eliot and Pound:

Eliot lives like a snail in his shell, pen protruding;
Pound struts like a cock, self-adored, self-deluding. (*CF* 91)[11]

Lowell's most scathing criticisms in *Fable* are, perhaps not surprisingly, reserved for male poets while her treatments of women poets are consistently favorable.

Lowell's section on Jean Untermeyer in *A Critical Fable* is of particular interest due to her focus on the erotic content of Untermeyer's poetry. In stark contrast to the "back-alley lust" and "smeary / And sticky . . . old amorous contacts" that Lowell somewhat prudishly attributes to Edgar Lee Masters's poetry (*CF* 35–36), Untermeyer's portrayal of an active, albeit acceptably heterosexual, female desire is celebrated:

> For woman possesses, it seems, an atomic
> Attraction for man, and his serio-comic
> Pretence of pursuit is a masculine blind
> To keep up his prestige within his own mind.
> If the lady appears to be fleeing, the stroke
> Is a masterly one and just her little joke.
> But when this same woman, in some bright confection
> Of boudoir attire, gives herself to reflection
> And writes down her heart in a freak of exposure,
> The result will most certainly jar the composure
> Of elderly persons brought up more demurely
> While youth retire, with doors locked securely. (*CF* 84)

This female "atomic attraction" is active, not passive, and the old script of woman as the prey hunted by man is presented as a "masterly . . . joke" or farce. Untermeyer's boudoir declarations reveal the sexual double standard by which women are judged: if the woman doesn't appear to be fleeing, readers' expectations are uncomfortably disturbed—their composure is jarred. Even though Lowell presents Jean Untermeyer as married, safely ensconced in the conventions of normative heterosexuality, there is something persistently perverse about a woman who speaks of her desire. Nevertheless, the contrast between elderly and youthful attitudes also suggests a progressive acceptance of woman's sexuality—the youth retire to read behind locked doors. Untermeyer's admission that women do have desire is heralded in the following lines by Lowell as one of her day's "pure revelations," likened to "the puritan night / Swallowed up in a gush of approaching daylight": "What the Orient knew we are learning again / For the next generation to laud with 'Amen!'" (*CF* 84–85).[12]

In addition to the exploration of female desire in Untermeyer's poetry and to the covert challenges to her ancestor's sexist beliefs, and by extension to the male bias in literary criticism at large, *A Critical Fable* also contains references to classical sculpture that are characteristic of Lowell's writing about women poets and a female literary tradition. In her section on H.D., Lowell writes:

> No pompous Victorian gush ever jeopards
> Her reticent, finely-drawn line. No Greek marble
> Has less of the pueril and less of the garble. (*CF* 53)

These images of classical sculpture recur in her description of Sara Teasdale, whose poetry is saved from becoming a prurient striptease by the addition of "stout railing":

> For Sara, if singer, is also a woman,
> I know of no creature more thoroughly human.
> If woman, she's also a lady who realizes
> That a hidden surprise is the best of surprises.
> She seems a white statue awaiting unveiling,
> But raised on a platform behind a stout railing. (*CF* 70)

Lowell's several references to Greek statuary warrant unfolding, linked as they are to Lowell's promotion of women's writing. Earlier, in her nonsatirical book of criticism, *Tendencies in Modern American Poetry* (1917), Lowell introduced H.D.'s poetry to a much wider audience and defended H.D.'s verses from charges that they were "cold," inconsiderably small, and imitative. H.D.'s poems have the "coolness of marble," she wrote; "let me liken [H.D.'s] poetry to the cool flesh of a woman bathing in a fountain—cool to the sight, cool to the touch, but within is a warm, beating heart."[13] Though short, H.D.'s poems are "as carefully done as that of a statue of Parian marble."[14] While resembling the precise lines of Greek statuary, H.D.'s poetry is nevertheless original. She does not simply imitate Greek models: "Often employing Greek names, still the poems have no real Hellenic prototype. Rather is it that 'H.D.' dwells in a world of her own longing, builded of remembered things, or things read of and delighted in. With this, with that, she makes her picture; and, when finished, it resembles nothing but itself."[15] Lowell's defense of H.D.'s poetry here bears a strong resemblance to her descriptions of women's writing elsewhere. In particular, the allusion to Greek models, the connection between a woman's poetry and a woman's body (the "cool flesh of a woman bathing in a fountain"), and a woman poet's use of Greek names to construct a "world of her own longing" constitute a set of images that Lowell returns to repeatedly.

Potentially the most significant Greek allusion that Lowell makes in the context of women's writing is the connection between modern women poets and Sappho. For example, in *A Critical Fable*, Lowell places Teasdale in a family of women poets ultimately descended from Sappho:

> "This poet," I went on, "is a great niece of Sapho,[16]
> I know not how many 'greats' laid in a row
> There should be, but her pedigree's perfectly clear;
> You can read it in 'Magazine Verse' for the year.
> She's also a cousin, a few times removed,
> Of dear Mrs. Browning, that last can be proved." (*CF* 67)

This is a lineage Lowell will revisit in "The Sisters," collected in the posthumously published *What's O'Clock* (1925) and to date her best known and most examined poem dealing with a female literary tradition.[17] In "Sisters" Lowell places herself within a makeshift family of three women writers—Sappho, Elizabeth Barrett Browning, and Emily Dickinson. "The Sisters" begins with the memorable lines: "Taking us by and large, we're a queer lot / We women who write poetry."[18] As Mary Galvin explains, Lowell's choice of words—"queer lot" to describe women writers—is at the very least "amusing" for readers today: "Even if Lowell was not referring directly to the sexual identities of her poetic 'sisters,' she did find that a certain unconventionality, a strangeness from the 'norm' of heterosexually defined 'femininity,' marked the lives of her poetic predecessors."[19] By placing Sappho, the eldest sister, at the beginning of this genealogy, Lowell roots her female tradition in Greek culture and the original lesbian poet. When Lowell promotes or analyzes her favorite modern women poets, these references to Greek statuary and an idealized classical aesthetic subtly reinforce this homage to Sappho and Lowell's frequently veiled recognition of a Sapphic poetic tradition.

Significantly, Lowell's characterization of each of the writers in "The Sisters" does not focus primarily on the content of their written works, but instead emphasizes their positions as women writing in a particular sexual and textual economy. Sappho is simply "Sapho—not Miss or Mrs." (128). Browning, on the other hand, is always "Mrs. Browning" and "very, very woman," which doesn't quite seem to be a compliment; her poems are "fertilized" and called into existence by Robert Browning (132). Dickinson is first "Miss Dickinson" and thereafter "Emily" (133). These titles are important to Lowell because they are a crucial part of a poet's identity, and the identity of a modern woman poet, Lowell points out, is subject to the dictates of the marriage market in ways that a male poet's is not. Elsewhere, in *A Critical Fable*, Lowell comments on Sara Teasdale's unfortunate transformation to Mrs. Filsinger:

> On taking a husband, the law's masculinity
> Would seem to demand a perpetual virginity
> For all married poets of the down-trodden sex.
> To forfeit the sale of a new volume checks
> Even marital ardour, to say nothing of cheques. (*CF* 68)

In "The Sisters" Lowell openly acknowledges Sappho's position outside this heterosexual traffic in women: she is "not Miss or Mrs."

Since Lowell's speaker in "The Sisters" admits to knowing only "a single slender thing about" Sappho, her character remains loosely sketched and somewhat obscure (127). Browning and Dickinson, on the other hand, appear in more detail, and Lowell's portrayals of the two emphasize a pathological connection between sexuality and writing. The body and the brain compete, and the woman poet suffers. Browning appears as a pathetic creature, passive and immobile, reclining on a sofa and barely able to lift her head. She seems the stereotypical Freudian patient—the hysteric on the couch. Trapped "within the body she believed so sick," Browning suffers from a psychosomatically induced physical illness: "when [words] take the place / Of actions they breed a poisonous miasma / Which, though it leave the brain, eats up the body" (120). Browning's words, her poems, actually consume her body.

In a similar vein, Dickinson discards her body, her sexuality, "her womanhood":

> The lonely brain-child of a gaunt maturity,
> She hung her womanhood upon a bough
> And played ball with the stars—too long—too long—
> The garment of herself hung on a tree
> Until at last she lost even the desire
> To take it down. (135)

Dickinson achieves disembodiment through her poetry (playing ball with the stars), and this sense of disembodiment is in keeping with her inability to appear in public. In *Poetry and Poets*, Lowell describes Dickinson as "sinking under the weight of an introverted imagination to a state bordering upon neurasthenia; for her horror of publicity would now certainly be classed as a 'phobia.' The ignorance and unwisdom of her friends confused illness with genius, and, reversing the usual experience in such cases, they saw in the morbidity of hysteria, the sensitiveness of a peculiarly artistic nature."[20] Lowell, perhaps not so surprisingly, takes Dickinson to task for lacking the very quality that Lowell herself had in abundance (or, her critics might say, in overabundance)—a penchant for publicity. All Dickinson needed, Lowell states, was "to be pushed into the healthy arena of publicity, a little assistance over the bump of her own shyness and a new, bright, and vigorous life would have lain before her."[21]

In her depictions of both Browning and Dickinson, then, Lowell showcases issues of female embodiment and associates poetic production with the regulation of sexual energy. She introduces potential binary body/mind and child/poem relationships at the beginning of "The Sisters": women poets are "mother-creatures, double-bearing, / With matrices in body and in brain" (127). Yet, despite the capacity to be double-bearing, "The Sisters" is remarkably mother-free. Sappho, after all, is never imagined as the "mother" of women's poetry. Lowell's sisterhood, as Galvin notes, establishes "an intimacy without a hierarchy, a familial simultaneity of existence."[22] And this sisterhood, I would add, also establishes a pregnant absence of mothers and of mothering. The matrix in the body spawns sexual pleasure rather than children. In this way, Lowell writes against the heteronormative scripts that conceive of women's desire only in terms of biological reproduction or childbearing. Lowell stresses the importance of the sexual economy of literary production in the poem's conclusion:

> Sapho spent and gained; and Mrs. Browning,
> After a miser girlhood, cut the strings
> Which tied her money-bags and let them run;
> But Emily hoarded—hoarded—only giving
> Herself to cold, white paper. (135)

The originating Sappho spent and gained, exchanging the erotic and the poetic freely in the idyllic Greek (Lesbian) past. After a "miser girlhood," Browning cashes in her virginity (marries), cuts loose her money bags (writes), and lets her self run out (dies). She is fatally heterosexual. Emily, the autoerotic hermit spinster, hoards her poetry and her sexuality, never spending or gaining. Lowell, I would argue, isn't using these financial terms simply figuratively; she knew the business of literary production, and what it demanded from women, far too well.

While "The Sisters" focuses on an elite group of women writers—what might be called the great men of women's poetry—"To Two Unknown Ladies" takes as its subject somewhat coarser fare and has thus far escaped the notice of most Lowell scholars. The writers Lowell focuses on in "To Two Unknown Ladies" are remarkable for their seeming lack of talent and dedication to serious literature:

> You wrote, but, Great Saint Peter, tell me how!
> With half a destiny . . .
> . . . .
> A book tossed off between two sets of tennis
> Or jotted down some morning of hard frost
> When the hounds could not run. Pale Jesus Christ,
> Is this an effort worthy to be classed
> Beyond the writing of cake recipes? (563)

Far from a celebration of the domestic crafts and of women's work, Lowell's reference to "cake recipes" is designed to trivialize by comparing these books with a gendered and devalued type of writing: cake recipes, everyone knows, are not literary epics.[23] The books "tossed off" and "jotted down" are doubly superfluous, second-rate amusements, produced when the writers take time off from their primary leisure activities of tennis and fox hunting. The ladies are not portrayed as serious, professional writers, but as dilettantes, and Lowell's criticism extends beyond their literary productions:

> One of you painted. Well, you have no shame
> To call such trash a picture. Years and years
> You studied with the patient, stupid zeal
> Of every amateur, and to this day
> You never guess how badly you have done. (563)

Lowell culls from a well-established, all-too-recognizable vocabulary. These are critical terms often wielded against women artists. The ladies are amateurs, they lack discipline, their efforts are trivial and, of course, sentimental:[24]

> You speak of music, and my nerve-ends sting
> Thinking of Chopin sentimentalized
> By innocent young ladyhood; of Liszt
> Doted upon, his tinsel rhodomontade

Held for high romance. And the ghastly nights
On cracked hotel pianos! (563)

"Innocent young ladyhood" is indiscriminate, incapable of discerning the good from the bad, or the lofty from the lowly. In the hands of the young ladies, and with their substandard borrowed instruments, Frédéric Chopin is unwittingly denigrated and just plain misunderstood. During this litany of complaints, Lowell almost seems inspired by the spirit of Ezra Pound.

However, it is not Lowell's intent to wholeheartedly reject the work of these women. In fact these criticisms act as a foil for her attraction. Lowell is "haunted" by the two:

. . . is there not
A strange absurdity in being haunted
By ghosts who crack one's jaws upon a yawn?
If that were all of it! But nothing's all.
For just as I am oozing into sleep,
See-sawing gently out of consciousness,
A phrase of yours will laugh out loud and clang
Me broad awake. (563)

The ladies appeal to Lowell not only with the clanging phrase, but also with "the faintest whiff of flutes" (563) and a "surprising . . . almond taste" (564). Lowell's visceral response to the women is a mystery she seeks to explain:

The puzzle grows as I unravel it,
For all these feelings come out of a book
And you, who cannot write, have written it. (564)

The puzzle consists primarily of two parts: the ladies themselves and the nature of their influence on Lowell.

To Lowell, the two ladies are unknown: "all our contact lies in printer's ink" (562). Although she herself never names them, in his biography of Lowell, S. Foster Damon identifies the two as "Irish Authors." Based on Lowell's descriptions of their lives, and especially the references to hounds and horses, they must certainly be E. Œ. Somerville and Martin Ross, the pen names of Edith Somerville and Violet Martin.[25] Somerville and Ross were best known for their stories collected in *Some Experiences of an Irish R.M.* (1899), about a somewhat bumbling Anglo-Irish resident magistrate (RM) and a cast of colorful Irish locals who test his authority. The two authors were apt ghostly figures for Lowell for a variety of reasons. All women were part of an aristocratic, privileged class: Somerville and Ross as part of an Anglo-Irish Ascendancy in decline; Lowell as part of what David Heymann has described as an "American Aristocracy."[26] Lowell's family estate, Sevenels (for the seven L's, the seven Lowells), might be considered an American version of the Irish big house, the life of which Somerville and Ross both satirized and celebrated. However, Somerville and

Ross did not write under the same conditions as Lowell. As James Cahalan notes, "The common and persistent view of Somerville and Ross as two wealthy Ascendancy 'ladies' writing comic tales for a lark could not be further from the truth. With rents withheld during the Land War era . . . they wrote the RM stories in order to survive."[27] Lowell's characterization of the two taking time off from tennis games to write reinforces this misconception of their collaboration. Though the RM stories, sold to various periodicals and collected in three volumes, were the most popular and most financially successful of their works, Somerville and Ross considered the earlier novel *The Real Charlotte* (1895) to be their masterpiece.[28] *Charlotte* tells the story of a love triangle involving a man and two female cousins—one who is young, beautiful and naive, and the other, Charlotte, who is older, homely, and cunning. Although Charlotte is often portrayed in an unflattering light as an embittered spinster, she is nevertheless a strong, dynamic character with an admirable will to survive, and the novel, with its depictions of disreputable men and undesirable marriages, can be read as a feminist indictment of the limited choices available to most women of this class.

Yet, other than the texts themselves, perhaps the most interesting aspect of Somerville and Ross's literary career was their collaboration. Somerville described their writing process as driving the pen in "double harness."[29] This image of the double is significant in Lowell's own work. In "To Two Unknown Ladies" Lowell writes,

> I see you double,
> Each one beheld in profile, as it were.
> And yet the full-face view is not composite,
> But shows two totally specific halves
> Which do not blend and still are not distinct. (562)

Lowell imagines the two as "a lighted candle, split / Upon an oculist's dissecting spectacles" (563), and she tries to draw these two profiles and candle flames together. It is possible that Lowell's lines may refer to actual photographs of the two women. Somerville and Ross's *Irish Memories* (published in 1918, three years after Ross's death) contains numerous photographs and drawings.[30] The frontispiece is a profile of Martin Ross, the smaller and less athletic of the two women, in a very feminine dress. The volume also contains a remarkably complementary portrait of Edith Somerville, also in profile but facing the opposite direction, wearing a riding habit and holding a crop. Lowell returns to the image of the "double" later in the poem:

> Two halves, I said, and here I patterned rightly.
> A frail half and a virile, but both shoots
> Of one straight mother tree. (564)

Lowell's lines, therefore, may have a literal counterpart in *Irish Memories*, or in another one of the several collections of Somerville and Ross's essays. Even if her conceit is coincidental, rather than literal, her imagery here is particularly evocative when one considers the close nature of Somerville and Ross's collaboration. When biographers describe the pair's early attempts at writing together, they describe their families' "perverse delight in preventing them from writing" and the pair's constant struggle "to eke out writing time."[31] The prevailing image is one of two women, sequestered in an attic room of their own, skirting family and social obligations in order to write. Their first book, *An Irish Cousin*, was nicknamed "The Shocker" by family members, and a January 1888 diary entry by Martin Ross describes the intensity of their writing process: "Terrible stress of the Shocker. At it all day, except when we went down to help at the Christmas tree. Shockered far into the night."[32]

Somerville and Ross shockered through fifteen more books until Ross's death in 1915. And then, with some necessary alterations to their collaborative process, they shockered through fourteen other books after her death. Edith Somerville attended Ross's deathbed, drew a final portrait of her companion, and wrote the following about her deep grief on the loss of her friend: "It is ungrateful to say I have no future left . . . but the innermost part, 'my share of the world,' has gone with Martin, and nothing can ever make that better. No one but ourselves can ever know what we were to each other."[33] Somerville had a lifelong interest in spiritualism and when a medium reported a message from Ross—"You and I have not finished our work"—it is not so surprising that Somerville would seek to continue their collaboration.[34] Somerville communicated with Ross through automatic handwriting sessions, often using the aid of a medium and sometimes directly receiving messages herself, and she kept publishing under both their names for more than thirty years.[35]

Somerville's ghostly contact with Ross is of particular interest to a reading of Lowell's "To Two Unknown Ladies" and to a discussion of the female literary lineage that Lowell imagines. Lowell uses images of spectral contact and haunting to describe the pair's influence on herself, stating in the final line of the poem, "I only write to exorcise a ghost" (565). Like Somerville's exercise in automatic handwriting, Lowell's exorcism is designed not to banish but to conjure the spirits. Somerville, Ross, and Lowell's connection transcends death and collapses distance:

> And death is nothing to vitality
> Swinging across a second heart. . . .
> . . . .
> Why, I'm not dead but merely gone in space
> And that you slap away with easy hand
> Drawing me closer much than you intend (565).

This poem itself is a "little pinch of incense" that Lowell offers in homage to Somerville and Ross (565). Yet, keeping in mind that Lowell has taken great pains earlier in the poem to register her disaffection with the pair's literary productions, one might reasonably ask what exactly she is paying homage to here. As she states in the beginning of the poem, "the thing is really not so simple /

As A.B.C., or Keats, or 'Christabel'" (563). In other words, this is not a simple act of reading the alphabet, or a great poet, or a great poem: nothing is spelled out and there is no preexisting rubric to guide her interpretation. Lowell tries to read the two ladies, who she sees "double," as "two totally specific halves / Which do not blend and still are not distinct" (562). Though she examines carefully this double image, "what it is drifts out / Beyond the surf-line of my consciousness / And blurs in a dazzle so I lose its edge" (564). She speaks here of the inscrutable, spectral presence of lesbian desire in women's writing.[36]

Though phantom-like, this desire is palpable. Lowell uses the almond, an image common to her lyric poetry to describe the effect of reading Somerville and Ross's text: "why should I go back to you again / Evening and evening, in a kind of thirst, / surprising my tongue upon an almond taste" (563). The almond taste is a moment of recognition: "So what's the truth . . . ? Almonds, I said / Smooth, white, and bitter, wonderfully almonds" (564). Lowell's use of the almond is in keeping with what Paula Bennett describes as clitoral imagery—representing woman "not as a space to be entered but as a presence to be uncovered and adored."[37] This imagery is typical of Lowell's love lyrics and a well-versed reader of Lowell would recognize, in turn, the almond and what it connotes. For example, Lowell's short poem "Aubade" makes the erotic, female context of the almond image more explicit:

> As I would free the white almond from the green husk
> So would I strip your trappings off,
> Beloved.
> And fingering the smooth and polished kernel
> I should see that in my hands glittered a gem beyond counting.[38]

Somerville and Ross's book evokes the surprising taste of almonds, they ghost Lowell, and she returns to them "with a kind of thirst" all because Lowell seeks an identifiably lesbian literary tradition. Lowell finds new "sisters" in the unlikely Somerville and Ross, and this is the puzzle Lowell begins to unravel.

In addition to her characteristic use of the almond in "To Two Unkown Ladies," Lowell also returns to her stock references to Greek statuary, situating the two ladies in a female, Sapphic-inspired lineage combining the erotic and the poetic. Of Somerville and Ross she writes,

> You might have posed for caryatides,
> With wind-drawn garments sucking round your limbs,
> Your beauty blushing through their flattened gauze,
> Before a temple, on a sunny day. (564)

The caryatides themselves get their name from the columns of the temple of Artemis Caryatis. Yet before the caryatides were transformed into columns or reduced to static representations of women, they existed as living models—the young women who danced at the festivals of Artemis. The caryatides' original relationship to Artemis is of particular importance here. Artemis, the virgin huntress, is associated with women's rites of passage (including childbirth and sudden death) and with animals.[39] These are noteworthy contexts for Lowell's poem, especially considering Somerville and Ross's love of hunting and Somerville's unusual role as MFH (master of fox hounds) of the West Carbery Hunt.[40] But most significantly, Lowell evokes a lost history and, by positioning Somerville and Ross as potential models for statues, reveals the peculiar double role which women writers may simultaneously fulfill as muses and as artists. Somerville and Ross "might have posed for caryatides" but Lowell resists the compulsion to transform them into these immobile figures:

> I wonder I am Greek enough to feel
> Such solace in mere outline. But again,
> As always where I find you concerned,
> This does not finish your effect. For when
> I write down Greek, it is inadequate.
> Marble you are, but there's that jet of fire
> Like a red sunset on a fall of snow.
> I feel a wind blowing off heather hills,
> Am vaguely conscious of the moan of waves,
> And seaweed fronds pulsating in a pool.
> Now this, of course, is anything but Greek. (564)

Greek is inadequate and Lowell is not Greek enough: male classical conventions fall short of accurately portraying the lesbian poetics Lowell as a woman writer seeks to describe. Lowell speaks of a "bay of tears" and quickly regrets using this traditional and clichéd language: "That figure is so old, I feel a twinge / Of hot compunction at using it again" (564).

However, in spite of her discomfort with this poetic tradition and her feeling that this language is inadequate, Lowell finds herself firmly entrenched in its conventions because of her desire for women. Women are typical objects of art and particular women can become iconographic: after all, "Helen / Was much considered by the youth of Troy" (564). She must then speak of a conventional subject (woman) from an unconventional position (lesbian writer). In "To Two Unknown Ladies," Lowell's Greek allusions reveal this crisis of the female poetic voice. In an earlier poem "A Bather: After a Picture by Andreas Zorn," Lowell rather neatly maneuvers from classical representations of women to a more vernacular, contemporary representation: "Oread, Dryad, or Naiad, or just / Woman, clad only in youth and in gallant perfection."[41] Patterned after a male-authored model (Zorn's original picture), Lowell's lesbian refiguring of the bather shows a woman in motion, with a dynamic relation to a sexually charged landscape. Yet, as Damon notes, audiences might loudly object to Lowell's public performance of such poetry.[42] Lowell's movement from Oread, Dryad, and Naiad to Woman in "A Bather" parallels the movement in "To Two Unknown Ladies" from Greek caryatides to the "unknown," the spectral, haunting, lesbian double (or, the lesbian couple that cannot be pictured). Somerville and Ross are not art, not caryatides, but are fragmentary "pigment, line" and split into "parts and parts" (564). As a lesbian writing within a literary tradition structured by male heterosexual desire, Lowell evokes but cannot resolve this problem of female representation. Yet at the same time, it is this problem of representation, the "puzzle" of Somerville and Ross, that prompts Lowell to write.

Somerville and Ross's spectral influence on Lowell in "To Two Unknown Ladies" is all the more poignant when one considers Lowell's relationship with her companion Ada Dwyer Russell and the conditions of this poem's publication. Though their working relationship had a different, seemingly more hierarchical dynamic than Somerville and Ross's, Lowell and Russell were also collaborators: "[Russell] criticized the latest poems; she listened to every composition before it was pronounced finished, standing proxy for the public; and so well did she act as comrade in art that Miss Lowell once suggested they put out a sign: 'Lowell & Russell, Makers of Fine Poems.'"[43] Russell, often the inspiration for Lowell's love lyrics, eventually became her literary executor, and Russell alone compiled *Ballads for Sale*, which contains the poem "To Two Unknown Ladies," after Lowell's untimely death. Russell, therefore, fashions Lowell's final literary productions: she is not simply Lowell's passive muse. In the context of Lowell's own attempts to translate lesbian desire into a literary tradition that all too often silences women, transforming them into static caryatides, Russell's collaboration is a particularly fitting legacy.

Notes

1. Amy Lowell, "To Two Unknown Ladies," in *The Complete Poetical Works of Amy Lowell,* intr. Louis Untermeyer (Boston: Houghton Mifflin, 1955), 563. Subsequent references appear parenthetically in the text.
2. Lillian Faderman's brief but insightful reading of Lowell's love lyrics in *Surpassing the Love of Men: Romantic Friendship and Love Between Women from the Renaissance to the Present* (New York: Morrow, 1981) is an early example. See also Judy Grahn, *The Highest Apple: Sappho and the Lesbian Poetic Tradition* (San Francisco: Spinster's, 1985); Jane Snyder, *Lesbian Desire in the Lyrics of Sappho*; Mary E. Galvin, *Queer Poetics: Five Modernist Writers* (Westport, Conn.: Praeger, 1999); Gillian Hanscombe and Virginia Smyers, *Writing for Their Lives: The Modernist Women 1910–1940* (Boston: Northeastern University Press, 1988).
3. Faderman, *Surpassing,* 392–393.
4. E. Claire Healey and Keith Cushman, eds., *The Letters of D. H. Lawrence and Amy Lowell 1914–1925* (Santa Barbara: Black Sparrow, 1985), 105.
5. Ibid., 67.
6. See, for example, Andrew Thacker, "Amy Lowell and H.D.: The Other Imagists," *Women: A Cultural Review* 4, no. 1 (1993): 49–59; Cary Nelson, "The Fate of Gender in Modern American Poetry," in *Marketing Modernisms: Self-Promotion, Canonization, Rereading,* ed. Kevin J. H. Dettmar and Stephen Watt (Ann Arbor:

University of Michigan Press, 1996), 321–360; and Sandra M. Gilbert and Susan Gubar, *No Man's Land: The Place of the Woman Writer in the Twentieth Century,* vol. 1, *The War of the Words* (New Haven: Yale University Press, 1988).

7. E. Claire Healey and Laura Ingram, "Amy Lowell," in *Dictionary of Literary Biography,* 3d series, vol. 54, *American Poets, 1880–1945, Part 2* (Detroit: Gale, 1987), 252–260.

8. In this essay I will read from Lowell's criticism in *Tendencies in American Poetry* (New York: Macmillan, 1917) and *Poetry and Poets* (1930, reprint New York: Biblo and Tannen, 1971), but my primary focus will be the poems *A Critical Fable* (see note 9, below), "The Sisters" in *What's O'Clock* (New York: Houghton Mifflin, 1925) and "To Two Unknown Ladies."

9. A Poker of Fun [pseud. of Amy Lowell], *A Critical Fable* (Boston: Houghton Mifflin, 1922); hereafter cited in the text as *CF.*

10. S. Foster Damon, *Amy Lowell: A Chronicle with Extracts from Her Correspondence* (New York: Houghton Mifflin, 1935), 616–617.

11. See also Lowell's depiction of Pound and his hyperphallic cane in "Astigmatism," in *Complete Poetical Works,* 34.

12. Lowell's association of the Orient with the secrets of women's desire is especially noteworthy given her interests in translation and Asian lyric forms.

13. Lowell, *Tendencies in Modern American Poetry,* 276.

14. Ibid., 256.

15. Ibid., 257.

16. Lowell preferred this particular spelling for Sappho's name.

17. See, for example, Snyder, *Lesbian Desire,* 125–135; Galvin, *Queer Poetics,* 21–36; and Susan McCabe, "'A Queer Lot' and the Lesbians of 1914," in *Challenging Boundaries: Gender and Periodization,* ed. Joyce W. Warren and Margaret Dickies (Athens: University of Georgia Press, 2000), 62–90.

18. Amy Lowell, "The Sisters," 127. Subsequent references appear parenthetically in the text.

19. Galvin, *Queer Poetics,* 26.

20. Lowell, *Poetry and Poets,* 89–90.

21. Ibid., 91.

22. Galvin, *Queer Poetics,* 26.

23. This denigration of the domestic and women's work is, of course, not characteristic of all of Lowell's poems. For example, in "Interlude," Lowell depicts the simple act of baking cakes in a much more complex and erotically charged context. See Lowell, "Interlude," in *Complete Poetical Works,* 212.

24. Jane Tompkins's analysis of the sentimental in *Sensational Designs: The Cultural Work of American Fiction 1790–1860* (New York: Oxford University Press, 1985) provides a necessary reevaluation of this feminized term. Also, Nelson's "The Fate of Gender" examines how modernist aesthetic values were inflected by bias against women.

25. Damon, *Amy Lowell: A Chronicle,* 715. I thank Adrienne Munich for calling this reference to my attention and for naming Somerville and Ross as the likely originals. Their pen names were originally designed to conceal their identities and the fact that they were women: Edith Somerville's first pseudonym was Geilles Herring, but it sounded too fishy and was quickly discarded and replaced with her own name, degendered though the use of her initials; see Somerville and Ross, *Irish Memories*

(New York: Longmans, Green, 1918), 137. Violet Martin, though, seemed to prefer her pen name and was increasingly addressed by her friends and by Edith Somerville as Martin Ross after their print debut. I will therefore refer to the two as Somerville and Ross hereafter.

26. C. David Heyman, *American Aristocracy: The Lives and Times of James Russell, Amy, and Robert Lowell* (New York: Dodd, Mead, 1980).

27. James Cahalan, "Humor with a Gender: Somerville and Ross and *The Irish R.M.*" in *The Comic Tradition in Irish Women Writers,* ed. Theresa O'Connor (Gainesville: University Press of Florida, 1996), 64.

28. Edith Somerville, in *Irish Memories,* noted that *Charlotte* "remains the best of our books" (238).

29. Ibid., 131.

30. Edith Somerville's collaboration with Martin Ross continued even after her death, a point I will discuss in greater detail later.

31. Gifford Lewis, *Somerville and Ross: The World of the Irish R.M.* (New York: Viking, 1985), 65; Cahalan, "Humor with a Gender," 61.

32. Ross, quoted in Maurice Collis, *Somerville and Ross: A Biography* (London: Faber and Faber, 1968), 45. Both Somerville and Ross described the act of collaboration in particularly evocative terms that, as Lewis points out, "suggest indulgence in the forbidden": "we conflagrote [*sic*]," wrote Somerville, and "we shockered," wrote Ross; see Lewis, *Somerville and Ross,* 31–32.

33. Lewis, *Somerville and Ross,* 185.

34. Ibid., 193.

35. For Somerville's philosophy of automatic writing, see her "Extra-Mundane Communications," in *Stray-Aways* (London: Longmans, Green, 1920). See also Lewis, *Somerville and Ross,* 181–193; John Cronin, *Somerville and Ross* (Lewisburg: Bucknell University Press, 1972), 76–78; and Collis, *A Biography,* 176–184.

36. Terry Castle discusses the "spectral lesbian subject" in *The Apparitional Lesbian: Female Homosexuality and Modern Culture* (New York: Columbia University Press, 1993), 8, and notes that lesbianism "cannot be perceived, except apparitionally" (31). Though her focus is fiction, Castle's discussion is wonderfully in keeping with the dynamic of Lowell's poem: "One woman or the other must be a ghost, or on the way to becoming one. Passion is excited, only to be obscured, disembodied, decarnalized" (34).

37. Paula Bennett, "Critical Clitoridectomy: Female Sexual Imagery and Feminist Psychoanalytic Theory," *Signs* 18, no. 2 (1993): 244.

38. Amy Lowell, "Aubade," in *Complete Poetical Works,* 73.

39. See "Artemis" and "Caryatides," in *Oxford Classical Dictionary,* 3d ed., ed. Simon Hornblower and Antony Spawforth (New York: Oxford University Press, 1996).

40. The MFH is traditionally a man; see Collis, *A Biography,* 135.

41. Amy Lowell, "A Bather: After a Picture by Andreas Zorn," in *Complete Poetical Works,* 223.

42. For the uproar caused by another bathing poem, see Damon, *Amy Lowell: A Chronicle,* 292–294.

43. Ibid., 264.

A Transatlantic Affair

AMY LOWELL AND BRYHER

JEAN RADFORD

Family Romance

I cannot write like you, I cannot think
In terms of Pagan or of Christian now.
I only hope that possibly some day
Some other woman with an itch for writing
May turn to me as I have turned to you
        —Amy Lowell, "The Sisters"

Since Amy Lowell wrote these lines, many women have turned to her, and in feminist critical theory, "The Sisters" has become a locus classicus of the woman writer's struggle to establish a tradition from which to write.[1] Whereas "sisters" are literally part of the same generation, are siblings, Lowell, by looking back at Sappho, Elizabeth Barrett Browning, and Emily Dickinson, and looking forward to "some other woman," positions herself as part of a cross-generational group. The sisters metaphor is used to dramatize the creative writer's search for both individual and group identity for, as Judith Butler reminds us, the question of kinship is not simply one of blood, but of *recognition*.[2]

The very title of Lowell's poem offers a challenge to what Suzanne Juhasz calls the "double-bind situation" of the woman writer, since "a woman's identity is not defined by a profession, such as a poet, but by her personal relationships as daughter, sister, wife, mother. Her 'life' is family life."[3]

In titling a poem that deals with her professional relation to other poets in terms of the feminine sphere, of "family life," Lowell signals her engagement with the affiliation issue and anticipates Virginia Woolf's similar move in *A Room of One's Own* (1929). As a modernist, her notion of a female literary tradition includes rupture and acknowledges difference ("I cannot write like you"); she is not in search of some essentialist notion of female subjectivity. Equally important, perhaps especially so for the sister of a president of Harvard University, the claim to belong to this "strange, isolated little family" offers an alternative to her own historically specific family, so that the poem is, in Sigmund Freud's term, a "family romance," a fantasy "by means of which the subject invents a new family for himself."[4]

When this poem first appeared in *North American Review* in 1922, a young woman from England with "an itch for writing" had already turned to Lowell, written to her and about her, and finally met her on the New York docks in September 1920. The story of Bryher's discovery of Amy Lowell's writing is outlined in both S. Foster Damon's and Jean Gould's biographies of Lowell, while Bryher's study of Lowell, in 1918, one of the earliest recognitions published in England, features on all Lowell bibliographies. It is, according to Gould, "almost embarrassingly full of adulation" but for Lowell a welcome antidote to Lytton Strachey's derisive reaction to her *Six French Poets* (1915). Lowell responded by writing a generous preface to Bryher's first autobiographical fiction *Development* (1920) in which she considers the novel as "the granddaughter of *Jane Eyre* or of *Obermann*."[5]

After Bryher's initial letter to Lowell in September 1917 asking for a reading list, the two women remained in close contact until Lowell's death in 1925.[6] Bryher meanwhile repeated the gesture she had made to Lowell, by reading, writing to, and meeting with H.D., whose *Sea Garden* Lowell had recommended to her. (She had also recommended the first volumes of Dorothy Richardson's *Pilgrimage*, which Bryher had already read.[7]) Finding from Lowell's *Tendencies in Modern American Poetry* (1917) that H.D. was a woman and lived in England, she "at once began to meditate an attack on her" as she wrote to Lowell,[8] obtained H.D.'s address from May Sinclair (another champion of H.D. and the New Poetry) and finally met her on 17 July 1918—a date the two women celebrated until H.D.'s death in 1961. Bryher's account of her first meeting with H.D is written into her novel *Two Selves* (1923), while her account of meeting Lowell in New York is fictionalized in her third novel *West* (1925), where the heroine Nancy and her companion Helga Brandt (H.D.), encounter a formidable New England poet Miss Lyall (Lowell), before meeting with Anne Trollope (Marianne Moore) and her mother. Bryher's later memoirs, *The Heart to Artemis* (1962) return to this encounter several times, as I shall discuss later.

Bryher (born Annie Winifred Ellerman in 1894) belongs to what Celeste Schenk calls "the dispersive underside of the modernist monolith"[9] and is still known mainly as the life partner of H.D. (Alice B. Toklas, on hearing of H.D.'s death, reportedly said, "It is impossible to believe in Bryher without H.D."[10]) Reading Bryher in relation to Amy Lowell not only takes her out of the shadow of H.D. but casts light on both Bryher's and Lowell's struggles to establish a poetic identity within modernism. Both started as late Victorian/Edwardian poets who underwent a conversion to imagism and played a major entrepreneurial role in modernism. Both were financially independent and sexually autonomous, identifying with what Sandra Gilbert and Susan Gubar call "the masculine position," and intensely concerned with issues of power and identity. If Lowell is, in her own words, "the last of the barons," then Bryher, according to Thornton Wilder, "is Napoleonic; she walks like him, she talks like him, she probably feels like him."[11] Bryher, could not, or did not, write like her mentor, but what she learned from her early identification with Lowell sheds light on Bryher's development and Lowell's achievement. Their relationship serves as a case study in the intertextual network of women writers in this period.[12]

Muses, Mentors and Ego Ideals

We can see only that identification endeavours to mould a person's
own ego after the fashion of the one that has been taken as a model.
—Sigmund Freud, "Group Psychology and the Analysis of the Ego"

In Freud's work the concept of identification has, or comes to have, a central importance that makes it not simply one psychical mechanism among others, but the operation itself whereby the human subject is constituted.[13] Identification—which Freud distinguishes from introjection, incorporation or internalization—is a psychological process whereby the subject assimilates an aspect, property or attribute of the other and is transformed, wholly or partially, after the model that the other provides. It is by means of a series of identifications that the personality is constituted and specified.[14] As Peter Gay comments in *Freud For Historians*, Freud emphasizes that "each individual is a component part of many crowds, tied in manifold ways by identifications, and has constructed his ego ideal on the most varied models."[15]

That is, the individual is constructed not only in relation to the family but to the race, class, religion, and nation to which she belongs. Freud's theories of identity and identification were developed during and after the First World War, the same period in which so many modernist women were struggling to forge a new identity.[16] Freud also maintains that there is no artist, scholar, writer, or thinker who has not had some model, some mentor, or some spiritual "father." Although his work was produced in a different context and he has little to say that is specific to women's creative identity, Freud's theories are as relevant, I would argue, to Lowell and Bryher's political and literary self-constructions as they were to be to H.D.

The initial catalyst for Lowell's turn to poetry was not a poet but the Italian actress, Eleonora Duse.[17] In the familiar story, Lowell, inspired by the performance of Duse in Gabriele d'Annunzio's plays in Boston in October 1902, returned home to write the poem "Eleonora Duse" in order to register the experience:

> For she whom we have come to see tonight
> Is more to be divined and felt than seen,
> And when she comes one yields one's heart perforce,
> As one might yield some noble instrument
> For her to draw its latent music forth.[18]

Published in 1923 in *Poetry* magazine as part of a special issue containing juvenile poems by established poets, the poem was sent with a letter describing Duse's impact on Lowell: "I went to see her, as I always went to see everything that was good in the theatre. The effect was tremendous. What really happened was that it revealed me to myself . . . it loosed a bolt in my brain and I found out where my true function lay."[19]

Both poem and letter stage the emergence of the writing self as an encounter with the other; it is recognition of the other that calls a new self into being—"draw(s) its latent music forth" or, as the letter claims, "revealed me to myself." The moment of revelation is also a moment of liberation—obstacles are removed to reveal, or actualize, what is potentially present. In Lowell's later poem, the sequence of Spenserian sonnets entitled "Eleonora Duse," written to commemorate her meeting with the dying actress in 1923, the speaker remembers and repeats the act of recognition:

> Seeing you after these long lengths of years,
> I only know the glory come again,
> A majesty bewildered by my tears,
> A golden sun. (479)

Within the I/you structure of the poem, the role of the other ("Lady, to whose enchantment I took shape") is acknowledged as engendering the "I" who writes and who renews her tribute with gratitude and "tears." An act of identification, originally unconscious, is brought to consciousness in poetry and the poem draws its power from the ways in which the emotional complexities of the experience are presented in tightly organized sonnets as an act of commemoration.

The title poem of Bryher's first collection of poetry, *Regions of Lutany* (1914), financed by her father and her only work published under the name W. Ellerman, dramatizes not the finding but the search for a muse, a "Mistress imperious" to engender the poet:

> Where is the way to thee,
> Region of Lutany? . . .
> I sought of my soul if the pathway lay there,
> Song vanished away, as the bird in the air, . . .
>
> I cannot reach to thee,
> Mistress imperious
> O thou mysterious
> Region of Lutany.

The poem has some of the weaknesses (cliché/inversion/archaism) that Lowell later criticized about her own first poem to Duse, but it is, I think, crucial to an understanding of Bryher's next work, *Amy Lowell: A Critical Appreciation* (1918).

Lowell's first contact with imagism and the New Poetry (via Harriet Monroe in Chicago) triggered her recognition that "I too am an Imagiste" and a trip to London in the summer of 1913.[20] Bryher, in her short critical study, recounts the younger poet's discovery of Lowell's work in the middle of the First World War, how her *Six French Poets* (1915) and *Tendencies in Modern American Poetry* (1917) opened the world of modern poetry, introduced her to imagism and led her to H.D. and what became a life-long partnership with the American poet: "I wanted a new world, and in the Imagist writers—particularly in Miss Lowell—all I needed lay before my eyes."[21] However, despite the claim to be "dumbed with admiration," the hero of the essay is not the poet Lowell, but the first-person critic Bryher, who casts herself as a sailor, a voyager adrift in seas of traditional verse until she encounters the peaks of Lowell's modernism. Reading Lowell's *Men, Women and Ghosts* (1916), the explorer metaphor transmutes into an eroticized image of Bryher as the fairytale prince who stumbles on a beautiful princess:

> To believe loveliness to be on the point of death and find she was but sleeping—to falter upon her in the stir of her early wakefulness and touch the fluttering petals as they slip from her unused arms. (8)

Unlike Lowell's poems about Duse, where the object of the poem (the addressee/Duse/"you") remains distinct from the subject she inspires and the poet she creates, the idealized object of Bryher's critical appreciation becomes a part-object of the narrating "I." This narrator-critic identifies particular themes (loneliness, solitude, "the hunger for escape," the desire "to be some other person for a day" [13]) and when contrasting Lowell's poetry with that of Robert Frost, finds Frost too "acquiescent," while "Miss Lowell is vital with protest, so aware of injustice and repression" (31). Although these elements are present in Lowell's poetry, Bryher's emphasis on them seems to be a case of finding what she is looking for—or what Melanie Klein would call "projective identification."[22] The essay ends with the claim that "among all poets, Miss Lowell is essentially an explorer"(48)—that is, an ideal image of the writer-critic herself.

After commenting on "how little trace of personal childhood Miss Lowell's poetry contains" (32), Bryher moves on to the historical poems in the *North American Review*, the final section of *Men, Women and Ghosts*, and *Can Grande's Castle*. What she admires in "Malmaison" (1916), which portrays Lowell and Bryher's hero Napoleon Bonaparte as a great liberator, is Lowell's ability to actualize the past in poetry: "only the intuition of a poet . . . could regather a vanished age and make it seem the present as we read" (31). In "Guns as Keys; and the Great Gate Swings" (1917), which she calls "an epic of modernity" (39), she finds two concepts of liberty, as Isaiah Berlin was later to describe them: negative liberty, which is freedom from constraint, and positive liberty, which is the freedom to realize one's ideal self. Lowell's historical poetry was to have a profound influence on Bryher's writing, but before she wrote her own "polyphonic" representations of the past as historical fiction, Bryher set out to engage with her own history. Encouraged by Lowell and H.D., she produced a trilogy of autobiographical fictions which address the theme she had found so powerfully dealt with in Lowell's poem "Pickthorn Manor"(1916) that "[r]epression is an evil thing" (22).

Divided Selves

The female voice may be universally described as divided, but it must be recognized as divided in a multitude of ways.
—Barbara Johnson, *A World of Difference*

Bryher's *Development* (1920) and *Two Selves* (1923) chart in imagist prose the growing consciousness of a woman and a writer through childhood and adolescence. The heroine, Nancy, has an epic childhood, full of travel and adventure, before entering, at the age of fifteen, into an oppressive schooling in conventional femininity. *Development*, like Lowell's essay "Poetry, Imagination, Education" (1917), is, among other things, a diatribe against utilitarian and vocational education that stresses the crippling effects of repressing a child's freedom to develop according to its own emotional and intellectual needs. It speaks to the ongoing debates in England around the1918 Education Act,[23] which give it a certain topicality. A narrow, powerful novel, *Development* offers a vivid contrast between the imaginative value of travel and the freedom of intellectual exploration, and the regimented, impoverished schooling available in middle-class girls' schools of the period. It stems directly from Bryher's own experience (her "personal childhood"), whereas Lowell's essay, which includes her research into the contents of a "large public library near Boston," makes the case for imagination in more impersonal terms.[24] Allowing that "facts are most important things, but fancies are important too" (39), Lowell argues for the importance of "literature, and more especially poetry, and more especially still, contemporary poetry" (34) in the development of individuality and imagination. She supports her argument by appeals to American individualism against "such a man-made people as the Germans" but also stresses the importance of extending access to education ("A democracy can only succeed through an enlightened proletariat"; 33). Despite differences of form, there is a remarkable convergence between Bryher's and Lowell's positions: both are passionate about educational reform, both pose the question of access, and both see poetry as central to the development of the imagination.

The protest element in *Development* supports an oppositional construction of the self—as outside or against—the institutions of family, race, class, and nation. Bryher's *Two Selves*, which Susan Stanford Friedman suggests took the idea for its title from Lowell's "The Sisters," continues this theme:

Two selves. Jammed against each other, disjointed and ill-fitting. An obedient Nancy with heavy plaits tied over two ears that answered "yes, no, yes, no," according as the wind blew. A boy, a brain, that planned adventures and sought wisdom.[25]

Bryher's fictional persona, Nancy, is presented as a divided self—yes/ no, girl/boy, conformist/rebel—and this splitting provides an alter ego, gendered male, with which to escape a subordinate feminine position: "She, herself, could escape into her other self. Swing her legs over a chair, and shout 'to hell with marriage, patriotism, duty, they are lies, lies, lies.'"[26]

In this novel, set during the First World War, Nancy identifies "freedom" (to think, to write, to travel, to find a friend) with the other gender. In terms of Freud's definition of identification cited above, she "assimilates an aspect, property or attribute of the other and is transformed, wholly or partially, after the model the other provides." Only at the end of the novel, in a chapter entitled "Meeting," when she encounters a same-sex love-object, can the split-off feminine side of herself be reembraced. Throughout the novel, freedom from internal conflict is linked to writing. "I want to be free," she writes, "To win freedom I must write a book";[27] the words *free* and *freedom* are repeated throughout the text, and their importance for the fictive persona, Nancy, can be traced through to the writing persona that Winifred Ellerman constructed for herself as Bryher.[28]

The theme of freedom is continued in *West* (1925), the third and last of Bryher's autobiographical fictions, which narrates Nancy's face-to-face encounter with Miss Lyall (Lowell) in the land of the free. The difficulties and delays of entering the country provide the first check on Nancy's idealization of America, and she is soon forced to recognize that it is not just the other of England— freedom to its lack of freedom—but that it has its own rules and regulations. The long postponed meeting with the muse/idealized other occupies a single chapter but is central to the affiliation drama staged in this novel. While they share an appreciation of New York as "Punic," "barbaric," and "epical,"[29] Nancy's uncritical identification with Miss Lyall receives a check when the latter urges her to go back to England as an ambassador for the New American Poetry: "No, Miss Lyall. I came to America to get away from what people expected me to do. Their life and the old code of thought hasn't any meaning for me. I've been through the war. And now I must find a new path."[30]

In this dialogue, the older poet urges the younger not to associate with the Greenwich Village bohemians and not to be "wild," since "the 'greatest poet is the man who lives as other people live. Conventional in all save words. For what scope of freedom there is, after all, in rhythm . . .' But that was not correct. One had come to America for freedom. For a new outlook if not a new world. Poets seldom lived a conventional life. Because they could not live lies. The ordinary life was a lie. . . . To save anything now there had to be rebellion."[31]

Nancy is presented here as the young pretender, arguing the connection between literary and political radicalism that Miss Lyall's social conservatism seemingly will not admit. At the simplest level, this is a clash between two strong women, and in terms of characterization the scene can be read as a necessary step in Nancy's development. At another level, the dialogue and passage of interior monologue echo the scene from "The Sisters" in which the poet-speaker rejects Elizabeth Barrett Browning's conformism and moves to her declaration of difference—"I cannot write like you." As an autobiographical fiction and roman-à-clef, *West* recounts a confrontation between the ego ideal of Bryher's construction, and the "reality" of the poet she encounters in New York, for the fictional exchange denies the precise qualities ("vital with protest, so aware of injustice and repression") that Bryher had identified in her *Amy Lowell: A Critical Appreciation.* However, the dogmatic reaction ("that was not correct") signals not so much reality testing as the denigration that lies on the other side of ide-alization. As Freud says, "[i]dentification, in fact, is ambivalent from the very first; it can turn into an expression of tenderness as easily as into a wish for someone's removal."[32] The repudiation of Miss Lyall is a necessary part of Nancy's self-construction, for the "removal" of the older poet enables the younger to move on, or in psychoanalytic terms, to reclaim that part of herself (the ego ideal) that she has invested in the other in order to strengthen her identity as a poet.

Identity in Question

> The unspeakable nevertheless makes itself heard through borrowing
> and exploiting the very terms that are meant to enforce its silence.
> —Judith Butler, *Antigone's Claim*

Recent discussions of Lowell's sequence "Planes of Personality: Two Speak Together" in *Pictures of the Floating World* (1919), focus in different ways on the encoding of lesbian desire. Bryher's *Arrow Music* (n.d.; 1922?), the sequence of poems written during her early relationship with H.D., reveals Bryher's different strategies. Borrowing from Greek lyric forms, Bryher exploits late nineteenth-century classicism to evoke same-sex desire, as seen in her poem "Myiskos," where we read of

> the white Lesbian boy
> with his arched and polished lyre;
> the girl with quince-buds
> thrust to match her breasts . . .[33]

Myiskos was the addressee of a number of love poems by the second century B.C.E. poet Menander, and the poet takes his name ("Only your name, Myiskos, they must leave / for me to keep") to present her own modern dilemmas. This classicizing strategy is one that Lowell herself deliberates in a poem entitled "The On-Looker" (1925):

> Suppose I plant you
> Like wide-eyed Helen
> On the battlements
> Of weary Troy,

Clutching the parapet with desperate hands,
She, too, gazes at a battle-field. . . . (46)

As in many of Lowell's poems, an ambiguously gendered speaker addresses a distinctly female "you" linked to history or myth, using images of war and battlefield to stage sexual and emotional conflicts. However, other voices in the poem suggest that restraint may be necessary:

The ancients at her elbow counsel patience and contingencies;
Such to a woman stretched upon a bed of battle,
Who bargained for this only in the whispering arras
Enclosed about a midnight of enchantment. (46)

Paul Lauter, in a brilliant reading of the poem, takes "the bed of battle" to refer to the psychosexual conflicts between same-sex lovers.[34] I would want to argue that it also stages the writer's struggles with various discursive options: "Suppose I plant you" —that is, where will this classical metaphor take me, take my reader? What is gained or lost in the parallel?

While Bryher's love poems generally voice a male position, the identity positions assumed in Lowell's "Two Speak Together" are much more unstable or variable. And this is perhaps the relevance of the Miss Lyall/Nancy dialogue in Bryher's *West*, cited earlier: that while Bryher, both in social and sexual contexts, identifies with an oppositional strategy ("there had to be rebellion"), Lowell, as one of the "ancients at her elbow," seems to "counsel patience and contingencies." While championing the new verse and freedom from metrical straitjackets, Lowell did not share Bryher's rebellious imperatives. She was to find different ways of negotiating her self-divisions, including those of gender and object choice, through the modification of existing conventions.

As Diana Collecott argues, since love poems have for centuries been addressed from "I" to "you," with the sex of both partners often unidentified, the conventions of the traditional lyric have always allowed the expression of same-sex love—as with William Shakespeare, W. H. Auden, and others. Collecott speaks of Lowell's "masculine impersonation" in her love poems to Ada Dwyer Russell,[35] and while this describes some poems in "Two Speak Together" (e.g., "Preparation"), in some the position of the speaker is marked as feminine (e.g., "Interlude"), and in many other poems it is not gender marked. Within the sequence, and sometimes within individual poems, there are shifts between masculine and feminine personae. Whether this variability is read as self-censorship, disguise, or as a camp strategy, it keeps questions of identity and identification open. In Lowell's poetic practice, the erotic frees rather than fixes sexual identity or, as psychoanalytic theory would claim, "At the height of being in love the boundary between ego and object threatens to melt away."[36]

"Two Speak Together" is a highly structured sequence and the opening poems function as an overture to foreground the question of writing. Thus the first poem, "Vernal Equinox," invokes the difference between presentation and representation, ironically recapitulating Lowell's point in *Tendencies* that "Imagism is presentation, not representation."[37] It presents the absence of the beloved as an effect on the present speaker, ending, "Why are you not here to overpower me / with your tense and urgent love?" (209). The next poem, "The Letter," treats the gap between representation and the real, playfully contrasting writing—"Little cramped words scrawling all over / the paper / Like draggled fly's legs"—with "the want of you" (209). In successive poems, this "you," the object of desire, is addressed through a series of self-consciously traditional tropes, as the beloved, spring, Madonna, Venus, a flower, a color—heart of silver"—and so on. The addressee is constituted through these, and through the cadence and tone of the speaker's voice, rather than as the object of gaze, for Lowell's visual imagery is supplemented by appeals to sound, scent, and touch. The erotic and the body, although sometimes directly evoked ("A Sprig of Rosemary"), are more often represented metonymically—in a shawl, a white flower, a bud—"There is nothing to equal a white bud" ("Weather-Cock," 211). Exploiting the convention of representing the female body through landscape,[38] the poet reshapes images of the natural world into different, more cultivated forms: "a smooth and stately garden / With parterres of gold and crimson." Lowell takes the tropes and idioms of romantic love—nature, the seasons, the elements—and deploys them allusively, ironically, and, for the most part, very effectively.

The lyric, expressive mode of "Two Speak Together" has led critics to read these poems as autobiographical, addressed to a particular lover or other—the Ada Russell to whom Amy Lowell wished to dedicate the volume. This, it seems to me, is only part of the story. For Lowell in "Two Speak Together" and in the later sequence of poems in the same volume, entitled "As Toward One's Self," is critically concerned with self/other relations, the modifications of consciousness made in relation to a series of real and imaginary others. The very titles signal these issues to the reader: who are "these two" who speak together? Are they one and the same? Who is speaking to whom? And what is it to write "toward one's self"? The lyric, in Lowell's use, is an encounter with the other, but the apostrophized other is not always or simply the "outside other" (the beloved who tells her the peonies need spraying); it may also present an "inside other," a part of the speaker that the poem seeks to address—hence "as toward oneself."

As Jonathan Culler argues, citing Percy Bysshe Shelley, the apostrophe may involve an internal drama where "I," "you," and "they" are "merely marks to denote the different modifications of the one mind."[39] Lowell's use of the apostrophe, I would argue, is complex in this sense. Not only is the identity of the subject-speaker unstable or variable, so too is that of the addressee, the object of the apostrophe. And if the object of desire can be, and in this sequence *is*, represented in so many different images from classical, religious, romantic and domestic contexts, it raises questions about the identity of the loved one and the identity politics of the lyric. In one reading, the multiple images serve simply to intensify the expressive function, to magnify the significance of the loved one. In another—Shelleyan—reading, it enacts the transformations and activity of the internal world, the mind's dialogue with itself. One might also say, at another level of reading, that the plethora of images gestures toward what escapes or is beyond representation—what the romantics might call the "ineffable" or what Jacques Lacan would call "the real." Lowell's poems admit all these readings.

So while, like Bryher's *Two Selves*, Lowell's "Two Speak Together" can be read as a coded coming out—a number of poems are superb examples of a lyrical celebration of the beloved and the state of being in love—the sequence also offers a much fuller taxonomy of emotional states. Love in these lyrics is not simply a resolution of conflict (as at the end of *Two Selves*) but is itself generative, and many of the poems in "Two Speak Together" dramatize the intricate ways in which love generates other emotions, such as fear, loss, and anxiety— see "Nerves," "Strain," and "The Wheel of the Sun." As Longinus says of Sappho's poetry, it deals with "not one emotion but a concourse of emotions."[40]

While dealing with love, sentiment, and "feeling," the poetry actively rethinks the materials it works with, for in Lowell's poetic practice, thinking and feeling are not alternative but linked human activities. Her struggle to hold the two together against the standard (gendered) opposition is thus a radical one. She is a poet of ideas not only in her narrative and symbolic poetry but also in her use of the lyric where indeterminacy and paradox link it to specifically modern conceptions of subjectivity: the interactive nature of identity; the language-based nature of consciousness; the embodied nature of being and the temporality of different states of being. As Suzanne Clark notes in *Sentimental Modernism*, "The degradation of sentimental writing, made to represent the emotional fakery of women's pleadings, has covered over the transgressive content of the sentimental, its connection to a sexual body, and its connection to the representations of consciousness."[41]

So while Ezra Pound feared that sentiment would dilute imagism into "Amygism" and D. H. Lawrence warned Lowell about the dangers of "uttering pure sensations *without concepts*," both, it seems to me, missed the crucial point that, as Anna Karina puts it in *Pierrot le Fou,* "il y a des idées dans les sentiments."

Beyond Imagism

> *Someday you will have an emotion that the "image" will not carry:*
> *then where are you?*
> —May Sinclair to Richard Aldington, c. 1915

Bryher and Lowell's friendship began with their discovery of imagism, which they supported as a movement and assimilated as a technique, but both moved beyond it—perhaps for the reasons suggested in May Sinclair's question to Aldington. Lowell's commitment to registering the complexities of "emotion" took her back into a lifelong engagement with the romantics—from Shelley, from whom she had taken the title of her first volume, to Keats, whose biography she finished shortly before her death. She uses the legacy of the romantics, as I

have argued above, to rethink and modernize categories of thinking and feel-
ing, self and other, masculine and feminine, becoming in the process a poet of
modern consciousness—rather like Dorothy Richardson, whom Lowell, like
Bryher and May Sinclair so much admired.[42] Louis Untermeyer, in a comment
on Lowell's early imagist poetry, calls her "a poet of the external world," but
that description—though in accord with her own theories of "externality" and
the "unrelated method" in earlier critical writing—upholds the very oppositions
that her later poetry calls into question.[43]

     Although in one of her poems ("The Doll," 1926), the speaker claims to
"thank God I had read Freud," Lowell was evidently a resistant reader; as she
wrote in 1917, "To suppose that all life under the surface consists of violent
sexual desires crushed out or sublimated, that all personal relation is a war of
sexual antagonisms is to see life through a perfectly distorted medium."[44] Skep-
tical about Freud and psychoanalysis, Lowell worked on different kinds of an-
tagonisms in and through her poetry. Horace Gregory claims that Lowell used
her writing as a self-imposed therapy and despite the hostile tenor of that com-
ment, it is true that Lowell chose a writing cure rather than "the talking cure"
that Bryher embarked upon.[45] While H.D.'s analysis and her account of it in
Tribute to Freud have been the subject of considerable attention from both lit-
erary critics and historians of psychoanalysis, the full story of Bryher's involve-
ment with psychoanalysis in the 1930s has only recently come to light. Using
unpublished letters between Bryher and H.D., among others, Maggie Magee and
Diana Miller provide a fascinating account of Bryher's training analysis with
Hanns Sachs in Berlin, her reservations about the English analytic community
and their attitudes toward homosexuality, her extensive financial support for
friends in analysis, and the endowment of a fund for analytic candidates and
refugee analysts arriving in America.[46]

     But if what Bryher did for psychoanalysis is becoming increasingly clear,
what it did for her is less so—a study of the psychoanalytic elements in her writ-
ing is yet to be written. And despite her Freudian analysis and the fact that she
almost became an analyst herself, Bryher's definition of her own sexual iden-
tity remained in some ways pre-Freudian, closer to that offered her by Have-
lock Ellis in 1919 when he agreed that "apparently I am quite justified in
pleading I ought to be a boy,—I am just a girl by accident."[47] It would appear
that her problematic relationship with Amy Lowell also remained unresolved;
she returns to it several times in *Heart to Artemis*, writing, "I was a disappoint-
ment to her eventually" and "Amy Lowell was disappointed in me."[48] While
this might mean, as the *West* portrait seems to suggest, that Bryher was in fact
disappointed with the older poet, it bears a curious resemblance to Lowell's com-
ment in "The Sisters" that her literary sisters left her feeling "sad and self-
distrustful / For older sisters are very sobering things."

     Heart to Artemis goes on to describe a later moment, in 1938, when Bryher,
after years of relative silence, found a new direction for her writing: "We crossed
the Arctic Circle on a bus," she writes, "and as I watched the reindeer moving

between the birches, I knew that, apart from my refugees, I had been following the wrong path. I did not belong to the literary movements nor even to a particularly intellectual group. I was an Elizabethan who needed action and the sea. I should only become a writer when I had returned to my proper material."[49]

The return of the swashbuckling Elizabethan! By switching genres and material, Bryher found a new voice and the cross-gendered personae of her historical fiction anticipate many practices adopted by later generations of the "queer lot." Action-packed, with atmospheric detail and anachronistic dialogue, her eight historical novels were read as children's fiction by her contemporaries. Like her *Arrow Music* poems, most of them are set in time of war: World War II in *Beowulf* (1952), and war between Saxons and Normans (*The Fourteenth of October,* 1952), Greeks and Lucanians (*Gate to the Sea,* 1958), and Romans and Carthaginians (*The Coin of Carthage,* 1963). Although generally narrated from a male point of view, as Ruth Hoberman points out,[50] in these and her other novels, (*The Player's Boy,* 1953, *Ruan,* 1960, and *The January Tale,* 1966) she reworks traditional male plotlines by creating multiple—sometimes conflicting—narrative perspectives. Undermining a single, authoritative notion of history, her narrative strategies stress the constructed nature of historical discourse and the possibility of alternative versions.

Bryher's revisionist treatment of the past, like H.D.'s view of history as protean and palimpsestic, is informed in part by Jane Harrison's feminist anthropology, but arguably also draws on her experience of the psychoanalytic process—the ways in which events are selected to tell different stories about the past. Concerned with histories of the defeated rather than the victors, the novels feature the bystanders as well as the main actors of traditional histories. An identification with conquered peoples is evident in *Roman Wall* (1954), which contrasts the enslaved feminine figures of Greeks, women, and traders with their masculine, law-ridden Roman conquerors. Bryher returns to the Romans in *The Coin of Carthage* and the author's preface makes her historical aims clear: since the Romans destroyed the Carthaginian libraries, the familiar stories about Hannibal are based on Roman sources and that this is "as if England had been defeated in 1940 and we were trying to describe the last hours of London only from enemy accounts." Like the work of Walter Benjamin, whom she tried to help escape as the Germans advanced on Paris, Bryher's postwar historical fiction can be read as an attempt to articulate the connection between her own era and the conflicts of the past, and to give voice to those who have been silenced in mainstream accounts. These are the very qualities that forty years earlier she had found so compelling in Lowell's historical poems. Had she been able to read Bryher's later writing, Lowell would not, I think, have been disappointed.

Notes

1. See, particularly, Betsy Erkkila, *The Wicked Sisters: Women Poets, Literary History, and Discord* (New York: Oxford University Press, 1992), 8–14.

2. Judith Butler, *Antigone's Claim: Kinship between Life and Death* (New York: Columbia University Press, 2000), 74.
3. Suzanne Juhasz, *Naked and Fiery Forms: Modern American Poetry by Women: A New Tradition* (New York: Harper and Row, 1976), 1.
4. Sigmund Freud, "Family Romances" (1909), in *The Standard Edition of the Complete Psychological Works of Sigmund Freud,* vol. 9, ed. James Strachey (London: Hogarth Press, 1959), 237; the *Standard Edition* is hereafter cited as *SE.*
5. Jean Gould, *Amy: The World of Amy Lowell and the Imagist Movement* (New York: Dodd, Mead, 1975), 244.
6. There are seventy-five letters from Bryher in the Lowell correspondence files at the Houghton Library, Harvard University.
7. Gillian Hanscombe and Virginia L. Smyers, *Writing for their Lives: The Modernist Women, 1910–1940* (London: The Women's Press, 1987), 35.
8. Ibid., 36.
9. Celeste Schenk, "Exiled by Genre: Modernism, Community and the Politics of Exile," in *Women's Writing in Exile,* ed. Mary Lynn Broe and Angela Ingram (Chapel Hill: University of North Carolina Press, 1989), 231.
10. Hanscombe and Smyers, *Writing,* 46.
11. Gould, *Amy,* 304.
12. Such networks are currently being studied by the (specifically modernist) project Reti di Donne/Networking Women centered in Italy: women modernists "considered in their role of founders of journals and publishing houses, . . . critical junctions of a complex network of human, political, cultural and literary relations." Website: http://reti.unimc.it/index1.asp.
13. See J. Laplanche and J.-B. Pontalis, *The Language of Psycho-analysis,* trans. Donald Nicholson-Smith (London: Hogarth Press and the Institute of Psycho-analysis, 1973), 206–207.
14. Ibid., 205.
15. Sigmund Freud, "Group Psychology and the Analysis of the Ego" (1921), in *SE* vol. 18 (1955), 129.
16. See Sigmund Freud, "On Narcissism" (1914) in *SE* vol. 14 (1957); "Group Psychology" (1921), in *SE* vol. 18 (1955); and "The Ego and the Id" (1923), in *SE* vol. 19 (1961).
17. Bryher found a parallel source of inspiration in the 1920s German film actress Elisabeth Bergner, whose long career was coincidentally crowned by the Eleonora Duse Prize in 1982.
18. Amy Lowell, "Eleonora Duse," in *The Complete Poetical Works of Amy Lowell* (Boston: Houghton Mifflin Company, 1955), 593. All quotations from Lowell's poetry are from this volume and are cited parenthetically in the text.
19. Amy Lowell, note accompanying the poem "Eleonora Duse," *Poetry: A Magazine of Verse* 22 (1923): 271–272.
20. S. Foster Damon, *Amy Lowell: A Chronicle with Extracts from Her Correspondence* (Boston: Houghton Mifflin, 1935), 196.
21. Bryher, *Amy Lowell: A Critical Appreciation* (London: Eyre and Spottiswoode, 1918), 9. Further references to this work in the section are by page number.
22. Laplanche and Pontalis, *Psycho-analysis,* 356.
23. This, the so-called Fisher Act, provided, among other things, for universal schooling

up to age fourteen; see A.J.P. Taylor, *English History 1914–1945* (Harmondsworth, England: Penguin, 1970), 241.

24. Amy Lowell, "Poetry, Imagination and Education," *North American Review* 206 (1917), reprinted in Lowell, *Poetry and Poets* (Boston and New York: Houghton Mifflin, 1930); page numbers in this paragraph refer to the latter. The case for educational reform arguably covers another set of repressions in Bryher's childhood, as Susan Stanford Friedman suggests in *Psyche Reborn: The Emergence of H.D.* (Bloomington: Indiana University Press, 1987), 35–36.

25. Bryher, *Two Selves* (Paris: Contact, 1923), 5.

26. Ibid., 82.

27. Ibid., 218.

28. H.D. wrote to Amy Lowell in 1918 that Bryher had changed her name because her father was reputed to be "the richest man in England." Lowell's reply, while describing Bryher's self-consciousness as "extremely foolish," admits that "it is a handicap to be even well-off." Correspondence quoted in Barbara Guest, *Herself Defined: The Poet H.D. and Her World* (London: Collins, 1985), 109.

29. Bryher, *West* (London: Jonathan Cape, 1925), 23.

30. Ibid., 29.

31. Ibid., 31–32.

32. Freud, "Group Psychology," 105.

33. Bryher, "Myiskos," in *Arrow Music* (n.p., n.d.—1922?). Bryher's two books of poetry are posted by the Women Writers' Research Project online at http://chaucer.library.emory.edu/wwrp/ index.html.

34. Paul Lauter, "Amy Lowell and Cultural Borders," in this volume and in *Speaking the Other Self: American Women Writers,* ed. Jeanne Campbell Reesman (Athens: University of Georgia Press, 1997), 288–294.

35. Diana Collecott, "What Is Not Said: A Study in Textual Inversion," in *Sexual Sameness: Textual Differences in Lesbian and Gay Writing,* ed. Joseph Bristow (London: Routledge, 1992), 101.

36. Sigmund Freud, "Civilization and its Discontents" (1930), in *SE* vol. 11 (1957), 66.

37. Amy Lowell, *Tendencies in Modern American Poetry* (New York: Macmillan, 1917) 245.

38. According to Sigmund Freud, "The complicated topography of the female genital parts makes one understand how it is that they are often represented as landscapes." See Freud, "Introductory Lectures on Psycho-Analysis" (1916), in *SE* vol. 15 (1961), 156.

39. Jonathan Culler, *The Pursuit of Signs: Semiotics, Literature, Deconstruction* (London: Routledge and Kegan Paul, 1981), 148.

40. Longinus, "On the Sublime," in *Classical Literary Criticism*, trans. and intro. by T. S. Dorsch (Harmondsworth, England: Penguin, 1965), 114–115.

41. Suzanne Clark, *Sentimental Modernism: Women Writers and the Revolution of the Word* (Bloomington: Indiana University Press, 1991), 7.

42. Bryher used the label "a poet of consciousness" to describe Richardson. See also Jean Radford, *Dorothy Richardson* (Bloomington: Indiana University Press, 1991).

43. For a useful account of Lowell and "externality" see Richard Benvenuto, *Amy Lowell* (Boston: Twayne, 1985), chapter 2.

44. Amy Lowell to Helen Bullis Kizer, 23 October 1917, cited in Damon, *Amy Lowell: A Chronicle,* 431.

45. Ibid., 431; see also Horace Gregory, *Amy Lowell: Portrait of the Poet in Her Time* (New York: Thomas Nelson and Sons, 1958), 208–209.
46. Maggie Magee and Diana C. Miller, *Lesbian Lives: Psychoanalytic Narratives Old and New* (Hillsdale, N.J.: Analytic Press, 1997), chapter 1.
47. Bryher to H.D., 20 March 1919, cited in Magee and Miller, *Lesbian Lives*, 5.
48. Bryher, *The Heart to Artemis: A Writer's Memoirs* (New York: Harcourt, Brace and World, 1962) 184, 203.
49. Ibid., 287.
50. Ruth Hoberman, *Gendering Classicism: The Ancient World in Twentieth-Century Women's Fiction* (Albany: State University of New York Press, 1997).

"Which, Being Interpreted, Is as May Be, or Otherwise"

ADA DWYER RUSSELL IN AMY LOWELL'S LIFE AND WORK

LILLIAN FADERMAN

Amy Lowell first met Ada Dwyer Russell, an actress, in 1909, when Russell appeared in Boston in *The Dawn of a Tomorrow*. Three years later Russell returned to Boston to play the character lead in *The Deep Purple*, and their intimate relationship ostensibly began. Russell, at forty-nine Lowell's senior by eleven years, was charming, cultured, poised, intelligent, and feminine—in short, everything Lowell sought in a muse, a lover, and, as she expressed it in "A Fairy Tale" (1912), a travel companion "along the parching highroad of the world." She invited Russell to spend the summer of 1912 on her country estate in New Hampshire and then to accompany her to England where Lowell, who had recently discovered the imagist movement, planned to meet with Ezra Pound. Russell did not go to England because she was committed to a road company tour, but she did spend the following summer with Lowell, again on Lowell's country estate. As S. Foster Damon, a personal friend of the couple's and Lowell's first biographer, suggests, it was then that Lowell proposed a permanent relationship. Russell refused for the short term and continued touring but promised to reconsider Lowell's proposal once the tour was over. Clearly, Lowell had difficulty bridling her impatience. At one point, in February of 1914, she sought Russell out when the actress was playing in Chicago and again proposed that she give up the stage and come live with her.[1]

What passed between them cannot be determined with absolute certainty since Lowell asked that their letters to each other be destroyed upon her death, but it is possible to conjecture Lowell's emotional state during these years from the apparently autobiographical poems of her second volume, *Sword Blades and Poppy Seed* (1914). The poem "Patience," for example, appears to answer Russell's plea for more time. Lowell's response is that Russell is so perfect, so much what the poet needs, that she cannot help her impatience. As in many of her love poems to Russell, she represses what Margaret Anderson described as her "Roman emperor" persona,[2] presenting herself as imploring, apologetic, and entirely at the mercy of the beloved who, in a series of images, is depicted as goddess, mother, healer, and holder of the sole and elemental power to rescue the speaker from alienation and pain:

> Be patient with you?
>   You! My sun and moon!
> My basket full of flowers!
>   My money-bag of shining dreams! My hours,
>   Windless and still, of afternoon!
> You are my world and I your citizen.
>   What meaning can patience have then?[3]

Other poems of this volume continue Lowell's suppliant lover's tone. In "Apology," a poem in which she employs the imagery of chivalry, Lowell is a young knight who is ecstatic that (s)he has been granted her beloved's favors, but (s)he has been sworn to silence:

> You blazon me with jewelled insignia
> . . . And yet
>   You set
> The word upon me, unconfessed
>   To go unguessed. (36)

The poem itself is, of course, an instance of her loving disobedience. Not only does she admit here that she has been shouting the secret of her good fortune everywhere, but the poem publishes the secret for posterity to see:

> Be not angry with me that I bear
>   Your colours everywhere,
>   All through each crowded street,
>   And meet
>   the wonder-light in every eye,
>   As I go by. (36)

The "Apology" of the title is therefore wittily undercut by her demonstration that she glories in divulging their secret—though by omitting gender reference and relying on what has been a universal assumption of heterosexuality in love poetry she does keep its lesbian content closeted. (Readers who wish to be unaware of it can permit themselves to be charmed by the role reversal: a female knight addressing a presumably male beloved.)

Lowell's uncertainties in the course of her courtship are revealed in this volume as well. "The Taxi," for example, expresses confusion and anger at the separations from Russell that are imposed on her:

> When I go away from you
> The world beats dead
> Like a slackened drum.
> I call out for you against the jutted stars
> And shout into the ridges of the wind.
> Streets come fast,
> One after the other,
> Wedge you away from me,
> And the lamps of the city prick my eyes
> So that I can no longer see your face.
> Why should I leave you,
> To wound myself upon the sharp edges of the night? (43)

But this demanding tone is rare in these courtship poems, even those that hint at Lowell's unhappy struggle as she sought commitment from Russell before the actress was ready to give it. Typically, Lowell is apologetic, turning her anger inward, criticizing herself for her impatience. In "A Blockhead" she is furious with her own "too hasty hand," which she holds responsible for threatening that which had brought her joy (36). Perhaps Russell delivered an ultimatum at this point, insisting that Lowell cease pressuring her or risk losing her. The same self-castigation is reflected in her short poem, "A Bungler":

> You glow in my heart
> Like the flames of uncounted candles.
> But when I go to warm my hands,
> My clumsiness overturns the light,
> And then I stumble
> Against the tables and chairs. (41)

In "Stupidity" Lowell depicts herself as a lover who bruised her beloved's fragile rose by her "clumsy touch," and she chides herself, swearing she is even more grieved by her action than the beloved (37).

In May 1914, Russell accepted another invitation to accompany Lowell to Europe, and there the two agreed to a trial arrangement upon their return: for six months Russell would share Lowell's home, Sevenels, in a business arrangement, assisting the poet with her literary pursuits and receiving for her work the same sum she would have earned had she continued on stage during those months.[4] The great success of the trial period is attested to by the fact that Russell remained to trudge "the parching highroad of the world" (albeit in grand style) with Lowell until Lowell's death eleven years later. She became not only Lowell's muse and lover, but also, as the nickname that Lowell coined for her suggests, her rock: Ada was Pete, Peter, or Mrs. Peter (the latter perhaps in deference to her essential femininity). Elizabeth Sergeant, an intimate of the two, observed in 1927, shortly after Lowell's death, that the poet had accomplished ten times more in the last decade and a half of her life than most do in a half century.[5] Sergeant was surely aware that the preponderance of Lowell's vast accomplishments dated from 1912, the year Russell came into her life. Lowell's literary output during those years include nine books of poetry, four books of prose, the editing of five anthologies, and numerous appearances all over the country as a popular reader of her own work. And, as Lowell acknowledged, it was Russell who made that prodigious output possible, not only in her roles of mate and muse but also in her vast variety of other functions: overseer of the estate, wifely presider over Lowell's table and cocktail parties, virtual bodyguard, governess to Lowell's ill-mannered youth persona, literary assistant, and consultant. Russell critiqued Lowell's poems, read page proofs, supervised her secretaries, soothed her ruffled feathers over bad reviews or literary disputes, soothed the ruffled feathers of others when Lowell had been too brusque with them, got rid of intrusive guests, and even coached Lowell in preparation of the dramatic monologues she read in public and on which so much of her reputation was (unfortunately) based. Russell was as lovingly solicitous of Lowell's welfare and as much a cheerleader of her success as Alice B. Toklas was of Gertrude Stein's.

Lowell admitted that she "owed everything to Ada," and she even suggested, only half-joking, that they erect a sign above the doorway at Sevenels: "Lowell and Russell, Makers of Fine Poems."[6] In lieu of that charming but perhaps too-telling gesture, Lowell hoped at least to dedicate her books to Russell, who forbade that tribute, finally relenting only with the last book Lowell saw to publication, her biography of John Keats. It may be that Russell gave permission for this dedication because, unlike most of Lowell's books, the Keats biography contained no love poetry to her and therefore could not have identified her to the public as the lesbian beloved and muse. But Lowell, like the knight in her poem "Apology" who cannot keep herself from boasting of her good fortune despite her promises to her beloved to maintain their secret, dedicated her Keats biography, "To A.D.R., This, and all my books. A. L."

The effect of Russell's presence on Lowell is the subject of numerous poems, some that were published during the poet's life; others—which may have been considered too revealing to be published while Lowell lived—were included in *Ballads for Sale* (1927), a posthumous volume edited by Russell two years after Lowell's death. These poems often reflect Lowell's view of their domestic bliss. In "Thorn Piece," for example, Lowell talks about the world being dark, but her beloved, who is gendered here by her bright dress, carries a lantern. The autobiographical details in the poem make it clear that the ungendered speaker is Lowell, who thanks Russell for having given her "fire, / And love to comfort, and speech to bind, / And the common things of morning and evening" (556). In another poem from *Ballads for Sale*, "On Christmas Eve," she again thanks the beloved other woman for having

lifted my eyes and made me whole,
And given me purpose, and held me faced
Toward the horizon you once had placed
As my aim's grand measure" (557).

Another poem, "A Decade," which reflects on their years together, concludes, "I am completely nourished" (217).

The greatest conflict in their relationship seems to have stemmed from Lowell's jealousy of Russell's visits to her daughter, who married soon after Russell came to live with Lowell. Lowell seems to have finally solved the problem of her beloved's periodic "desertions" by convincing her to invite her daughter and son-in-law (and later, grandchild) to Sevenels for their vacations and ultimately making them her family, too.

With Russell presiding over Lowell's table and her drawing room the couple became this continent's counterpart of Gertrude Stein and Alice B. Toklas in the social realm as well as the personal. Their friends, who were lured not only by Lowell's force and power but also by Russell's graciousness and charm, included many of the leading Anglo-American literary lights: Conrad Aiken, Robert Frost, D. H. Lawrence, Compton Mackenzie, Archibald MacLeish, Sara Teasdale, Louis Untermeyer, Elinor Wylie, and, of course, numerous lesbian couples, including Margaret Anderson and Jane Heap, and Bryher and H.D.

It is interesting to note that many of their heterosexual friends were in fact homophobic (or, more specifically, "lesbophobic"), but like Ernest Hemingway in his relationship with Stein and Toklas, they made an "exception" for Lowell and Russell. Lawrence's loving correspondence with Lowell, in which he ended every letter by sending his and Frieda's love to both Amy and Ada, did not prevent him from writing his lesbian-hating novella *The Fox;* nor did Compton Mackenzie refrain from penning his lesbian satire *Extraordinary Women* despite his fondness for Lowell and Russell and the fact that Lowell came to his defense when one of his novels was censored in Boston. Perhaps they knew and did not know at the same time that Lowell and Russell were a lesbian couple. The era seems to have encouraged such willful denial, but that denial also made possible, in an era when censorship was rife in American literature, the publication of some of the most remarkable, barely encoded, lesbian poems since Sappho.

Warding Off the "Watch and Ward Society"

As a mover and shaker in the literary world, a position she merited by virtue of both her social status and her popular success as a writer, Amy Lowell pioneered in the battle against censorship. She fought the Comstock Society's efforts to suppress Theodore Dreiser's novel *The Genius*, and she opposed the Boston banning of works by Compton Mackenzie and D. H. Lawrence. She claimed to believe, as she wrote H. L. Mencken in support of his battle against censorship, "No country can hope to develop itself, unless its authors are permitted to educate it."[7]

But despite her expressed opposition to literary censorship, Lowell prided herself on being a pragmatist. In a 1915 letter to Richard Aldington she warned the novelist about the power and influence of the "Watch and Ward Society" and the necessity of eschewing in writing what it would find objectionable.[8] In 1918 she wrote D. H. Lawrence about his refusal to be practical about such matters. His novel *The Rainbow* had been suppressed because of two erotic passages—a heterosexual love scene between Ursula and Anton, and a lesbian scene between Ursula and Winifred. As Lowell admonished,

> I know there is no use in counseling you to make concessions to public opinions in your books and, although I regret sincerely that you cut yourself off from being published by an outspokenness which the English public does not understand, I regret it not in itself . . . but simply because it keeps the world from knowing what a great novelist you are. I think that you could top them all if you would be a little more reticent on this one subject [of sex]. You need not change your attitude a particle, you can simply use an india rubber [eraser] in certain places, and then you can come into your own as it ought to be. . . . When one is surrounded by prejudice and blindness, it seems to me that the only thing to do is to get over in spite of it and not constantly run foul of these same prejudices which, after all, hurts oneself and the spreading of one's work, and does not do a thing to right the prejudice.[9]

Needless to say, Lawrence did not take her advice seriously, but much of Lowell's own writing was predicated on such a view. With regard to lesbian subject matter in her poetry, she did not "change [her] attitude a particle," but she did "use an india rubber in certain places," though only perfunctorily, rubbing out of much of her love poetry only explicit references that would identify the gender of the speaker. She depended on the probability that her general public would read her love lyrics like her dramatic monologues—that is, assuming that the speaker was a (male) persona—and on the readers' habit of taking for granted heterosexuality in the absence of specific evidence to the contrary.

But her use of the "india rubber" was not more than perfunctory. Unlike her monologues, in her lyric poems the speaker is not characterized into a dramatis persona, and Lowell often furnishes abundant autobiographical facts (e.g., descriptions of her estate, her sheepdogs, her illustrious family name) that make it quite clear to one who knows the details of her life that the speaker and the author of these poems are not disparate. She thus provides a double discourse, revealing herself sufficiently to those who might welcome the revelation while avoiding what would get her into trouble. In this way, Lowell warded off the "Watch and Ward Society" though she produced the most explicit (as well as eloquent and elegant) lesbian love poetry to have been written between the time of Sappho and the 1970s. She thumbed her nose at the forces that would repress her while appearing to have no intention of violating their strictures.

If we can believe the confessions she makes about the way she worked as a writer in her poem "To a Gentleman Who Wanted to See the First Drafts of My Poems in the Interests of Psychological Research into the Workings of the Creative Mind" (1927) Lowell may have revealed even the speaker's gender and more autobiographical references in the early drafts of her love poetry. "To a Gentleman" is based on an actual incident: a professor at the Carnegie Institute of Psychology wanted to analyze, he said, her creative processes. Lowell suspected, as she says in this poem, that he wanted to see when she was using a persona and when she was speaking for herself: "What is I, and what that other? That's your quest." And she refused him access to her early drafts and any other revelations, hinting that only Russell was privy to such secret information: "If I did consent, to please you, I should tell you packs of lies / To one only will I tell it, do I tell it all day long. / Only one can see the patches I work into quilts of song." (Lest we feel guilty for our present dissections, she exonerates us: "Still I have a word, one moment, stop, before you leave this room. / Though I shudder thinking of you wandering through my beds of bloom, / You may come with spade and shovel when I'm safely in the tomb"[535].)

Yet Lowell's quite perfunctory encoding of lesbian subject matter was usually successful in throwing critics off the track, even after she was safely in her tomb. With few exceptions, commentators on her work appear to have believed that her poems of passion were literary exercises and that she revealed herself only in her poems of frustration. A notable exception is the hateful Clement Wood biography *Amy Lowell* (1926), in which he argued the year after she was placed "safely in the tomb" that her work was not "universal" because her love lyrics may "qualify [her] as an impassioned singer of her own desires; and she may well be a laureate of as many as stand beside her [i.e., other lesbians], [but] they do not word a common cry of many hearts."[10]

However, ironically, most critics who bludgeoned her work with an argumentum ad femina in the years after her death usually devalued it not because her passions were lesbian, but because she was an "old maid" who supposedly had no passions at all of her own. They observed that Lowell was overweight and unmarried and therefore, as one critic opined in the *Saturday Review of Literature* in 1927, her work is a "knell of personal frustration . . . an effort to hide the bare walls of the empty chambers of her heart."[11] Thirty years later, another critic wrote that Lowell confessed her lifelong sexual frustration in the opening lines of her monologue "Appuldurcombe Park"(1919) : "I am a woman, sick for passion."[12] Until Jean Gould's 1975 biography, the first book to deal openly with Lowell's lesbian relationships, such outrageous misreading of the poet and her work had been unchallenged—and even subsequent studies, such as Richard Benvenuto's 1985 biography, ignore the significance of her lesbian relationship with Russell. (Benvenuto suggests, for example, that Lowell's poetry expresses "loneliness and longings which she, a fat woman, knew keenly."[13])

Indeed, hundreds of Lowell poems contradict such a reading. Even dramatic monologues and long poems such as "Appuldurcombe Park," "Pickthorne Manor"(1916), and "The Cremona Violin" (1916) may be seen not as expressing the author's personal frustration but rather as a demonstration of her interest in, and experience with, passions that society considered "illicit." Though these poems are about heterosexuals, they provide some commentary on homosexuality inasmuch as they have their source in Lowell's "outlaw" lesbian sensibility. Lowell even teases the reader on this point at times, as with the wittily titled "Which, Being Interpreted, Is as May Be, Or Otherwise," a poem that is ostensibly about a man's illicit lust for a fantasmic married female.

But far more interesting, from the perspective of lesbian reading, are Lowell's many lyric poems that do not rely on the metaphor provided by illicit heterosexuality, as her dramatic poems do, but deal more directly with her passionate interest in another woman. In her numerous long monologue poems, she created always ostensibly heterosexual personae. Unlike her dramatic poems, her lesbian poems are invariably quite short, perhaps because short lyrics excuse the poet from presenting a characterized persona. Her selection of the length of her lesbian poems may indeed have been another means to enable her to encode her forbidden subject matter, to apply the india rubber, to ward off the "Watch and Ward Society."

Amy Lowell as a Poet of Eros

Amy Lowell's lesbian love poems are often fresh, vivid, powerful, and (unlike many of her long poems, such as the famous "Patterns" (1916), with its clichéd heterosexual fantasy scene of a pink and silver female surrendering her soft and willing body to a heavy-booted man in a dashing uniform) they reflect their source in felt emotion. The lesbian poems in *Sword Blades and Poppy Seed* (1914), *Pictures of the Floating World* (1919), *What's O'Clock* (1925), and *Ballads for Sale* (1927), comprise one of the most detailed records in literature of an emotional and erotic relationship between two women, from their sometimes ecstatic, sometimes painful courtship; through the highs and lows of the life they built together; to Lowell's anticipation of its end by her premature death.

Although Lowell admitted in correspondence to friends such as John Livingston Lowes that Russell was the subject of her love poetry, many critics continued to have difficulty acknowledging that Lowell had a real-life source for the impassioned eroticism in her poems, that it was based on feelings she actually experienced.[14] In his 1975 study of Lowell, Glenn Richard Ruihley articulates what may be a major reason for their bafflement: Russell was "past middle age" when Lowell met her, he says, and "not graced with loveliness of face and form." Russell was, in fact, forty-nine when their relationship began, and she was quite beautiful if one's standard does not run to Hollywood starlet types. Ruihley, however, concludes that what Lowell must have loved in Russell was merely her "spiritual beauty," and he asserts that the relationship was therefore "removed . . . to a rare and platonic plane."[15] Under such assumptions one could easily miss the sexual meaning of many of the Ada poems.

Despite her vague attempts at disguise and the heterosexually biased critical obtuseness she could have counted on, Lowell may have felt that some of her lesbian poems were indeed too revealing for publication during her life, though after her death Russell published them in *Ballads for Sale*. Several such poems in the volume, including "Thorn Piece," "On Christmas Eve," "Hippocrene," and "Grievance," offer glimpses into the Lowell-Russell household. Other poems in the volume are astonishingly explicit in their sexual meaning. "Paradox," for example, establishes Russell as the beloved through images that have come to stand for Russell in the body of Lowell's poetry. Here, as in many of the lesbian poems, Russell is associated with amethyst and purple, torches and snow, gardens and moonlight. The opening image, "You are an amethyst to me, / Beating dark slabs of purple," hints at an eroticism that becomes more insistent and even preemptory as the poem progresses:

> Open your purple palaces for my entertainment . . .
> And keep in your brazier always
> One red hot coal;
> For I come at the times which suit me,
> Morning or evening,
> And I am cold when I come down the long alleys to you.
> Clang the doors against the multitude who would follow me.
> Is not this my chamber where I would sleep? (555)

The speaker's baronial tone as she addresses her beloved is offset and undercut by one of the several paradoxes of the poem—the other woman's subjugation of her: "You oversweep me with the splendid flashing of your darkness" (556).

Amy's stated position on sexual subject matter in literature was perhaps as disingenuous as that of Gertrude Stein, who warned the young Ernest Hemingway, much as Lowell warned D. H. Lawrence, that his story, "Up in Michigan," contained too much sexual detail, which made it impractical: it was *inaccrochable*, like a painting with salacious subject matter, which one could never exhibit. "There is no point" in such a work, Stein famously told Hemingway;[16] yet she herself wrote detailed, though encoded, descriptions of lesbian sex and even orgasm in works such as "As a Wife Has a Cow: A Love Story." And so did Lowell: One five-line poem from *Sword Blades and Poppy Seed*, for example, presents bold clitoral imagery that suggests lesbian sex:

> As I would free the white almond from the green husk
> So would I strip your trappings off,
> Beloved.

And fingering the smooth and polished kernel
I should see that in my hands glittered a gem beyond counting. (73)

Although the poem could be interpreted otherwise, Lowell hints at her inten-
tion to give the sexual meaning primacy by titling it "Aubade"—a dawn piece
in which, traditionally, the poet thanks the beloved with whom he has spent the
night for her sexual favors. "A Rainy Night" is explicit about the speaker's erotic
tension in the moments that precede their lovemaking and about her trick for
prolonging the delicious excitement of anticipation. Lowell sets the scene in a
bedroom she shares with her beloved, which is illuminated only by an electric
lamp in the street:

In its silver lustre
I can see the old four-post bed,
With the fringes and balls of its canopy.
You are lying beside me, waiting.
But I do not turn.
In the silver light you would be too beautiful,
And there are ten pleats on this side of the bed canopy,
And ten on the other. (591)

Other poems by Lowell may be read as lesbian primarily by virtue of their per-
spective: the gaze revealed in these poems is erotic and focused exclusively on
a female, such as "In a Garden" (1914) in which the first-person speaker fanta-
sizes that she could see her beloved "White and shining in the silver-flecked
water / While the moon rode over the garden, . . . / Night, and the water, and
you in your whiteness, bathing!" (73)

"On a Certain Critic," the concluding poem of *Pictures of the Floating
World*, teases the reader into believing the literality of such poems by revealing
Lowell's humorous disdain for those who confuse the poet's real lust with meta-
phor. In this poem John Keats (Lowell's alter ego) climbs Box Hill and there
makes love to the Lady of the Moon (Lowell's frequent name for Russell). Keats
and the Lady of the Moon are so close that he confuses his tears for hers. She
is absolutely real to him. Lowell then depicts the poet going home and writing
a poem in memory of the experience. But in years to come, Lowell says, a "sprig"
little gentleman will "turn over your manuscript with his mincing fingers." He
will tabulate places and dates and conclude that Keats could not possibly have
lain with Mistress Moon, that she was only "a copy-book maxim." The critic
will then pontificate "about the spirit of solitude, / And the salvation of genius
through the social order." Lowell wishes that Keats would be there to damn the
critic's density with oaths. And she concludes the poem with a slap at Keats's
critic and very possibly at her own critics as well:

But just snap your fingers,
You and the moon will still love,

When he and his papers have slithered away
In the bodies of innumerable worms. (242)

Two Speak Together

Lowell's most sustained effort at writing lesbian poetry resulted in a forty-three-poem sequence published under the heading "Two Speak Together" in her best-selling 1919 collection, *Pictures of the Floating World*. Judging from internal evidence such as changing and recurring season references, the poems seem to have been written over a four-year period, beginning not long after Lowell and Russell began living together. "A Decade," a poem in which she seems to celebrate their ten-year relationship, is confusing until it is remembered that Lowell first set eyes on Russell in 1909.

The autobiographical content of these poems is seldom disguised. Lowell admitted to friends that Russell was her inspiration, her "Madonna of the Evening Flowers," as one of the poems in this series is entitled;[17] and the poems are rife with references—to Sevenels and its lavish gardens, her animals, her habits such as writing while the rest of the household sleeps—that identify Lowell as the speaker. In "Preparation" a shopkeeper addresses the speaker as "Sir," but this attempt at "drag" is barely perfunctory and the speaker is often revealed to be a woman. For example, in "The Garden by Moonlight" the speaker thinks back through her mother in reflecting on her childless state (and it is impossible not to believe this is Amy Lowell in the garden of Sevenels):

> Ah, Beloved, do you see those orange lilies?
> They knew my mother,
> But who belonging to me will they know
> When I am gone? (212)

In other poems as well, the speaker's gender is identified as female. Sometimes Lowell employs the metaphor of childbirth to describe her literary creations: in "April" she tells her beloved that her happiness with their life together will overflow into poetry:

> I will lie among the little squills
> And be delivered of this overcharge of beauty,
> And that which is born shall be a joy to you
> Who love me. (213)

In "Interlude" she uses the metaphor of traditional female tasks to describe her creation of imagist poems: she is baking cakes and "smoothing the seam of the linen I have been working" (212). Obviously Lowell does not try overly hard to disguise the speaker's gender in this poem, despite the fact that her beloved here is specifically associated with the moon, which is an Ada image in "Two Speak Together" and throughout the Lowell canon.

There is little question that the speaker in all these poems is female, and there is no question whatsoever that the beloved is also female. In several of the poems the beloved is compared to other women of great virtue or beauty such as the Madonna or Venus (and Lowell's role of poet becomes analogous to those of the early modern artists who painted them). In others, Russell is depicted in seductively feminine dress, as in "The Wheel of the Sun": "I see your lifting silks and rejoice" (212). Russell's pastimes are also invariably feminine. In "A Sprig of Rosemary," for example, she sews. In many of the poems she is described in passively feminine terms, protected or made love to by the speaker.

The forty-three poems in "Two Speak Together" tell the story of Lowell and Russell in their first years as a couple. As a poetic sequence that reveals a lesbian relationship to any reader who would care to understand it, "Two Speak Together" was unprecedented in literature and had no equal until Adrienne Rich's sequence, "Twenty-one Love Poems," which was published in 1976. In "Two Speak Together" Lowell reflects the complexity of this relationship: their dyad nourishes Lowell, inspires her work, and arouses her passion, but it also creates great anxieties in her. Her loneliness when Russell leaves her periodically—usually to visit her daughter—is depicted as maddening. In the opening poems, "Vernal Equinox" and "The Letter," which concern the first year, Lowell already finds Russell's brief absence unbearable. Her missing of Russell has clear erotic overtones. In "Vernal Equinox" she demands to know, "Why are you not here to overpower me with your tense and urgent love?" (209). In "The Letter" she laments, employing tropes that will be central to the sequence, "I scald alone, here, under the fire / Of the great moon" (209).

In the next twenty poems of "Two Speak Together" Lowell is happier and fulfilled. She celebrates Russell's beauty in some of her very best work, including "Venus Transiens," in which Lowell compares herself trying to capture Russell on paper with Botticelli's attempt to capture Venus on canvas. Another poem in this sequence, "Madonna of the Evening Flowers" has been, after the far inferior "Patterns," the Lowell poem most likely to be anthologized, though its lesbian source is seldom discussed. It is a seminal poem in which Lowell, who was by no means conventionally pious, introduces the religious metaphors that were to become prevalent in many of her Ada Russell poems:

All day long I have been working,
Now I am tired.
I call: "Where are you?"
But there is only the oak tree rustling in the wind.
The house is very quiet,
The sun shines in on your books,
On your scissors and thimble just put down,
But you are not there.
Suddenly I am lonely:

Where are you?
I go about searching.

Then I see you,
Standing under a spire of pale blue larkspur,
With a basket of roses on your arm.
You are cool, like silver,
And you smile.
I think the Canterbury bells are playing little tunes.
You tell me that the peonies need spraying,
That the columbines have overrun all bounds,
That the pyrus japonica should be cut back and rounded.
You tell me these things.
But I look at you, heart of silver,
White heart-flame of polished silver,
Burning beneath the blue steeples of the larkspur,
And I long to kneel instantly at your feet,
While all about us peal the loud, sweet *Te Deums* of the Canterbury
    bells. (210)

Many of the love poems in the final volume of poetry Lowell prepared before her death, *What's O'Clock*, draw on the religious metaphor that she established in "Madonna of the Evening Flowers." She manages, in the best Jacobean tradition, to combine metaphors of religious worship with metaphors of Eros, but unlike those early poets, in her poems Eros is central. In "In Excelsis," for example, Russell is the Eucharist, Christ, and the beloved of the Songs of Solomon, but she is especially the beautiful woman the speaker longs to devour sexually as well as to worship:

As the perfume of jonquils, you come forth in the morning.
Young horses are not more sudden than your thoughts,
Your words are bees about a pear-tree . . .
I drink your lips,
I eat the whiteness of your hands and feet.
My mouth is open,
As a new jar I am empty and open.
Like white water are you who fill the cup of my mouth . . .
How have you come to dwell with me,
Compassing me with the four circles of your mystic lightness,
So that I say "Glory! Glory! and bow before you
As to a shrine? (444).

In "Prime" (the morning prayer) Russell's voice moves Lowell to worship; in "Vespers" (the evening prayer) Russell herself becomes the object of worship (as well as of lust):

>Last night at sunset,
>The foxgloves were like tall altar candles.
>Could I have lifted you to the roof of the greenhouse, my Dear,
>I should have understood their burning. (444)

Similar religious-erotic images can be found in the posthumous *Ballads for Sale*. In "Thorn Piece," for instance, her beloved is again an object of both reverence and sexual passion. Russell's dress here is "red as a Cardinal's cloak. / I kneel at the trace of your feet on the grass" (556).

In the "Two Speak Together" sequence the worshipful "Madonna of the Evening Flowers" is followed by a number of poems that are patent celebrations of Lowell and Russell's sexual relationship. Some of these poems, however, suggest that Russell sometimes withholds herself. In "Wheat-in-the-Ear," for instance, the speaker declares, "My hands are flames seeking you, / But you are as remote from me as a bright pointed planet / Set in the distance of an evening sky" (211). Another poem in the sequence, "The Artist," chides Russell, demanding to know, "Why do you subdue yourself in golds and purples? / Why do you dim yourself with folded silks?" Lowell fantasizes her nakedness:

>How pale you would be, and startling,
>How quiet. . . .
>You would quiver like a shot-up spray of water,
>You would waver, and relapse, and tremble.
>And I too should tremble,
>Watching. (211)

In "Bullion," Lowell orders her beloved, "Come, You! and open my heart; / That my thoughts torment me no longer, / But glitter in your hair" (212).

As much as those poems suggest some sexual reluctance on Russell's part, there are other poems in the "Two Speak Together" sequence that hint that she amply fulfilled Lowell's erotic desires. The poems repeatedly capture an intimate physicality between Lowell and Russell: "as you lean against me" ("July Midnight"), "as you press against me" ("A Shower"). "Summer Rain," like "A Rainy Night," places the two women in bed together, listening to the rain:

>But to me the darkness was red-gold and crocus-coloured
>With your brightness,
>And the words you whispered to me
>Sprang up and flamed—orange torches against the rain.
>Torches against the wall of cool, silver rain! (213)

While most of these poems suggest a sexuality and sensuality that is diffused and generalized, the most remarkable erotic poem of "Two Speak Together" can be read through its metaphoric language as an extended description of a sexual act. The title of this poem, "The Weather-Cock Points South," with its slang reference to male genitalia, may have been Lowell's device here for telling the truth "slant." It also hints at a lesbian sexual act, "going *down*" (the slang term for cunnilingus that seems to have come into the language about 1905):[18]

> I put your leaves aside,
> One by one:
> The stiff broad outer leaves;
> The smaller ones,
> Pleasant to touch, veined with purple;
> The glazed inner leaves.
> One by one
> I parted you from your leaves,
> Until you stood up like a white flower
> Swaying slightly in the evening wind.
>
> White flower,
> Flower of wax, of jade, of unstreaked agate;
> Flower with surfaces of ice,
> With shadows faintly crimson.
> Where in all the garden is there such a flower?
> The stars crowd through the lilac leaves
> To look at you.
> The low moon brightens you with silver.
>
> The bud is more than the calyx.
> There is nothing to equal a white bud,
> Of no colour and of all,
> Burnished by moonlight,
> Thrust upon by a softly-swinging wind. (211).

The entire person of Russell may be seen to be a flower in this poem, just as she is represented to be in other poems, such as "Song for a Viola D'Amore," or the description here may suggest much more particularly the genitalia of the beloved. The poem may describe the act of disrobing the beloved—or it may be seen as graphically localized in its sexual meaning. But while Lawrence's graphic sexual passages landed him in trouble with the censors, Lowell landed on the best-seller list, perhaps because many readers refused to understand her metaphor; yet it is not difficult to see the flower image of "The Weather-Cock Points South" as an evocative and descriptive symbol for female genitalia: the labia major ("broader outer leaves"), the labia minor ("the smaller ones . . .veined with purple"), pubic hair ("stiff"), sexual secretions ("glazed inner leaves"), female tumescence ("you stood up like a white flower"), and the clitoris ("the bud"). Phrases in the poem also suggest knowledge of female sexual sensitivity ("the bud is more than the calyx") and the breath of the lover in an oral-genital act ("thrust upon by a softly-swinging wind"). Perhaps many of Lowell's readers thought this was a poem about the soft south wind as it played on the flowers, but its sexual code is hardly difficult to crack. Thus deciphered, the poem is more frankly and joyously sexual than any of the works of Lowell's contemporaries who came under the strictures of the "Watch and Ward Society."

These poems of both frustrated and satiated love in "Two Speak Together" are followed by a series of poems that introduce a note of anxiety. They must have been written when Russell was preparing to leave again on a visit to her daughter, and also while she was gone. They include poems such as "Nerves," "Strain," and "Grotesque," with their nightmare imagery, their fear that Russell will die before she returns, and that Lowell will go—or has already gone—mad. Attempting to comfort herself with memories of Russell, the poet confesses in "A Sprig of Rosemary" (which Shakespeare's Ophelia tells us is the symbol of remembrance) that even though she cannot see her beloved's face, she remembers her hands,

> Sewing,
> Holding a book,
> Resting for a moment on the sill of a window.
> My eyes keep always the sight of your hands. (216).

The anxiety of separation is finally broken in the poem "Preparation," in which the speaker, awaiting her beloved, goes to a shop to buy smoke-colored glasses. When the shop man comments "What a world must be yours . . . / When it requires to be dimmed by smoked glasses," the speaker responds, "Not a world . . . / Certainly not a world." As the next poem in the sequence, "A Decade," makes clear, it is the beloved who is everything to her, and whose bright presence necessitates shaded glasses (217). While the novelty of their relationship may have worn off through the years, what remains is solid and complete:

> When you came, you were like red wine and honey,
> And the taste of you burnt my mouth with its sweetness.
> Now you are like morning bread,
> Smooth and pleasant.
> I hardly taste you at all for I know your savour,
> But I am completely nourished. (217)

The last two poems of "Two Speak Together" anticipate Lowell's early death. She was by 1919 suffering from various health problems and complications from obesity. In "Penumbra" a shadow falls over the two women's relationship as Lowell envisions the time she will no longer be there. Unmistakably autobiographical details in this poem—including a description of Lowell's home, Sevenels, "the old house which has known me since the beginning," and her intention to leave that house to Russell upon her death—figure prominently and help to confirm the inspiration and source of the poem sequence in the lives of the two women (218). The final poem of the sequence, "Frimaire," is a melancholy commentary on the inevitability of aging and death even when one has much for which to live. Lowell compares the lovers to two flowers in late autumn, "Blooming last in a yellowing garden." They have survived though many who kept them company have faded. Like the earlier verse in the sequence, "Frimaire" is a poem of anxiety and fear, as the speaker realizes that one or the other of them must soon die. Describing herself as a coward, she hopes she will be first and Russell, the purple flower, will outlive her, being better prepared to survive alone—"very splendid in isolation"—than Lowell is. The poem ends in both despair and affirmation: "Many mornings there cannot be now / For us both. Ah, Dear, I love you" (218).

Even those later biographers who have understood that these poems are autobiographical and that they reflect Lowell's life with Russell have refused to acknowledge that they are lesbian poems, that they picture not only the two women's spiritual relationship but their sexual relationship as well: "Graphic as it appears, there is an air of amorous innocence about [the poems]," C. David Heyman insists, and then goes on to say that these poems are "*too* graphic to be taken at face value," since, if we read them thus, they become "merely a description of lust."[19] But Amy Lowell appears to have seen "lust" as integral to the fullness of her love for Ada Russell. Once, in great anguish, referring to her obesity, Lowell called herself "a walking sideshow."[20] But no one reading her love poems could have that image of her. It was her ability to love, erotically as well as spiritually, and to record that love in her poems, that restored, and continues to restore to Lowell the dignity of which she was robbed by her appearance and by most of her critics.

Notes

1. S. Foster Damon, *Amy Lowell: A Chronicle with Extracts from Her Correspondence* (Boston: Houghton Mifflin, 1935), 35, 43–44, 56, 60, 65.
2. Margaret Anderson, quoted in Horace Gregory, *Amy Lowell* (New York: Thomas Nelson and Sons, 1958), 128.
3. Amy Lowell, *The Complete Poetical Works of Amy Lowell* (Boston: Houghton Mifflin, 1955), 35. All quotations from Lowell's poetry are from this volume and hereafter are cited parenthetically in the text.
4. Jean Gould, *Amy: The World of Amy Lowell and the Imagist Movement* (New York: Dodd, Mead, 1975), 123.
5. Elizabeth Shepley Sergeant, *Fire under the Andes* (New York: Knopf, 1927), 30.
6. C. David Heymann, *American Aristocracy: The Lives and Times of James Russell, Amy, and Robert Lowell* (New York: Dodd, Mead, 1980), 209.
7. Gould, *Amy,* 244.
8. Damon, *Amy Lowell: A Chronicle,* 306–307.
9. Ibid., 482–483.
10. Clement Wood, *Amy Lowell* (New York: Harold Vinal, 1926), 13, 173.
11. Hervey Allen, "Amy Lowell as a Poet," *Saturday Review of Literature* 3, no. 28 (1925), 557.
12. Glenn Richard Ruihley, *A Shard of Silence: Selected Poems of Amy Lowell* (New York: Twayne, 1957), xvii.

13. Richard Benvenuto, *Amy Lowell* (Boston: Twayne, 1985), 11.

14. Damon, *Amy Lowell: A Chronicle,* 441. See also Gillian Hanscombe and Virginia L. Smyers, *Writing for their Lives: The Modernist Woman, 1910–1940* (London: The Women's Press, 1997), 70–71.

15. Ruihley, *A Shard of Silence,* 38.

16. Ernest Hemingway, *A Moveable Feast* (New York: Bantam, 1969), 15.

17. Damon, *Amy Lowell: A Chronicle,* 441.

18. "Going Down," in Eric Partridge, *A Dictionary of the Underworld* (London: Routledge and Kegan Paul, 1950), 294.

19. Heymann, *American Aristocracy,* 251.

20. In his introduction to *The Complete Poetical Works of Amy Lowell* Louis Untermeyer remembers Lowell describing herself in these terms.

Lesbian Chivalry in Amy Lowell's *Sword Blades and Poppy Seed*

JAIME HOVEY

Feminist critics have written for nearly twenty years about the influence of Sappho's poetry, much of which was rediscovered in the late nineteenth century, on modernist lesbian writing, lending her name to a tradition variously characterized as "Sapphistry,"[1] "Sapphic modernism,"[2] and, in a variation on Henry Louis Gates's renowned work on African American aesthetic practices in *The Signifying Monkey*, Sapphist "'signifyin'."[3] But while feminism recognized the lesbian identification and formal innovation made possible in literary modernism by the discovery in the 1890s of a substantive number of lost Sapphic fragments, the theme of unrequited desire that is most often the subject of Sappho's poetry was largely ignored. Lesbian criticism, especially, has seen in representations of lesbian desire the fulfillment of sexual possibilities realized by the sexual revolution, the women's movement, and gay liberation, downplaying for the most part the long tradition of shame and thwarted love that was often the outcome of pre-Stonewall lesbian attraction. Lesbian modernism, however, recognized in its own tradition of oft-unrequited longing an aesthetic of feminine idealization worth celebrating, a desire whose articulation possessed classical antecedents in the greatest lyric poetry of ancient times, and whose elements could later be found in the courtly love poetry and romances that flourished in medieval, Renaissance, and modern Europe.

Indeed, Sapphic modernist poets such as Amy Lowell saw in the unrequited desire that infuses both Sappho's poetry and the European courtly love literature that followed it a longing that spoke to them, a longing that seemed to offer a lesbian tradition stretching back to antiquity. This tradition combined Sapphic longing for the love of an indifferent woman with the courtly love tradition of service to an idealized and unattainable lady. This unrequited and devoted longing was echoed in the songs brought from the Holy Land by crusaders, the ballads of the troubadours, and medieval, Renaissance, and nineteenth-century courtly love tales and poems. In these, knights pine for the ladies they serve, often without hope of reward or favor, as Lancelot pines for the married Guinevere in Chretien de Troyes's romances, and as Pelleas pines for the cruel Etarre in Alfred, Lord Tennyson's *Idylls of the King*. In chivalry, Sapphic modernist poets and novelists found inspiration to create a modernism that was both solidly grounded at the heart of European literary tradition, and was able at the same time to constitute an aesthetic and moral challenge to early-twentieth-century bourgeois sexual respectability.

Consider how desire for an unattainable feminine ideal introduces the problem of the artist's relationship to the market in Amy Lowell's "The Captured Goddess," the second poem in her 1914 volume *Sword Blades and Poppy Seed*.[4] "The Captured Goddess" concerns the artist's quest for beauty in the modern city, but takes the form of the ambiguously gendered speaker's desire for a female divinity, who in this case has been carried off as a war trophy and sold as a slave in the marketplace. The speaker first suspects the existence of this goddess because her beauty stands apart from the urban landscape:

Over the housetops,
Above the rotating chimney-pots,
I have seen a shiver of amethyst,
And blue and cinnamon have flickered
A moment,
At the far end of a dusty street. (31)

These colors appear above the ordinary elements of domestic existence such as "chimney-pots"; they are dynamic colors that "shiver" and "flicker"; they are exotic colors such as "amethyst" and "cinnamon," with names suggesting the value of jewels and spices. The value of these colors and the words that describe them increases with the revelation that they are "her wings, / Goddess!" The ambiguously gendered speaker then recounts following this vision in worshipful adoration, "With gazing eyes and stumbling feet. / I cared not where she led me, / My eyes were full of colors." These colors and images are the sensuous jewels of poetic language:

Saffrons, rubies, the yellows of beryls,
And the indigo-blue of quartz;
Flights of rose, layers of chrysoprase,
Points of orange, spirals of vermilion,
The spotted gold of tiger-lily petals,
The loud pink of bursting hydrangeas. (32)

The poem thus establishes aesthetic value in several ways. Poetic value is found in the "Flights of rose" and "loud pink of bursting hydrangeas" that explode off the page with their strange fusion of sound, movement, and color. Emotional value is expressed in the love of the speaker for the goddess who creates these images. And the courtly values of submission, devotion, and service are shown in the tireless journey of the speaker in pursuit of the goddess, a journey that leads the speaker to discover ever more beauty in following her.

But the aesthetic values of poetic language emotional expression, and artistic devotion are cast into doubt when the speaker discovers the goddess "in the market-place," "naked and cold," with "Her fluted wings fastened." For the first time, gender enters the poem:

> Men chaffered for her,
> They bargained in silver and gold,
> In copper, in wheat,
> And called their bids across the market-place.

> The Goddess wept. (33)

Now value is assigned by men, who measure the goddess by the exchange value of their commodities rather than the power of poetry, with "copper" and "wheat" rather than "Flights of rose" or "the loud pink of bursting hydrangeas." As a result, divinity, art, and beauty are debased. The artist speaker feels helpless in such a world: "Hiding my face I fled. / And the grey wind hissed behind me, / Along the narrow streets" (33). The speaker's acknowledgment of impotence and guilt is marked by the hiss of the wind, and the sound of the hissing wind in the last lines of the poem. The rest of the poems in *Sword Blades and Poppy Seed* address the question of whether art, desire, and the idealized feminine can be valued in a world where men seek to subdue and possess women.

"The Captured Goddess" gestures to an alternative set of moral and aesthetic values built upon idealized femininity and unrequited or sublimated desire. This desire is common to most of the poems in the volume, whether the speaker is a man, the poet, or a sexually ambiguous subject, and echoes the complaint of the self-identified speaker in Sappho's ancient poetic fragments, a speaker who sometimes pines for a man but often pines for a woman. One sees this speaker revealed in a charming moment of self-deprecation in one of Sappho's poems, where she humorously impersonates Aphrodite, the goddess of love, in a moment of exasperation at yet another of Sappho's pleas for assistance with some unreciprocated passion: "Whom *this* time should I persuade to / lead you back again to her love? Who *now*, oh / Sappho, who wrongs you?" The poem offers its solaces to Sappho, however, as the goddess agrees to help her, and promises eventual victory:

> If she flees you now, she will soon pursue you;
> if she won't accept what you give, she'll give it;
> if she doesn't love you, she'll love you soon now,
>   even unwilling.[5]

Like the captured goddess who flees the artist in *Sword Blades,* Sappho's beloved is often unavailable. And like the captured goddess, she serves as inspiration to the artist, but Sappho clearly longs to possess her beloved, while Lowell's poetry finds a certain satisfaction in desire itself. *Sword Blades* takes up the theme of Sapphic longing and celebrates it as art, as valuable as John Keats's Grecian urn is valuable to his speaker, more for its attenuation of desire and suspension of time than for realized sexual gratification. Similarly, Lowell's ambiguously gendered speakers value the art that springs from a desire suspended in its moment of longing. The humble courtly champion of "Apology" recognizes that desire for the beloved, as much as the presence of the beloved herself, creates beauty and value, and entreats her lady:

> Be not angry with me that I bear
> Your colours everywhere,
> All through each crowded street,
> And meet
> The wonder-light in every eye,
> As I go by. (57)

Here it is both the beloved's "colours" and the pride and passion of the gallant speaker that elicits the acknowledgement of value, the "wonder-light in every eye." Both of these elements together make the beautiful object that is the subject of the poem, as well as the poem itself. The adoring speaker seems laminated by desire, suspended in a dreamy world where time is stopped by love:

> Around me is the sound of steepled bells,
> And rich perfuméd smells
> Hang like a wind-forgotten cloud,
> And shroud
> Me from close contact with the world.
> I dwell impearled. (58)

Elsewhere, the Sapphic plaint balances inspiration, desire, and poetry, as in "The Taxi," where the poem's composition echoes the literal and poetic vehicle that forces the speaker to articulate the anguish of separation from a beloved:

> When I go away from you
> The world beats dead
> Like a slackened drum.
> I call out for you against the jutted stars
> And shout into the ridges of the wind.
> Streets coming fast,
> One after the other,
> Wedge you away from me,
> And the lamps of the city prick my eyes
> So that I can no longer see your face.

Why should I leave you,
To wound myself upon the sharp edges of the night? (96)

The answer to the speaker's question is, of course, the poem itself, which trans-
forms the pain of separation into an eloquent tribute to the beauty of desire—a
beauty which requires separation as the condition of its existence.

As these poems suggest, Lowell's *Sword Blades and Poppy Seed* fuses Sap-
phic longing and an unrequited, courtly love that requires service to a lady as
its own reward into a kind of lesbian chivalry. Lesbian chivalry is one of the
most striking aesthetic strategies that appears in modernism as a way of think-
ing through the relationship of sexuality to art; Djuna Barnes's *Nightwood*,
Radclyffe Hall's *The Well of Loneliness,* and Virginia Woolf's *Orlando* are some
of its best-known fictional works, while the poems of both Renée Vivien and
H. D. also suggest a lesbian version of courtly love.[6] Foregrounding the artis-
tic, cultural, and ethical value of lesbian emotion and lesbian desire, lesbian chiv-
alry often, though not always, also uses traditional Gothic elements such as
knights, castles and manor houses, medieval towns, paganism, alchemy and
magic, and sexual suspicion and violence, to emphasize the romantic and af-
fective elements of lesbian desire, celebrate the beauty of that desire, and con-
test the values of a mechanistic, rational, indifferent, commodified normative
culture. Medieval fantasies of courtly love provided a model for lesbian mod-
ernists of lovers who could not marry. In courtly love, devotion perfects the vir-
tue of both the lover and the beloved, and secures social status for both lovers
as a tested and legitimate couple. Nineteenth-century courtly love literature fur-
ther attenuates, slows down, and delays the inevitable coupling of the hetero-
sexual pair. Tennyson especially, but also William Morris, Walter Scott, and many
of the Gothic writers (and writers who used Gothic elements in their fiction and
poetry) emphasized the courtly love situation as a state where satisfaction was
delayed, derailed, or denied. In the Victorian fantasy of courtly love, as in its
medieval version, consummation is usually dangerous and often impossible, and
at least one of the partners, and usually both, is married to someone else, or
must eventually marry someone else.

When lesbian modernist writers appropriated the stylized gender roles of
courtly love, they emphasized the illicit and passionate nature of the courtly love
situation, and made the gender of the desiring speaker female, indeterminate,
or youthfully boyish, suggesting a lesbian version of chivalry and courtly de-
sire. By inserting a stigmatized subject—the lesbian—in the place of the courtly
lover, or suggesting that the lesbian could be in this place, and making an art
out of the drama of lesbian desire, lesbian chivalry makes a degraded love hon-
orable, much as the poet's love for the captured goddess makes an ugly land-
scape beautiful, and a language degraded by the bourgeois marketplace valuable
again. Since it was widely held by many fin-de-siècle and progressive-era writ-
ers, critics, physicians, and moralists that homosexuality was a sterile and patho-
logical impulse that needed to be cured or hidden from public view through

repression or sublimation, the poetic celebration of a desiring aesthetic that was both lesbian and valuable would have operated to undermine these attitudes, which reflect what critics and historians have come to recognize as the "norms" of bourgeois sexual respectability.

Lesbian chivalry reworks cultural notions of sublimation that erase homosexuality, and emphasizes instead the aesthetic and cultural significance of lesbian desire. Lesbian chivalry emphasizes the beauty of feminine idealization, unrequited longing, amorous servility, and patient fidelity, showing it as a wellspring of creativity and inspiration, a model of discipline and ethical reciprocity, and a critique of a culturally fetishized heterosexuality. Sublimation as theorized in psychoanalysis conserves certain Victorian attitudes about sexual normativity as valuable and sexual abnormality as useless in and of itself. It is one of the most well-known mechanisms for containing deviant sexuality and enforcing "norms" of bourgeois sexual respectability, and though its existence precedes the work of Sigmund Freud, his early theorization of it seems chiefly interested in seeing sublimation as a dynamic of reconciliation, one where the abnormal becomes the normal. In Freud's 1910 *Leonardo da Vinci and a Memory of His Childhood,* sublimation is the unconscious transformation of the sexual drive into other creative drives, whereby "the libido evades the fate of repression by being sublimated from the very beginning into curiosity."[7] Indeed, he refers to Leonardo's combination of "overpowerful instinct for research" and "atrophy of his sexual life" as "ideal [sublimated] homosexuality." In calling a withered homosexuality "ideal" because it finds outlets other than sexual ones, Freud attaches an ethics to sublimation, suggesting that the moral homosexual is the homosexual who finds better things to do with himself than have sex, or even think or talk about it. Homosexual creativity is mystified as a kind of magical transformation that erases the homosexual and yields art or science cleansed of abnormal influences. Heterosexuality remains in ascendance as the only sexuality that is allowed public representation as itself. Homosexual desire must be veiled, transformed, or erased.

By using the feudal dynamic of courtly love, lesbian chivalry as an aesthetic practice exposes the cultural fetishization of heterosexuality and of heterosexual fantasies of romantic love by exaggerating these fantasies, denying their fulfillment, and showing their perversity. In lesbian chivalry the relationship between homosexual desire and culture does not have to be mystified, transformed, or erased in order to have value. Instead, the conscious, foregrounded emotion of unrequited courtly love, a courtly love that can be read as an exaggerated heterosexuality, but also recognized as a possible lesbian desire, contests the unconscious practices of exchange and misrecognition upon which both sublimation and commodity exchange depend.

In order to see how lesbian chivalry might operate as a transformative mechanism that both invokes and critiques heterosexuality, and with it, the mystifications of bourgeois sexual respectability and commodity culture more generally, I wish to return to Lowell's *Sword Blades and Poppy Seed.* Produced at what was arguably the center, or at least *a* center, of the American imagist movement, Lowell's 1914 volume theorizes a lesbian homoartistic aesthetic as a counterethics to those of bourgeois heterosexual normative culture. Her audience did not have to look far to see the violence of normal and normative society. *Sword Blades and Poppy Seed* was published in 1914, the year World War I broke out in Europe. Paul Fussell has read the "high" courtly diction of patriotic British poetry and newspaper essays during the Great War as symptomatic of both national innocence and the longing for moral stability: "Everyone knew what Glory was, and what Honor meant."[8] Courtly language for Fussell is an unconscious expression of conventional mores. Lowell's invocation of courtly passion in the United States in *Sword Blades* makes the opposite argument, that the noble passions of courtly love inspire the artist to imagine life in new and potentially more transgressive ways. Courtly love also requires the degendering of the masculine poet as part of the price of art. Consider the lines from the framing poem, where an old man who deals in words warns a young poet about the price he will pay for art:

Who buy of me must simply pay
Their whole existence quite away:
Their strength, their manhood, and their prime,
Their hours from morning till the time
When evening comes on tiptoe feet,
And losing life, think it complete. (23)

Rather than gain masculine honor from this kind of sacrifice, the poet loses all the accouterments of normal and successful manhood. Not only does he give up honor and glory, but he is cheated of love as well, especially the kind of love that will bind him to things other than his art:

Must miss what other men count being,
To gain the gift of deeper seeing;
Must spurn all ease, all hindering love,
All which could hold or bind. (23)

If this renunciation of love seems at odds with the argument about courtly love and lesbian chivalry I have outlined, it is because *Sword Blades and Poppy Seed* views heterosexual masculine desire as having a tendency toward possessiveness and ownership of women, as well as an insistence on the embodiment and accessibility of the beloved, that lesbian desire and more ambiguous passions seem to escape. Men in the poems who see in women an inspiration for their lives and art find only tragedy when they insist that those women be physically real and available only to them. In "The Great Adventure of Max Breuck," a man who thinks he has courted a beautiful young girl for two years awakes from an opium trance to find his whole romantic life has been nothing more than a hallucination, and commits suicide. In "The Shadow," a watchmaker is driven to madness and suicide when a shadow he imagines is a cruel and unyielding woman disappears from the wall of his workshop. In "The Basket," a writer neglected by the girl he loves imagines her "quietly sitting on the window-sill, eating human eyes" (170). In "In a Castle," a Crusader returns home to find his lady in bed with a page, kills both of them, has sex with her dead body, then kills himself. These last two poems, among the longer narrative poems of Lowell's "polyphonic" prose that form the most innovative work in the volume, specifically critique the unattainable lady and the gallant lover by emphasizing the masochistic and sadistic elements of courtly love, as well as the lurid, violent, and emotional excesses that can also be the products of unrequited desire. Here the volume critiques chivalry in its unproductive aspect of thwarted exchange, while still celebrating its strange, sublime beauty. At the same time, it exposes the dark excesses of heterosexuality, showing that its celebrated normativity and respectability is actually comprised of violence, rape, murder, and all manner of suffering. Lowell's lurid chivalry undermines the mechanism of sublimation by invoking the heterosexual elements of gothic tradition—women with magical powers, cruel ladies, passionate knights, heroines trapped in castles and in loveless marriages—in all their decadence. The violent passions of this gothic heterosexuality inevitably lead to cannibalism, murder, necrophilia, and suicide.

   Sword Blades and Poppy Seed is divided into two sections, but the tensions in the volume are less between the "Sword Blades" and "Poppy Seed" sections than they are between the lurid, tragic, violent, and decadent heterosexuality of many of the poems and the aestheticized lesbian or ambiguous erotic appreciation one finds in others. In spite of the differences the volume draws between its two sections, nearly all of its poems explore either courtly love or a more generalized theme of unrequited passion. Physical consummation is beside the point; what matters is the queer emotion elicited by the anguish of impossible love, an emotion that is not turned into something else, but is valued as its own currency, produced by the particular situation of a lover existing in an excruciating but ultimately untraversable proximity to a beloved woman. This desiring aesthetic, where the "middle" of the story of love takes up more room and more meaning than does the climax and denouement,[9] is queer both in its perverse insistence on lingering within an endless dynamic, and queer because within the terms of its courtliness, roles matter more than bodies. *Sword Blades and Poppy Seed*'s emphasis on courtly manners, devotion, and unrequited sexual passion also plays with the central place heterosexual desire holds in culture. The ability of courtly love to signify both lesbian and heterosexual desire allows *Sword Blades* to simultaneously celebrate lesbian desire and expose the way heterosexuality functions as a cultural fetish. While the volume's spare imagism celebrates the beauty of the poet's love for an unattainable feminine ideal, the longer and more experimental poems in the volume explore the doubleness of the heterosexual fetish, emphasizing the excessive emotion, violence, and paranoia of "normal" heterosexual longing.

The speaker in "The Basket," who is a writer, berates the woman he loves, whose art is her embroidery, for her diligence which excludes him from her attentions:

> "My God, but you keep me starved! You write 'No Entrance Here,'
> over all the doors. Is it not strange, my Dear, that loving, yet you deny
> me entrance everywhere. Would marriage strike you blind, or, hating
> bonds as you do, why should I be denied the rights of loving if I leave
> you free? You want the whole of me, you pick my brains to rest you,
> but you give me not one heart-beat. Oh, forgive me, Sweet! I suffer in
> my loving, and you know it. I cannot feed my life on being a poet. Let
> me stay." (169)

Fearing her stronger allegiance to her art, he dreams that she has found the color red she has been seeking, cracking open human eyes and throwing them out the window onto the roof. The poem closes with his nightmare vision of her house as a "ruin" with "Deflowered windows, sockets without sight" (171). The writer's courtly infatuation has become an obsessive and possessive love, turning his desire into a hellish fever. The "deflowered sockets" of the windows suggest that he has resorted to rape. This, and his inability to accept her devotion to something other than him and to appreciate her for herself, makes his beloved disappear from his sight forever.

"In a Castle" is similarly concerned with courtly love run to possessiveness and violence. This time the woman is killed because she fails to abide by the contractual monogamy of courtly love. Her lover reasons away their adultery by imagining that their love is more ethical than her loveless marriage: "Is it guilt to free a lady from her palsied lord, absent and fighting, terribly abhorred?" He develops this line of reasoning further, justifying their love as a better version of the marriage she seeks to escape:

> She is so pure and whole. Only because he has her soul will she resign
> herself to him, for where the soul has gone, the body must be given as
> a sign. He takes her by the divine right of the only lover. He has sworn
> to fight her lord, and wed her after. Should he be overborne, she will
> die adoring him, forlorn, shriven by her great love. (174)

The truth, as he soon discovers, is that she is in bed with someone else. The narrative cuts to the spectacle of two headless bodies on the bed, with notes addressed to the lady's husband attached to their hair. The first simply labels the man as the wife's lover. The second, however, invites the husband to ravish the wife's headless body:

> I have engaged that, on your return, she shall welcome you here. She
> will not spurn your love as before, you have still the best part of her.
> Her blood was red, her body white, they will both be here for your

delight. The soul inside was a lump of dirt, I have rid you of that with a spurt of my sword point. Good luck to your pleasure. She will be quite complaisant, my friend, I wager. (177)

Their love itself was a kind of fetish to the knight, a relationship that denied the transgressiveness of their adultery by turning it into something resembling conventional marriage. The knight's misogynist, necrophilic invitation to the absent husband, which also suggests the knight's own indulgence in necrophilia; the identification of the knight with the spurned husband; and the mad internal rhyme of the suicide note all suggest that the lady's sexual autonomy has destroyed his fantasy of her as a pure feminine ideal, and this has driven the knight violently insane. His transformation of the scene of murder into the sexual invitation of the marriage bed is a perverse and lurid expose of the brutal possessiveness that underpins normative heterosexual marriage, and serves as a warning that such brutality poisons all couplings, no matter how courtly, that imagine themselves in its image.

Ambiguously gendered and explicitly female speakers tend to fare better in the volume than men do, content to value desire as much as or more than its fulfillment. Most of the imagist poems in the volume are articulated by women and ungendered speakers, and sketch sharp, intense moments of passionate longing, such as "The Blue Scarf," where the speaker sees a scarf on a bench and imagines making love to the woman who owns it:

> Her kisses are sharp buds of fire; and I burn back
> > against her, a jewel
> Hard and white; a stalked, flaming flower; till I break
> > to a handful of cinders,
> And open my eyes to the scarf, shining blue in the
> > afternoon sunshine. (237)

Imagining the woman who wears the scarf is just as sexually and poetically satisfying as actually touching her body—perhaps more so, since the end of the poem brings readers right back to the scarf that was present at the beginning of the poem, enabling another endless cycle of pleasure in its contemplation. It might seem from the poem's emphasis on the scarf, and from the satisfactions possible from pure desire as an end in itself, that this poem celebrates and performs a kind of sublimation or fetishism, but if this desire is sublimated, it is certainly not transformed from a sexual desire into some other kind of creativity, as in psychoanalytic sublimation, nor does the synecdoche of the scarf replace the woman's absent penis in order to render her an acceptable object of male desire, as it would in Freud's model of fetishism. Indeed, "The Blue Scarf" manages to have it both ways, to have desire and fulfillment, possession and elusiveness, longing and satisfaction. The poem may suggest both sublimation and fetishism, but the hermaphroditic combination of the "stalked, flaming flower" suggests nothing so much as a phallic, lesbian femininity expressing its sexuality as its art, and its art as its sexuality. "Aubade" is even more spare, but nevertheless powerfully erotic:

> As I would free the white almond from the green husk
> So would I strip your trappings off,
> Beloved,
> And fingering the smooth and polished kernel
> I should see that in my hands glittered a gem beyond counting. (239)

In all of these, intense desire for a woman just out of reach creates alternative value—"a jewel / Hard and white," or "a gem beyond counting"—in addition to market value. Passion makes the lover hot, phallic, and valuable, and also makes the lover value the beloved for making the lover feel this way. In one of the last poems of the volume, aptly titled "A Lady," the speaker argues that this intense desire is a life force more valuable than money:

> My vigour is a new-minted penny,
> Which I cast at your feet.
> Gather it up from the dust,
> That its sparkle may amuse you. (242–243)

The speaker is humble, but also recognizes the worth of the vigor (s)he offers. It is something that is both valuable and beautiful as it is, not for what it can buy, but for the pleasure it can give the beloved. Sapphic complaint fused with courtly abasement suggests the medieval, Renaissance, and Victorian tradition of courtly longing, as well as the lesbian ancient antecedents and modern incarnations that frame that tradition on either side. The speaking "I" could be anybody, of course, but we also know Amy Lowell wrote these poems, and we know Lowell lived with a woman for years, and was a great admirer of women, and never married a man. We know that this Amy Lowell wrote poem after poem about female beauty and female grace and unrequited love for women. Because we know this, it is more than possible for readers to think of these poems as lesbian poems. And in them, one is struck by the intensity of a desire that creates value all around it—in the speaker, in the beloved, and in beauty of the poem itself.

If the volume seeks to expose the dark side of a fetishized heterosexual ideal, it also passionately celebrates the beauty of a queerer courtly desire, one that binds nature, sensuality, and poetic language together into poetry that pulsates with feeling. In the penultimate poem in the volume, "In a Garden," the speaker wishes an absent beloved were present in a garden that ripples with the energy of Samuel Taylor Coleridge's "Kubla Khan":

> Splashing down moss-tarnished steps
> It falls, the water;
> And the air is throbbing with it.

With its gurgling and running.
With its leaping, and deep, cool murmur. (244–245)

The sensuous language replicates the sound of water running over stones, filling up the air with music. The growing, insistent presence of the water sounds, and the crescendo of vibration that fills the air around the fountain, creates a corresponding echo in the speaker who responds to it, so much so that we are hardly surprised by the next lines of the poem:

And I wished for night and you.
I wanted to see you in the swimming-pool,
White and shining in the silver-flecked water.
While the moon rode over the garden,
High in the arch of night,
And the scent of the lilacs was heavy with stillness.

Night, and the water, and you in your whiteness, bathing! (245)

This suspended desire, aestheticized into one endless moment of tribute to female beauty, is in sharp contrast to its mirror poem, "Clear, with Light, Variable Winds," where a poet hears a naked woman call to him from a fountain to come to her, and he is found drowned in the morning. In "Clear," the male poet, the "master," has mistakenly tried to physically possess his feminine ideal, and pays with his life, while "In a Garden" celebrates only the moment of desire. In "In a Garden," the beloved is absent, but like "Clear," the beloved is not Coleridge's Abyssinian maid, but a white Artemis bathing, observed by Actaeon. The danger of this wish—Actaeon was, after all, turned into a stag by Artemis and torn to pieces by her hounds—suggests that something is more transgressive about the wish to see the beloved bathing than its simple voyeurism. In "In a Garden," the beloved is valuable because all of nature is missing something when she is absent, but she is most valuable because her beauty and the beauty of the poem are fused together into one element through the speaker's intense and palpable desire to see her naked in the moonlight, perfumed by lilacs. The dream of this desire, the intensity of it, cannot be made more complete except by the presence of the longed-for woman, a presence desired, then invoked, and finally insisted upon by the turn of the speaker to the beloved. With this address, the beloved becomes present, as the most perfect image in the poem, as art itself.

"I wished for night and you," the speaker insists, "I wanted to see you in the swimming pool, / Night, and the water, and you in your whiteness, bathing!" (245). The speaker wants to contemplate the beloved, aestheticize the beloved, admire the beloved, write a poem in tribute to the beloved, and celebrate the joy of the state of desiring the beloved. Neither sublimation nor consummation, this lesbian desiring address freezes the state of love into an eternal moment, and celebrates the freezing of that desire. With this address, Lowell's readers, too, are the beloved, invited by her speaker to delight in these poems, to watch the speaker watching her beloved or serenading her beloved, or to be the beloved whose naked beauty the watcher longs to admire. As lovers who might experience this longing as reciprocal and interchangeable, readers and speaker are obligated to create beauty for each other, inspire art, and elicit desire. Time stops; the "you" the poem invokes "are" permanently "bathing." Beauty exists in its unrequited eternity, in the space between address and listener. Readers become interpellated "yous" in a courtly lesbian dynamic where the poetic speaker overcomes impotence, sterility, violent appropriation, and degradation to offer desire as the living stuff of art.

Notes

1. See Pat Califia, *Sapphistry* (Tallahassee, Fla.: Naid Press, 1980); Susan Gubar, "Sapphistries," *Signs* 10, no. 1 (1984): 43–62; and Jane Marcus, "Sapphistory: The Woolf and the Well," in *Lesbian Texts and Contexts: Radical Revisions,* ed. Karla Jay and Joanne Glasgow (New York: New York University Press, 1990), 164–179.
2. See Shari Benstock, "Expatriate Sapphic Modernism: Entering Literary History" in Jay and Glasgow, eds., *Lesbian Texts and Contexts*, 183–203.
3. See Diana Collecott, *H.D. and Sapphic Modernism* (Cambridge: Cambridge University Press 1999), 11.
4. Amy Lowell, *Sword Blades and Poppy Seed* (New York: Macmillan, 1914). Hereafter, parenthetical page references are to this volume.
5. Sappho, *A Garland,* trans. Jim Powell (New York: Farrar, Straus and Giroux, 1993), 3.
6. See Karla Jay's discussion of courtly role-playing between lovers Renée Vivien and Natalie Barney in *The Amazon and the Page: Natalie Clifford Barney and Renée Vivien* (Bloomington: Indiana University Press, 1988).
7. Sigmund Freud, *Leonardo da Vinci and a Memory of His Childhood,* trans. Alan Tyson (New York: W. W. Norton, 1964), 30.
8. Paul Fussell, *The Great War and Modern Memory* (New York: Oxford University Press, 1975), 21.
9. Judith Roof has argued that narrative is infused with heterosexual ideologies, such as those that Freud articulates in his *Three Essays*, where normal sexuality is defined by its timely end of orgasm. Such ideologies, she writes, privilege the end of the story as that which gives meaning to everything that comes before it: "Without the expectation of an ending, we have difficulty discerning a story, its pleasures, terrors, lessons, its making sense of things, its usefulness as catharsis or panacea." See Roof, *Come As You Are: Sexuality and Narrative* (New York: Columbia University Press, 1996), 6.

Amy Lowell, John Keats, and the "Shielded Scutcheon" of Imagist Art

MARGARET HOMANS

Amy Lowell read, collected, and wrote about John Keats all her life. Her first published volume of poetry, *A Dome of Many-Coloured Glass,* takes its title from Percy Bysshe Shelley's elegy on Keats and its design and typography from Keats's 1820 volume *Lamia, Isabella, The Eve of St. Agnes, and Other Poems.* She wrote seven poems that are explicitly about Keats and other poems that allude to his works; the culmination of her writing career was the 1925 publication of her two-volume literary biography, *John Keats,* a work based in part on her own archive of Keats manuscripts and Keatsiana.[1] According to her friend and biographer S. Foster Damon, "she always claimed that she learned more about poetic composition from the manuscript of 'The Eve of St. Agnes' than from any book or human being. 'I think the constant studying of his manuscripts with his corrections, and seeing why he made them, has taught me more about writing poetry than anything else in the world.'"[2] While readers need not take these claims at face value, it is worth finding out what it meant for Lowell to make them. In Damon's view, her admiration for Keats came from his being "nearest to the Imagist ideals: none other had attempted so thoroughly to describe things as they appear to the senses."[3] But that view of Keats is made possible in large part by Lowell's careful molding of Keats's reputation. Indeed, William Marquess sharply criticizes Lowell's Keats biography for the author's tendency to identify with Keats, to "remake him in her own imagism, as a Modernist poet."[4] Lowell made Keats into her forebear as imagist poet to acquire an irreproachable pedigree for her own poetic practice. Keats's rising popularity in the U.S. made him an inspired choice for Lowell in the marketing of her version of modernist poetry.[5] Remaking him as an imagist, however, also meant dismantling the very authority Keats supplied, by treating Keats as ambivalently as Keats treated his poetic forebears, as sources for poetic fragments, beautiful but incoherent, in need of reassembly by her expert modern hands.

Lowell's treatment of the manuscript of "The Eve of St. Agnes" in her *John Keats* supports Damon's claim for its preeminence for her. Although she spends more time analyzing his *Endymion* (1818) and the odes, she selects as illustrations for her book (among assorted portraits, images of places Keats lived, and so on) Keats's draft of "On First Looking into Chapman's Homer" (1816) and a single sheet of the manuscript of "The Eve of St. Agnes," heavily corrected by Keats. The reproduced photograph of the sheet (two columns of verse that include the end of stanza 23 and stanzas 24 and 25) makes visible not only Keats's crossings out and rewritings but also the frailty of the paper itself, which is so thin that words written on the reverse show through. Calling attention in this way to the manuscript as a rare and valuable object that can be taken to pieces for the purpose of displaying its beauty underscores the point Lowell makes about the poem itself in her accompanying text when she writes, "No one of Keats's manuscripts which I have seen is so carefully worked over as this. A glance at the reproduction of two of the pages of the first draft will show how shrewdly and carefully he shaped and reshaped his material, always with the object of increasing some splendour, making clearer some manner of feeling, adding some brighter lustre to an image, captivating the ear with some stranger, more unexpected, harmony of sound."[6] Her emphasis on Keats's sensory effects as discrete elements, each of which can be heightened, like her subsequent reading of the poem as an assemblage of beauties, is supported particularly well by the stanzas she has selected for the illustration. Carved out from the rest of the poem, they epitomize the imagist Keats, for they comprise the description of the "casement high and triple arch'd" in stanza 24 whose diamond-shaped panes are decorated with "Innumerable of stains and splendid dyes" and "thousand heraldries, / And twilight saints, and dim enblazonings"; "in the midst" of these "A shielded scutcheon blush'd with blood of kings and queens." Through this colored glass, in Keats's famous error in stanza 25, the full moonlight "threw warm gules on Madeline's fair breast," in shades of "rose bloom," "soft amethyst," and perhaps gold, if that is what is indicated by the "glory" that falls on her hair.[7]

Much has been written about these gorgeous lines, which are important to arguments such as that of John Collick, who posits that Madeline and Porphyro cannot be united in the poem because the characters keep being displaced by the gothic decorations (of which the shielded scutcheon is his chief example), or Alan Boehm, who claims that "disturbing effects of fragmentation [and] a grotesque confusion of sculptured and human forms" undermine the conspicuous beauty of the poem's setting.[8] The "blood of kings and queens" that "blush[es]" or reddens the shield on the window seems to have more life than do Madeline (who seems an angel) and Porphyro (who grows faint); projecting lifelike color onto the humans, the window even seems more endowed with agency than they are.

The passage also dramatizes a recurrent effect in Keats, the transformation of an apparently allegorical figure freighted with metaphysical meanings into an image, pure and simple, that means nothing but its own beauty. As the moonlight falls through the stained glass, the potentially rich meanings of the shielded scutcheon and other "heraldries," which would serve in some other context as identificatory symbols, dissolve into pure colors that fall sensuously but meaninglessly onto Madeline's body. For Greg Kucich, this habitual move to fragment and dismantle allegory is part of Keats's ambivalent "Spenserianism"; Keats, he argues, endows "The Eve of St. Agnes" with "an allegorical machinery that turns out to have no clear allegorical meanings."[9] This antiallegorical reading of Keats, or the reading of Keats as antiallegorist, has a long history in Keats criticism: Earl Wasserman, writing in 1953, traces a lineage of readers including Algernon Charles Swinburne and Arthur Symons, who insisted that Keats's merit lay in his lack of ideas or morality and his exclusive attention to "sensuous riches."[10]

Wasserman includes Lowell in this tradition of Keats readers, citing her "repudiat[ion of] all allegorical interpretations of *Endymion*" and her insistence on Keats's focus on "'the beauties of a material universe.'"[11] And indeed, Lowell's account of the manuscript sheet she reproduces in her book is consistent with this view of her: as we have seen, her stated interest is in Keats's technical virtuosity as he revises the poem to heighten its sensuous effects one by one. George Ridley's careful technical study of the manuscript of stanza 24 supports her view: he finds that Keats "takes it all to pieces" and "begins to put the fragments together in a different design."[12] Lowell's overarching reading of the poem is that it is a "choral hymn" to Keats's love for Fanny Brawne, but this reading is consistent with her emphasis on sensory effects because for Lowell "the beauties of a material universe" include love and friendship as much as moonlight and statuary; she says she finds in the poem "no allegory."[13]

In titling her first volume of poetry *A Dome of Many-Coloured Glass*, Lowell both declares her allegiance to Keats's love of the material universe and expresses this loyalty by emptying an allegorical figure of the meaning it had in its original context, just the kind of gesture Lowell sees Keats making with the stained glass in "The Eve of St. Agnes." In stanza 52 of Shelley's *Adonais*, the dome is a distinctly ambivalent simile for the beauties of mortal life:

> The One remains, the many change and pass;
> Heaven's light forever shines, Earth's shadows fly;
> Life, like a dome of many-coloured glass,
> Stains the white radiance of Eternity,
> Until Death tramples it to fragments.—Die,
> If thou wouldst be with that which thou dost seek!
> Follow where all is fled!—Rome's azure sky,
> Flowers, ruins, statues, music, words are weak
> The glory they transfuse with fitting truth to speak.[14]

Whereas Shelley overtly prefers the "white radiance of Eternity" to the colorful world that "stains" it, the list of material things Shelley dismisses as inadequate to reveal "truth" ("sky, / Flowers, ruins, statues, music, words") is just the sort of collection that Keats lovingly elaborates in "The Eve of St. Agnes" and that Lowell adores him for making as he crafts his poem to heighten its beauties one sense at a time. Whereas Shelley links glory to eternity and opposes both to fragmentary earthly beauty, in "The Eve of St. Agnes" glory becomes visible only when light falls through colored glass onto human hair. Removing Shelley's phrase from its original context and placing it in the new context of her imagist book, Lowell emphasizes the satisfactoriness of the "dome" over its vulnerability to fragmentation in Shelley's verse; or rather, she expresses the satisfaction in that vulnerability that she believes she shares with Keats. Lowell deallegorizes Shelley's "dome of many-coloured glass" by taking it out of context. If Shelley used it as a figure for Keats's love of sensuous beauty because of the "shielded scutcheon" passage (and this seems likely given that *Adonais* shares with "The Eve of St. Agnes" its Spenserian stanzas), then the "dome" in Lowell's title is doubly deallegorized, since Keats had already emptied his glass "scutcheon" of its allegorical import in favor of the imagistic beauty it casts on Madeline.

"Beauties" and allegories emptied of meaning, such as illegible heraldries that serve only to color the heroine's flesh and hair, are among the "fragments" that critics have seen "The Eve of St. Agnes" comprising; also contributing to the effect that the poem is a compilation of fragments are the poem's literary allusions. Aileen Ward, dismissing source study as irrelevant, nonetheless acknowledges that "if one listens for them, echoes of the whole gamut of Keats's reading may be heard throughout the poem, from Spenser and Shakespeare and Milton to Boccaccio and Mrs. Radcliffe and the Arabian Nights."[15] Ward's lack of interest in sources comes from the apparent superficiality of these echoes, but their lack of integration into the poem is precisely what interests Marjorie Levinson. For Levinson, Keats leaves his literary allusions unintegrated on purpose so as to display his hard-won learning. According to Levinson he fills his poems with styles that are "imperfectly appropriated" and "heaped heterogeniously together."[16] In contrast to the way William Wordsworth "effortlessly reaps his memory of its rich and naturally integrated meanings," Keats deliberately displays the "careful inventories of his overdecorated psychic interiors." Levinson notes that in Keats, "whole and living speech is rendered a quotation, and everything is as an artifact in an overwrought cabinet: framed, spotlighted, exhibited as possessions that are also signs *of* possession."[17]

For Levinson, "The Eve of St. Agnes" epitomizes Keats's treatment of literary allusions; "each stanza is a sort of display case for the exhibition of fine phrases."[18] The "shielded scutcheon" passage is particularly important to her reading, as it thematizes her view that Keats attempts to authorize his own style by representing earlier writers as pure style or merely style. Levinson adopts the figure of the shield to describe Keats's simultaneous deference to and belittling of the earlier writers, particularly John Milton in this case. "The verbal exhibition is as a shield that Keats positions between himself and his subject, and between himself and his reader," she writes. "We grasp the function of this heraldic device by turning to Madeline for a moment, 'guled' by the blushed scutcheon. Madeline's own body—a blank field stained by heraldic insignia—legitimates her. [Yet] Madeline's device is only skin deep. . . . [T]o focus the relation between Madeline's blushed body and the 'shielded scutcheon' is to grasp Madeline as an alienated representation of a representation. She is literally the dissociated reflection of the window image. *That* image represents some 'actual' shield, itself the emblem of some absent genetic and social authority."[19] When Levinson writes that "Keats wears Milton's colors as a sort of reversible coat of arms," she means that Milton as the source for the banquet Porphyro prepares, which is a salad of allusions to Adam and Raphael's meal, legitimates Keats even while Keats, by absorbing only the color and surface of Milton's food descriptions and not their meanings, resists Milton's power over him.[20]

Lowell was very interested in source study too, and in a way that aligns her less with the mostly male, mostly Victorian Keats scholars with whom she often disagrees and more with so recent a reader as Levinson, for Lowell sees the literary allusions as she sees the other "beauties," as items in Keats's collection. Lowell identified with Keats as a collector even as she turned him into an object and source of objects for her own collection.[21] Her style imitations, including her poems about and in imitation of Keats, may derive from the same anxious source as his (in Levinson's compelling view), the wish to find a place among the English poets. Levinson argues that Keats's self-creation as a poet who lived entirely in and by art depended upon his defining his originality through his secondariness: "Keats . . . could not begin to invent an original voice without first and throughout establishing his legitimacy: roughly, his derivativeness."[22] She draws here on Leslie Brisman's account of minor romantic poets who made a virtue of their secondariness, and she makes Keats sound like a modern poet too, for her argument corresponds aptly to Elizabeth Gregory's account of T. S. Eliot's relation to literary authority.[23] Eliot, Gregory argues, established his originality by showing that all the major English poets established their originality by quoting earlier poets, and thus in *The Waste Land* Eliot can make a virtue of his indebtedness. Just as anxious as Keats or Eliot to prove her literary legitimacy (an American, writing after great forebears both British and American, and ill-educated because of her sex), Lowell found in Keats an especially appealing model for deriving originality from secondariness.

Diverging from the mainstream of Keats source study, Lowell quirkily identifies Francisco de Moraes's *Palmerin of England*, "a romance of chivalry . . . written in Portuguese about 1570," as an important source for all the poems Keats was working on in the first half of 1819 while he had the book on loan from his publisher—not only "The Eve of St. Agnes" but also "La Belle Dame sans Merci" and the great odes.[24] Since almost no one either before or after Lowell has taken *Palmerin* seriously as a source or influence for Keats, it is worth wondering what it means that Lowell does so so emphatically. As an appendix to her book *John Keats,* Lowell transcribes Keats's marginalia and underscorings in various books. The greatest amount of space is given to Keats's markings in Edmund Spenser's *The Faerie Queen,* but the marks in *Palmerin* are carefully transcribed too. Describing Keats's annotations in the main text of her book, Lowell emphasizes Keats's interest in *Palmerin*'s supply of "what I may call 'images of effect'" and in "the purely colour passages."[25] She argues that Keats got more for "The Eve of St. Agnes" from *Palmerin* than from Boccaccio and Shakespeare, the usual scholars' favorites; or, to put it another way, she claims that getting "colour" is more significant than getting plot, character, or dramatic situation.[26] By "images of effect" Lowell says she means Keats's lifelong reading habit of isolating images from their contexts and marking them for later borrowing. After giving several examples, Lowell writes, "A great many passages describing the colours and devices of armour are marked: 'A Knight mounted on a mulberry courser' who wears 'green armour'; white armour with 'golden fruit of the arbutus in a green field on their shields'; armour 'black and yellow with grey griffins thereon'; 'armour red, with black joints.'"[27]

Conceding that Keats marks other sorts of passages too, she still maintains, "it is his colour sense and his faculty of observation which I wish to lay stress on here" and that she stresses again when she describes how Keats used his marked-up *Palmerin* when composing. In the original context of Moraes's poem these "colours and devices" bear fairly clear allegorical meanings: for example, there is a knight of death whose shield depicts "a knight of sorrowful aspect, surrounded by many deaths, who all fled from him."[28] Lowell's quotation of such devices renders them, however, as pure, nonsignifying color.

In Lowell's reading, *Palmerin* thus supplies color for Keats's poems, just as the "shielded scutcheon" on the window in "The Eve of St. Agnes" supplies color for Madeline's flesh. In both cases, decodable allegorical figures are emptied of their previous content and transformed into the material components of imagery. Whatever the "colours and devices of armour" may signify in their original contexts, they become purely decorative when they reappear in a Keats poem. Writing of Keats's use of Geoffrey Chaucer, Levinson argues that Keats gets from his allusions an "authenticity effect":[29] Chaucerian phrases lend Keats's poems an air of solid Englishness even as their decontextualization robs them of their authority over Keats. Just so, *Palmerin of England* supplies archaic sounds and colors that can be recombined for Keats's fresh purposes, Lowell and perhaps Keats as well finding *Palmerin* all the more available for this sort of dissection (compared to Milton or Spenser) because of its lack of weight in the English canon. Reading as an imagist, Lowell sees Keats reading as an imagist too. Writing of "La Belle Dame sans Merci," which she praises hyperbolically and calls "essentially an experimental poem," Lowell identifies its revolutionary quality with its use of archaisms derived in large part, she claims, from fragments of *Palmerin* more than from any other sources.[30] "Working from Chartier's intriguing title, with a hint from one of Spenser's stories and the absolutely enchanting properties which were scattered for him all through the four volumes of *Palmerin,* Keats suddenly and unexpectedly produced one of the finest poems in all literature," she writes.[31] For Lowell, the most admirable experiment is not a combination of fresh images; it is a fresh recombination of old images pulled from their original contexts. In "The Eve of St. Agnes," "La Belle Dame sans Merci," and some of the odes (for example, Lowell believes that such key Keatsian ode words as "moan," "faery," and "perilous" all came from his reading *Palmerin*), Lowell sees Keats as a treasure seeker, collecting the forgotten and "scattered" beauties of *Palmerin* from where they lie on the dust heap of literary tradition. As "properties," these beauties and colors are both props (artificial constructions) and possessions, displayed (as Levinson says of Keats's allusions to more canonical authors) to demonstrate possession, and displayed again by Lowell to affirm her possession of his creative acts of possession.

In transcribing Keats's underlinings in *Palmerin* in the appendix of her book, Lowell does in her own voice roughly what she sees Keats doing when, pencil in hand, he marked his borrowed copy: she lets the indicated passages remain at least partially in their own context. In her interpretation of his underlinings in the main text of her book, however, Lowell's work resembles Keats's when he later reuses the passages in his poems. She recontextualizes *Palmerin*'s "images of effect" in an openly tendentious argument, just as Keats recontextualized them in "The Eve of St. Agnes" and "La Belle Dame sans Merci." The new context is nonetheless the relatively neutral one of scholarly prose. In her sonnet-like poem "On Reading a Line Underscored by Keats in a Copy of 'Palmerin of England'" (1922) written while she was at work on her book, Lowell goes one step further, taking a line out of both its prior contexts (in *Palmerin* itself and in Keats's underlinings and annotations) and placing it in an entirely uncongenial context, indeed making her own arbitrary act of recontextualization the subject of the poem. Here are the poem's first seven lines:

> You marked it with light pencil upon a printed page,
> And, as though your finger pointed along a sunny path for my eyes'
> better direction,
> I see "a knight mounted on a mulberry courser and attired in green
> armour."
> I think the sky is faintly blue, but with a Spring shining about it,
> And the new grass scarcely fetlock high in the meads.
> He rides, I believe, alongside an overflown river,
> By a path soft and easy to his charger's feet.[32]

At first Lowell seems to be reading passively, following Keats's guiding hand as his pencil marks the line for her attention and claiming to "see" more or less what Keats saw. But when in the fourth line she turns from "I see" to "I think," she signals that her reading has become not only more actively creative but aggressively reconstructive. Lowell's carefully prepared appendix allows any reader to see that the knight riding on a mulberry courser and wearing green armor already bears the scars of battle: he is "a knight mounted on a mulberry courser and attired in green armour, which was all hacked and hewed."[33] Lest there be any doubt here, in the appendix you can see that Keats underlined "hacked and hewed" along with the rest of the description.

Moreover, a look at the first volume of *Palmerin* itself (beyond the point where Lowell transcribes) reveals that this knight is about to participate in an unusually nasty battle scene, which he provokes and which he barely survives, his opponent being the heroic protagonist (Palmerin disguised as the Knight of Fortune). In this scene, the knight in green comes across as a prickly, overly sensitive, and depressive character. In the chapter just before the one in which this episode occurs, Keats underlined several passages; the Knight of Death, inconsolable over the death of his beloved and dressed "in black armour" and riding "a dark flame-coloured horse," fights other knights dressed in symbol-laden arms including a knight "whose armour was beset all with green spheres, bearing in his shield likewise a sphere of the same color; he rode upon a roan horse stained with blood, which made him look the fairer."[34] Even if one reads only Lowell's transcription of Keats's underlinings in the appendix to *John Keats*, it is clear that Keats sees the knight in green as part of a violent world. Keats perhaps was struck by Moraes's continued use of the green-red color scheme, and the "stain[ing]" of the one horse's flanks by blood makes the "mulberry" coloring of the horse in the next chapter join with the descriptors "hacked and hewed" to evoke an ominous mood. Whether Keats was interested in the colors alone or in the mood they evoke in context as well, Lowell's poem calls attention to her reorientation of the description away from both of its prior contexts in Moraes's writing and Keats's reading. To reimagine this knight riding on a "path soft and easy" by a full river on a sunny spring day is deliberately to forget the strife that surrounds him. It is to misrepresent both the original meaning of the knight's colors and Keats's interest in them. Indeed, since Keats also marked elsewhere in the book passages that are generically similar to the grassy "meads" and "overflown river" where Lowell has misplaced the knight (for example, someone else rides "in a green meadow beside a brook, which with its clear running waters might have gladdened hearts not disposed to gladness"), it may be that Lowell's misrepresentation rehearses what she sees as Keats's habit of making fresh combinations of "scattered . . . properties."[35]

As the poem continues, Lowell's interest in her own misreading as well as the extent of it increase: "My vision confuses you with the green-armoured knight: / So dight and caparisoned might you be in a land of Faery." Now it appears that Lowell has been "prettying up" the knight in green so that he can serve as a figure for her idea of Keats. Despite Keats's legible attention to the images of blood and suffering in these pages of *Palmerin*, Lowell represents Keats merging into the purely decorative scenery of what she likes to identify as one of his "images of effect." She makes Keats vindicate Symons's trivializing version of him, when he remarks that Keats's idea of poetry "imprisoned him as within a fairy ring, alone with his little circle of green grass and blue sky."[36] Lowell's misquotation of *Palmerin* and of Keats's reading of it does to Keats what Symons also does: it misremembers Keats as a poet of sweetmeats only. It helps to show why Wasserman thinks Lowell continues Symons's reading tradition, reading Keats as a fine crafter of beauties with no moral content, because Lowell's misquotation does the same. By means of ostentatious acts of recontextualization Lowell empties Keats's words and his reading of their authoritative content. Levinson argues that when Keats does the same to Chaucer or Milton, his motive is resistance to their power over him. To what end does Lowell resignify Keats?

Lowell's shifting pronouns suggest one way in which she gains from misrepresenting Keats's reading and Keats as a reader. In the process of "confus[ing]" Keats with the text he marks, Lowell shifts from addressing Keats as "you" to referring to him as "he." Moreover, in the poem's next line, the trajectory from "you" to "he" to "it" is completed: "Thus, with denoting finger, you make of yourself an escutcheon to guide me to that in you which is its essence." Keats, Lowell claims, transforms himself into the very figure he has collected from *Palmerin*: a heraldic shield or scutcheon. At first conflated with the knight in an authentic romance, Keats is then taken out of the romance context to become that knight's shield, a shield that Lowell resignifies as a figure for "that in you which is its essence." What is "it," and what could "its essence" be? Lowell's grammar is so attenuated that, although "land of Faery" may be the answer, other referents slide in between. Is "it" the escutcheon's own essence? Or Keats's essence, now that Keats has become an "it"? Allegorical signage is reduced here to tautology, as the allegorically potent "escutcheon," standing in here as an allegorical figure for allegory itself, guides the reader to its own unnamed, self-identical essence. Anticipating Levinson's view that Keats, lacking the "authority, authenticity, and ease" of the other romantic poets, made himself a poet by way of simulacra, imitation, and parody, Lowell transforms Keats into a collectible object of beauty empty of meanings except those with which she has filled him, an "escutcheon" that like the "shielded scutcheon" in "The Eve of St. Agnes" can only be admired but not read. Lowell resignifies Keats so that he—or rather, "it"—will authorize her brand of imagism.

As the poem concludes, it adopts a new tone and declares what purports to be a fresh start: "But for the rest, / The part which most persists and is remembered, / I only know I compass it in loving and neither have, nor need, a symbol." "But for the rest" indicates a further turn away from the allegorical. There is another and better part to Keats that can be loved and that rejects the idea of symbolism or allegory altogether, and this is the best part of Keats and the most enduring. Allegory is put aside in favor of human love, one of the "beauties of a material universe" that Lowell admires Keats for celebrating, a love that is no more legible or meaningful than the self-referencing escutcheon. Although making Keats a lovable human would seem to restore him to life, Lowell's love, like the escutcheon, by dividing Keats into "part[s]" renders Keats an "it."

"On Reading a Line Underscored by Keats" is among Lowell's last Keats poems and is informed by her immersion in the Keats archive. One of Lowell's earliest Keats poems, the 1912 sonnet "To John Keats," was published in *A Dome of Many-Coloured Glass* when Lowell was more a fan and less a scholar of Keats. Nonetheless it is consistent with the later poem's transformation of Keats into an object of art, an "it," and then back into an antiallegorical, lovable figure— in this case, "you":

> Great master! Boyish, sympathetic man!
>   Whose orbed and ripened genius lightly hung
>   From life's slim, twisted tendril and there swung
> In crimson-sphered completeness; guardian
> Of crystal portals through whose openings fan
>   The spiced winds which blew when earth was young,
>   Scattering wreaths of stars, as Jove once flung
> A golden shower from heights cerulean.
>   Crumbled before thy majesty we bow.
>   Forget thy empurpled state, thy panoply
> Of greatness, and be merciful and near;
>   A youth who trudged the highroad we tread now
>   Singing the miles behind him; so may we
> Faint throbbings of thy music overhear.[37]

Just as the implicit "you" of the first line awkwardly modulates into the implicit "he" of "whose" in the second line, the "man" addressed in the opening gives way to an arty but patronizing representation of "genius" that objectifies Keats. "Thy" returns but gives way to the third person "a youth," whose appealingly ordinary "trudg[ing]" transforms "him" into "thy" again in the last line. Keats is made into an allegorical object, this time not an "escutcheon" but something rather like one, a red orb that serves as "guardian / Of crystal portals," only to have that allegorical object emptied of its apparent significance ("Forget thy empurpled state") in favor of a claim for Keats's simple but unrepresentable humanity. The poem opens by signing on with Shelley's elegiac program to idealize and reify Keats: while Lowell makes Keats an orb, Shelley makes him first a delicate blossom and later a star. It departs from that program in the end, however, by insisting on Keats's humanity and restoring him to the position of interlocutor. This is what "loving" without a "symbol" means in "On Reading a Line Underscored by Keats" as well. Favoring the unintimidating, imagined man over his awe-inspiring work, Lowell can claim to make a new, whole man out of scattered literary pieces, but only by reducing him to his human, mortal "part."

Most of Lowell's Keats poems follow this pattern of favoring the lovable, meaningless man over his work. The early poem "Suggested by the Cover of a Volume of Keats's Poems" (1912) echoes Keats's "Ode to a Nightingale" in such a way as to render the bird allegorical, but it ends with a patronizing account of Keats's real illness and death. The later poems "On a Certain Critic" (1917) and "View of Teignmouth in Devonshire" (1923) cite fragmentary phrases from early, minor, nonpoetic sources and from them reconstitute the figure of Keats the authentic man, who resembles the "part which most persists" in "On Reading a Line Underscored by Keats" or the "[b]oyish, sympathetic man!" of "To John Keats," who should be loved and not read allegorically. "View of Teignmouth" invents lengthy conversations between Keats the man and some townspeople who cheer him up out of a despondent mood; "On a Certain Critic" puts words into the mouth of a bouncingly healthy-minded Keats who in Lowell's imagining would deliver a "good, round, agreeable oath" to what Lowell castigates as another critic's excessively textual version of Keats.[38]

Lowell's insistent returns to Keats the unallegorical man culminate in her choice to devote so many years to writing his biography. Neither by training nor by inclination a scholar, Lowell was nonetheless drawn to a project that would call upon her to reconstruct Keats the man from the fragmentary evidence of his works and that would license her to elevate the imagined man over his writing. *John Keats* is a psychobiography as well as a literary biography, and it depends heavily both on a Freudian framework and on knowledge of Keats's manuscripts to let Lowell "almost get inside his brain."[39] In reconstituting Keats as a lovable person, however, Lowell tends to transform him into a fictional character. She invents scenes, and she attributes thoughts and feelings to Keats; although she supplies plenty of evidence from Keats's letters, she often calls attention to her tendentious use of this evidence. Once, for example, she justifies an assertion about Keats's feelings for Fanny Brawne by means of "our intimate knowledge of his temperament."[40] Two pages before making this claim to "intimate knowledge" Lowell quotes (as she must) Keats's famous statement in a letter, "[a] Man's life of any worth is a continual allegory, and very few eyes can see the mystery of his life." Framing her quotation by referring to it as "a beautiful and wise observation, one of those observations which show us the very heart and core of his continual reflections," Lowell ignores the evidence of Keats's interest in allegory together with his clear warning to any future biographer.[41] Instead of yielding material for reflection on the difficulty of interpreting any richly significant life, Keats's remark becomes flattened out as yet another "beauty," one that steers Lowell and her readers to the "heart" she has made up for her lovable Keats.

Lowell's Keats poems and biography claim for her the favored role of the poet-creator on whom Keats's living reputation depends. Like Keats himself, in Levinson's words "turn[ing] the arrow of literary history backward," Lowell's use and invention of Keats allusions and quotations places him in her debt.[42] But her handling of Keats also differs in an important way from Keats's handling of Chaucer and Milton: whereas, in Levinson's view, he takes apart past literary masters to resist their power over him, Lowell takes her "great master" apart in order to grant him new life on her terms. Calling attention to her debts to Keats in her Keats poems and biography, she draws on her version of Keats as a fragmenter of prior texts to authorize her own fragmentation of the

Keats text into valuable pieces, and then to reassemble them into a humanized whole of her own devising. In so claiming to know the real Keats, Lowell does just what the "shielded scutcheon" does when it casts its moonlit colors onto Madeline's flesh and hair: words or colors still trailing an aura of authenticity from their original contexts are emptied and refilled with a new meaning, in this case the lifelike body of Lowell's Keats. This new Keats, the "youth" or "man" whose work can be reduced to its "beauty," replaces the infinitely complex Keats who can be found only in the lines of his poetry. Keats reconstituted as a human being becomes a prime example of those "beauties of a material universe"—once Keats's subject, now the identity to which he is reduced —that underwrite and justify Lowell's practice of imagism. Lowell's Keats would be the first imagist, were it not that his beautiful image is what enables Lowell to claim that role for herself.

Notes

1. I have argued elsewhere that Lowell's Keats (her reading, collecting, and writing on Keats) served both to form and to meet the needs of her own self-definition as a gendered and sexual being; see "Amy Lowell's Keats: Reading Straight, Writing Lesbian," *Yale Journal of Criticism* 14 (2001): 319–351. The present essay looks at two poems about Keats that I did not consider in the earlier essay, and it emphasizes Lowell's use of Keats to place herself in literary history rather than along a spectrum of social identities. The basic facts of Lowell's Keats interests and publications listed in this paragraph appear in that essay also; otherwise they do not overlap.

2. S. Foster Damon, *Amy Lowell: A Chronicle with Extracts from Her Correspondence* (Boston: Houghton Mifflin, 1935), 673.

3. Ibid., 674.

4. William Henry Marquess, *Lives of the Poet: The First Century of Keats Biography* (University Park: Pennsylvania State University Press, 1985), 97.

5. On the importance of reading Lowell's work in terms of her marketing of modernism and imagism, see Melissa Bradshaw, "Outselling the Modernisms of Men: Amy Lowell and the Art of Self-Commodification," *Victorian Poetry* 38 (2000): 141–169.

6. Amy Lowell, *John Keats* (Boston: Houghton Mifflin, 1925), 2:168–169.

7. John Keats, *The Poems of John Keats,* ed. Jack Stillinger (Cambridge, Mass.: Harvard University Press, 1978), 309.

8. John Collick, "Desire on 'The Eve of St. Agnes,'" *Critical Survey* 3 (1991), 37–43; Alan D. Boehm, "Madeline's Castle: Setting and Visual Discrepancy in John Keats's 'The Eve of St. Agnes,'" in *Spectrum of the Fantastic,* ed. Donald Palumbo (Westport, Conn.: Greenwood Press, 1988), 21–27, quotation on p. 21. Jack Stillinger lucidly presents and compares these readings together with numerous others in his masterful summary of "a token fifty-nine interpretations" of the poem, and I am indebted to his book for introducing me to these and other readings I had been unaware of. See Jack Stillinger, *Reading The Eve of St. Agnes: The Multiples of Complex Literary Transaction* (New York: Oxford University Press, 1999).

9. Greg Kucich, *Keats, Shelley, and Romantic Spenserianism* (University Park: Pennsylvania State University Press, 1991); my quotation is from Stillinger's summary in *Reading The Eve of St. Agnes,* 69.

10. Earl R. Wasserman, *The Finer Tone: Keats' Major Poems* (Baltimore: Johns Hopkins University Press, 1953), 97–98.

11. Ibid., 98, quoting Lowell, *John Keats*, 1:456.

12. George Ridley, *Keats's Craftsmanship* (1933), quoted in Walter Jackson Bate, *John Keats* (New York: Oxford University Press, 1966), 450.

13. Lowell, *John Keats*, 2:171.

14. *Shelley's Poetry and Prose,* ed. Donald H. Reiman and Sharon B. Powers (New York: W. W. Norton, 1977), 405.

15. Aileen Ward, *John Keats: The Making of a Poet* (New York: Viking, 1963), 245.

16. Marjorie Levinson, *Keats's Life of Allegory: The Origins of a Style* (Oxford: Blackwell, 1988), 95, 18.

17. Ibid., 21, 19.

18. Ibid., 186.

19. Ibid., 119.

20. Ibid., 120.

21. See my "Amy Lowell's Keats" for a reading of Lowell's activities as a Keats collector.

22. Levinson, *Keats's Life,* 8.

23. See Leslie Brisman, *Romantic Origins* (Ithaca, N.Y.: Cornell University Press, 1978); and Elizabeth Gregory, *Quotation and Modern American Poetry: "'Imaginary Gardens with Real Toads'"* (Houston: Rice University Press, 1996). Lynn Keller makes a similar argument about Marianne Moore in "'For inferior who is free?': Liberating the Woman Writer in Marianne Moore's 'Marriage,'" in *Influence and Intertextuality in Literary History,* ed. Jay Clayton and Eric Rothstein (Madison: University of Wisconsin Press, 1991), 219–244. In Keller's view, Moore may be "ambivalent about the patriarchal tradition" but "she nonetheless desires to claim her own place in its economy" and as a consequence quotes conspicuously from canonical literature: "the marginal writer has something to gain by establishing him/herself as securely enough within the tradition to be influenced by it" (224).

24. Lowell, *John Keats,* 2:592. The edition that Keats and Lowell read is Francisco de Moraes, *Palmerin of England,* translated by Anthony Munday and edited by Robert Southey, 4 vols. (London: Longman, Hurst, Rees, and Orme, 1807).

25. Lowell, *John Keats*, 1:103, 2:160. Among other major Keats studies, Claude Lee Finney's is almost alone in even mentioning *Palmerin* among the books that supplied Keats with the idea of medieval romance that he drew on for "The Eve of St. Agnes" and "La Belle Dame sans Merci"; see Finney, *The Evolution of Keats's Poetry* (Cambridge: Harvard University Press, 1933), 2:546, 596. Only a short essay by Charles I. Patterson takes Lowell's idea seriously and pursues in detail the substance and meanings of Keats's borrowings from *Palmerin*; see Patterson, "The Keats-Hazlitt-Hunt Copy of *Palmerin of England* in Relation to Keats's Poetry," *Journal of English and Germanic Philology* 60 (1961): 31–43. Two even briefer articles supply further information about but little interpretation of Keats's marginalia (Lowell was able to borrow the copy of *Palmerin* from its private owner only briefly); see Norman A. Anderson, "Corrections to Amy Lowell's Reading of Keats's Marginalia," *Keats-Shelley Journal* 23 (1974): 25–31; and Beth Lau, "Further Corrections to Amy Lowell's Transcriptions of Keats's Marginalia," *Keats-Shelley Journal* 35 (1986): 30–38.

26. Lowell also emphasizes that Keats had borrowed the volume and that he was irresponsible to deface someone else's property; the scholarly debate over whether the

volumes belonged to Keats or not literalizes the more substantive question of his literary borrowing.

27. Lowell, *John Keats*, 1:103–104. She is quoting from Moraes, *Palmerin*, 1:251, 1:320, and 1:319 (the last two quotations).

28. Moraes, *Palmerin*, 1:184.

29. Levinson, *Keats's Life*, 65.

30. Lowell, *John Keats*, 2:225.

31. Ibid., 2:226.

32. Amy Lowell, "On Reading a Line Underscored by Keats in a Copy of 'Palmerin of England,'" in *The Complete Poetical Works of Amy Lowell*, ed. Louis Untermeyer (Boston: Houghton Mifflin, 1955), 476. The poem was first published in the *Literary Review* of the *New York Post*, 7 October 1922, and was reprinted in Lowell's posthumous 1925 volume *What's O'Clock* (Boston: Houghton Mifflin, 1925).

33. Lowell, *John Keats*, 2:596; Lowell transcribes Moraes, *Palmerin*, 1:193.

34. Ibid., 2:596, transcribing Moraes, *Palmerin*, 1:184, 187; Keats marked these passages in the margins and, where indicated, also underlined particular phrases.

35. Moraes, *Palmerin*, 1:5.

36. Arthur Symons, *The Romantic Movement in English Poetry* (New York: E. P. Dutton, 1909), 312; quoted in Wasserman, *Finer Tone*, 97.

37. Lowell, "To John Keats," in *Complete Poetical Works*, 21.

38. See my "Amy Lowell's Keats" for a fuller reading of these three poems and of the biography. Quotation from "On a Certain Critic" is from *Complete Poetical Works*, 243.

39. Lowell, *John Keats*, 1:505.

40. Ibid., 2:180; Marquess complains of Lowell's inventive technique in *Lives of the Poet*, 96–100.

41. Lowell, *John Keats*, 2:178.

42. Levinson, *Keats's Life*, 85.

Unrelated Beauty

Amy Lowell, Polyphonic Prose, and the Imagist City

Andrew Thacker

Polyphonic Tides of Revolution

In the first manifesto of Italian futurism, composed in 1909, Filippo Tomasso Marinetti proclaimed that his protean movement would be devoted to an urban art of upheaval and many voices: "We will sing of great crowds excited by work, by pleasure, and by riot; we will sing of the multicoloured, polyphonic tides of revolution in the modern capital."[1] What interests me here are the links among the crowd, the metropolis, and the notion of polyphonic voices. While the first two features are well established as key emblems of modernity, it is only with the recent rereadings by, for example, feminist and historicist critics, that the canon of modernism has opened up to the plurality of voices that engaged socially, politically, and aesthetically with modernity; too often it is the monologic "men of 1914" that have dominated our sense of the artistic tides of revolution from this period.

In a quieter, less riotous and declamatory fashion, a number of poems by Amy Lowell also explore the connections among polyphony, the city and modernity. For Lowell, the modernist experimentation of her "polyphonic prose" is, I wish to argue, conditioned by two central factors. First, her commitment to formal literary innovation as an essential condition for being "modern"; and secondly, a sense that modernity, especially urban modernity, is itself "many-voiced," and that to capture this aspect of life requires a fresh form of poetic expression. This commitment to innovation is, of course, shared by all modernist poets, and is exemplified by Ezra Pound's slogan, "Make it new." Lowell's polyphonic prose, I suggest, is an interesting, and hitherto undervalued, form of modernist revolution; it cannot, however, be easily subsumed under Pound's version of imagism.[2]

Marinetti's polyphonic city is mainly characterized by industry and technology: arsenals, shipyards, railway stations, and factories are all praised, along with locomotives, steamers, and "the sleek flight of planes whose propellers chatter in the wind like banners and seem to cheer like an enthusiastic crowd."[3]

Lowell's image of the city is somewhat different, especially in her sequence of poems, "Towns in Colour," and the imagist poem, "Spring Day," both published in 1916. Not all of Lowell's poetry of the city is in the polyphonic form, and not all of her polyphonic poetry considers urban themes, but some of her most interesting work occurs when the city and polyphony are conjoined. Between 1914 and 1918 Lowell produced a number of texts that use polyphonic prose to explore both the individual protagonist in the city (such as "Spring Day") and the city as an historical entity in its own right ("The Bronze Horses" in *Can Grande's Castle,* 1918).

As a term, *polyphony* is perhaps best known to literary critics from its use by the Russian theorist Mikhail Bakhtin to characterize a certain form of novelistic practice. In the 1920s Bakhtin described Fyodor Dostoevsky's novels as being polyphonic, the creation of which form was, he felt, a major innovation in the history of the European novel: "What unfolds in his works is not a multitude of characters and fates in a single objective world, illuminated by a single consciousness; rather a plurality of consciousnesses, with equal rights and each with its own world, combine but are not merged in the unity of the event."[4] This polyphonic practice is described as a "plurality of independent and unmerged voices and consciousnesses, a genuine polyphony of fully valid voices" rejecting the "fundamentally monologic (homophonic) European novel."[5] As in Bakhtin's similar theories of heteroglossia and dialogism, the stress in the polyphonic novel is upon the many voices that merge, overlap and interact in Dostoevsky without ever being controlled or submerged beneath one controlling voice, even that of the author. It is worth emphasizing that Bakhtin's work here was carried out in a postrevolutionary context, where the opening-up of hitherto unheard voices was part, not just of a literary innovation, but of an experiment in the democratization of voices at the social and political levels. Each polyphonic voice, as Bakhtin writes, has "equal rights" and is independent and "fully valid."[6] As Julia Kristeva notes of the polyphonic novel, it rejects both law and hierarchy, as it consists of "a plurality of linguistic elements in dialogical relationships."[7] Marinetti's "polyphonic tides of revolution" would, therefore, be a very recognizable reality for Bakhtin in this period.

Polyphony in Bakhtinian terms is perhaps best summarized as an impulse or force within literary language that strives to create an open form in which multiple voices and discourses can mingle and be modified and reinterpreted, but without any overall closure within a unified point of view. Bakhtin found this Babel of voices in the novel and was quite hostile to poetic discourse for what he saw as its intrinsic impulse toward a unifying language, with a single point of view.[8] Arguably, Lowell's use of polyphonic prose for poetic expression shows an agreement with Bakhtinian principles. Like Bakhtin, Lowell employed the musical analogy of orchestration for the many voices of her polyphonic prose; and her shifting between different scenes for narrative in "The Bronze Horses" would perhaps be recognized by Bakhtin as an attempt to render a "plurality of independent voices." Clearly, the social and political context

Lowell operated within differed greatly from that of Bakhtin. However, the aesthetic ferment and excitements of modernism offered Lowell her own version of "tides of revolution," with the polyphonic voices of the modernist city and the traumas of World War I also providing a context of radical upheaval.

In the modernist period the term *polyphony* has a range of uses, and there is some evidence that in English usage the word seemed to undergo something of a revival in the late nineteenth and early twentieth centuries. The definitions of polyphonic and polyphony found in the *New Oxford English Dictionary* indicate three main usages. The earliest is for a musical instrument like a lute (1655, 1674), which is revived in the 1880s and early twentieth century to refer to a mechanical pianola-type device called a polyphone. The second main usage is again musical, and describes a type of composition for several voices, each with its own melody (1782, 1876), a form of music dating from the tenth and eleventh centuries and rising to its apogee with the works of Johann Sebastian Bach. The third usage is found in philology and linguistics to describe a written character with more than one phonetic value, and citations occur from 1870, 1891, and 1901. The dictionary then refers to a sense relating to prose, to sound pleasant and melodious, with the first reference being an article by John Gould Fletcher of 1916, followed by references to Lowell, Hart Crane, and I. A. Richards in the 1920s.

The implication is that Lowell has combined the two earlier senses of musical and linguistic polyphony. Though the musical references point backward, the 1880s "polyphone" indicates a technological invention that Lowell might well have been aware of. And then there was the pianola, a proprietary brand invented in 1901; it also worked without a player, but unlike the polyphone was attached to an actual piano. In *Hugh Selwyn Mauberly* Pound notes that "the pianola 'replaces' / Sappho's barbitos," a morbid symptom of the decline of modern aesthetics.[9] The link between music and language, explicitly poetic language, was also one that many writers explored in this period, perhaps prompted by Walter Pater's famous claim that "all art aspires to the condition of music." For instance, one of William Butler Yeats's semimystical friends, Florence Farr, had published a book in 1909 titled *The Music of Speech*. This suggested accompanying spoken poetry by a bare sounding of chords on a specially constructed instrument, a psaltery, to emphasize the natural "melody of words."[10] Accompanied by Arnold Dolmetsch, Yeats spoke some poems in a "subtly modulated monotone" in order to demonstrate what Farr called "song in speech" and that each single word "has its own significant music."[11] Farr's ideas were entertained widely, and in 1907 she toured North America, visiting New York; Cambridge, Massachusetts; Chicago; and Boston. One direct link with the imagists was that Farr was a member of T. E. Hulme's group, the Poets' Club, along with F. S. Flint.

Such experiments might have influenced Pound, who met Farr through Yeats and heard her recitals. Yeats came to believe that Pound's interest in the troubadours, another modernist association of music and poetry, was an improvement upon Farr's work: "it is more definitely music with strongly marked time and yet it is effective speech." The drawback with Pound, remarked Yeats, was that "he cannot sing, as he has no voice. It is like something on a very bad phonograph."[12] Nevertheless, Pound's interest, along with others in this period, perhaps led to his assertion in a 1918 essay that "Poetry is a composition of words set to music."[13] Poetry, argues Pound, must be read as if to imaginary music and not as oratory, a possible retort to Lowell's claim in the preface to *Can Grande's Castle* that polyphonic prose must resemble oratorical prose. However, only a few years earlier, in "A Few Don'ts by an Imagiste" of March 1913, Pound's section on "Rhyme and Rhythm" argued that it is not necessary that a poem rely upon its music, but if it does it must be good: "Let the neophyte know assonance and alliteration, rhyme immediate and delayed, simple and polyphonic, as a musician would expect to know harmony and counterpoint and all the minutiae of his craft."[14] This suggests that a poet must know the technical side of poetry as well as a trained musician; the idea of a polyphonic rhyme, however, is slightly puzzling, but might be understood in terms of complex rhymes, like near rhyme or internal rhyming.

Though there is no clear indication that Lowell knew of Farr's work, the invention of polyphonic prose might be understood as yet another experiment in the field of music and language in the early twentieth century. She had certainly read Pound's "A Few Don'ts," with its reference to polyphonic rhyme, and perhaps more significantly had an active interest in contemporary music.[15] In *John Gould Fletcher and Southern Modernism*, Lucas Carpenter argues that polyphonic prose was named and formulated by Fletcher, even though he gave Lowell the credit for inventing it.[16] This was outlined in Fletcher's article of 1915, "Miss Lowell's Discovery: Polyphonic Prose."[17] Most of Fletcher's poems in this form date from 1914 to 1916, but were not published until his 1921 volume, *Breakers and Granite*. In this volume polyphonic prose is often used to describe geographical entities, like the cities of Chicago or New Orleans, or the Deep South of the United States. Fletcher, like Lowell, credits the French poet Paul Fort for indicating the possibility of polyphonic prose, but saw antecedents in the "elaborately rhymed prose of Sir Thomas Browne, de Quincey, or Melville, with this addition: that all the wealth of English rhyme, assonance, verbal onomatopoeia, was deliberately woven into it exactly as the masters of polyphony, such as Bach, had woven over their simple chorales the most elaborate contrapuntal forms."[18] Other possible French antecedents, of whom Lowell and Fletcher were aware, included the prose poetry of Arthur Rimbaud and Jules Laforgue.[19]

Lowell's earliest experiments in polyphonic prose echo Fletcher's ideas and also date from 1914. In her volume of that year a number of poems utilized a prose format, including "The Basket" and "In a Castle," based upon vers libre, or what Lowell preferred to call "unrhymed cadence" or "the rhythm of the speaking voice."[20] In a later article Lowell said that her choice of polyphonic prose was designed "to find a new form for epic poetry. . . . The modern epic . . . should be based rather upon drama than upon narrative. This came partly from the greater speed and vividness demanded today of all the arts."[21] This latter comment shows clearly how Lowell conceived the form to be essentially linked to the modernity of her times, and that to compose a modern epic demanded a modern form, a principle also shared by Pound in *The Cantos*. Although in this article Lowell calls polyphonic prose "an orchestral effect," she is also keen to extend the term beyond its merely musical resonance: it will treat subjects "at once musically, dramatically, lyrically, and pictorially."[22] This indicates a sense of polyphony that is closer to Bakhtin's many-voiced conception. This is certainly borne out in Lowell's own poetry, which frequently extends away from the musical basis of polyphony toward a synesthetic approach that is perhaps most successful when its subject matter is that of the city. Her visits to London in 1913 and 1914 seemed to precipitate her most experimental verse, not only due to her contact with expatriate writers such as Pound and Fletcher, but also, I would argue, because of her sense of the modernity represented by London in this period. *Sword Blades and Poppy Seed* (1914) contains only a few poems, such as "A London Thoroughfare. 2 A.M.," that take the city "squalid and sinister" as its subject matter. But it is with her next volume, *Men, Women and Ghosts* (1916) and the imagist volume of this year, that we see Lowell combine the musical and formalist techniques of polyphonic prose with the many voices of the modernist city.

The Imagist Anthologies

The period of the imagist anthologies (1914–1917) coincides with the main years of Lowell's employment of polyphonic prose. The 1916 imagist anthology, the second to be produced under Lowell's stewardship, has perhaps her most significant exploration of the city using the format of polyphonic prose, the poem, "Spring Day." In this period the debate among Anglophone modernists over the status of vers libre was perhaps at its height, but unlike others Lowell shifts her interest from free verse to free prose verse.[23] The preface to the anthology contains a short set of remarks upon the difference between poetry and prose, comments that could only apply to Lowell, as no other contributor to the volume employs prose poetry. Throughout the imagist period Lowell was also the only regular user of prose verse forms. The 1914 *Des Imagistes*, edited by Pound, had included John Cournos's short prose poem "The Rose," and in this period other writers published a number of prose poems, such as Gertrude Stein's *Tender Buttons* (composed in 1911 and published in 1914) and T. S. Eliot's "Hysteria," in Pound's *Catholic Anthology* (1915).[24] Lowell, however, is alone among modernist writers in providing such a systematic and theoretical attempt to utilize prose for poetic purposes.

"Spring Day" enacts a sensual engagement with the hubbub of the city, before withdrawing to regard it from afar through the use of tropes of nature.[25] The city is not, however, negatively portrayed in comparison with the flowery garden, as the poet is "proud" to feel the pavement and is said to be "part" of the city, merged into its fibers. "Spring Day" is in five sections and follows the protagonist from an early morning bath to sleep at nighttime in a single day. This exploration of the day, and dailiness in all its mundanity is also of interest, as it is prior to James Joyce's Bloomsday setting in *Ulysses*. Though Lowell's poem is conceived on a much smaller scale than Joyce's work, it contains something of the same sense of the ordinary and quotidian as significant topics for modernism. And like Joyce, something of the heroic capacity to endure and flourish in the condition of modernity is also evident in this poem. In order to capture the sense of newness represented by modernity what better place to start than with the sensation of the everyday, rather than with the extraordinary?

Nothing remarkable happens in Lowell's poem—merely breakfast and a walk through the city—but the poem's attempt to transform the mundane into an instance of beauty is characteristically imagist and modernist. One of the devices Lowell uses to produce this is her focus upon synesthesia, with the "smell of tulips and narcissus in the air" a phrase that is repeated throughout the poem. The opening section describing the bath focuses upon the visual play of light upon water, as the sunshine pours through the window and "cleaves the water into flaws like a jewel, and cracks it to bright light."[26] The protagonist lies back in the bath and lets the "green-white water, the sun-flawed beryl water, flow over me," the sensuous qualities of the light and water being repeatedly stressed. In the next section, "Breakfast Table," this observing eye turns upon the everyday objects of the breakfast, attempting a kind of defamiliarization of the breakfast paraphernalia: "Wheels of white glitter in the silver coffee pot, hot and spinning like catherine-wheels, they whirl, and twirl." It is, of course, very easy for this kind of verse to spill over into parody, as it strives to perceive something like pats of butter in a fresh light: "A stack of butter-pats, pyramidal, shout orange through the white, scream, flutter, call: 'Yellow ! Yellow ! Yellow !'" But, as with Stein's efforts in *Tender Buttons* to depict roast potatoes, custard, and butter also, Lowell's verse can be read as a semiserious attempt to capture both the ordinariness and the absurdity of everyday objects, much as Pablo Picasso and the cubists represented traditional still-life subjects in startling new ways.[27] In another sense the use of prose for these images of mundane objects is appropriate, suggesting that poetry can and should describe the dull and overlooked, but that perhaps the ordinary typographical appearance of prose is best suited to this strategy. It is only when read aloud, as Lowell insisted of her polyphonic prose, that the full "poetic qualities" are evident, and the transformation of prose about pats of butter into something else becomes evident in the employment of aural devices such as alliteration and assonance.[28]

Much the most successful section of "Spring Day" is the section "Midday and Afternoon," which is set amid the bustling streets of the city. This is because the formal polyphonic devices Lowell utilizes find a more appropriate content in the phenomenology of the modern city:

> Swirl of crowded streets. Shock and recoil of traffic. The stock-still
> brick façade of an old church, against which the waves of people lurch

and withdraw. Flare of sunshine down side-streets. Eddies of light in
the windows of chemists' shops, with their blue, gold, purple jars,
darting colours far into the crowd. Loud bangs and tremors,
murmurings out of high windows, whirling of machine belts,
blurring of horses and motors. A quick spin and shudder of brakes
on an electric car, and the jar of a church bell knocking against the
metal blue of the sky. I am a piece of the town, a bit of blown dust,
thrust along with the crowd. Proud to feel the pavement under me,
reeling with feet. Feet tripping, skipping, lagging, dragging,
plodding doggedly, or springing up and advancing on firm elastic
insteps.[29]

Here the poetic effects of rhyme, assonance, alliteration and return enhance the
claims of polyphonic prose to be orchestral and many voiced, as Lowell creates
a kaleidoscopic urban panorama. The irregular rhymes of the opening lines
(Shock/stock; traffic/brick; church/lurch) add to what Lowell terms the "tonal
colour" of the aural picture of the city.[30] Arguably, a regular rhyme scheme can-
not represent the haphazard sounds, the "loud bangs and tremors" that one en-
counters when walking the streets of the city. This attempt to directly capture
the texture of the city derives from the imagist dictum that *presentation* rather
than *representation* was to be the aim of their poetry.[31] Lowell's argument that
polyphonic prose is "an orchestral form" that employs a contrapuntal logic rather
than a single melodic line seems ideally suited to the urban soundscape she de-
scribes here. One might recall T. S. Eliot's claim in 1921 that the music of Igor
Stravinsky's *The Rite of Spring* reminded him of "the scream of the motor-horn,
the rattle of machinery, the grind of wheels, the beating of iron and steel, the
roar of the underground railway, and the other barbaric noises of modern life."[32]
Lowell's "Spring Day" might be read with an ear for the noises of modern life,
albeit with the difference that barbarism is tempered with a certain pleasure in
the sounds of the city.

   In addition to the clatter of the city, Lowell's poem also uses the irregular
sentence lengths of polyphonic prose to capture another key aspect of urban life,
the effect of movement. Freed from the constraints of the metrical line we see
how the switching between long and short sentences apes the crabby progress
of the traffic and pedestrians in the city, shifting forward only to stop and "re-
coil" a moment later. Even in the childlike rhyming of the line "Feet tripping,
skipping, lagging, dragging, plodding doggedly" it is the physical patterns of
movement in the modern city that Lowell is trying to present. Pound would un-
doubtedly have derided this sort of verse, perhaps recalling his criticism of fu-
turism as "accelerated impressionism."[33] However, Pound's obsession with an
imagism of hard, clear lines (particularly in his vorticist phase) can be contrasted
with Lowell's form of imagist attention to the flux and blurred outlines of the
city. While Pound's rhetoric of poetic objectivity was designed to master and
control the energy of the city, Lowell's poem shows a protagonist happy to drift

through the town, like "a bit of blown dust, thrust along with the crowd." Lowell's corporal engagement with the city, emphasizing the contact of feet upon the pavements, does not try to bemoan or contain the urban, but quietly celebrate its powerful qualities. Again, unlike the visual thrust of Poundian imagism, Lowell's representation of the city equally, and perhaps more so, emphasizes sound and touch.[34]

The final section of the poem, "Night and Sleep," does, however, contain a predominantly visualized city, as Lowell describes the electric advertising signs that "gleam out along the shop fronts," such as an effervescent mug of beer. Again, however, Lowell tries to employ aural effects to describe these visual images. Some signs "grow, and grow, and blow into patterns of fire-flowers, as the sky fades," while of another Lowell writes, "Twinkle, jab, snap, that means a new play; and over the way: plop, drop, quiver is the sidelong sliver of a watchmaker's sign."[35] Raymond Williams once noted that many of the linguistic experiments of the modernist avant-garde could be traced back to certain kinds of "strangeness and distance" to be found in the metropolis that stemmed from "the inescapable new uses in newspapers and advertising" of even one's native language. Lowell's images of neon advertisements bear out Williams's claim that the metropolis itself not only stimulated such experiments as polyphonic prose, but also was "an intense and visually and linguistically exciting process in its own right."[36]

After this visual bombardment the protagonist retreats to the edge of the city, to where "the earth of my garden smells of tulips and narcissus." The repetition of this phrase, an example of what Lowell calls "return" in polyphonic prose, is interesting since it indicates that the garden is not a pastoral retreat from the sensations of the city. In fact there are "no flowers in bloom yet" in the garden, and the most pungent smells of tulips and narcissus have occurred in the city when, for example, the poet sees a boy on the street selling newspapers: "I smell them clean and new from the press. They are fresh like the air, and pungent as tulips and narcissus." Curiously, then, the odors generated in the city are more real than the smell of actual flowers. This confusion of city and nature continues as the poet looks out of her window: "I can see the distant city, a band of twinkling gems, little flower heads with no stems. I cannot see the beer glass, nor the letters of the restaurants and shops I passed, now the signs blur and all together make the city, glowing on a night of fine weather, like a garden stirring and blowing for the Spring."[37] City and garden are not contrasted, but seemingly merged, with the flowery smells of the city replacing those of the garden, and the lights of the city being transformed into "twinkling" flower heads.

Lowell had written in the preface to her volume *Men, Women and Ghosts* (1916) of how walking in the city was an experience informing poems like "Spring Day" and the sequence "Towns in Colour": "It is an enchanting thing to wander through a city looking for its unrelated beauty, the beauty by which it captivates the sensuous sense of seeing."[38] The idea of "sensuous seeing" is an intriguing one, and perhaps suggests that other senses are somehow included in the visual or that visuality must somehow be expanded to be more haptic. Certainly, the use of sound and smell in "Spring Day" supports a more tactile understanding of imagist "seeing" than even Lowell imagined in her claim that she was employing a "purely pictorial effect."[39] This expanded sense of sight might also help understand the concept of "unrelated beauty." Unrelated seems a link to the many voices of the polyphonic prose, a poetry of unrelated rhythmical and tonal effects, where the devices are not joined together by some overarching rhyme or meter but connect or interact in a seemingly random fashion. The prose mimics the beauty of the city, where images are constantly juxtaposed in an accidental fashion to the eyes of the passerby, and where people in the street mingle and meet in chance, unrelated encounters.

In the preface to *Men, Women and Ghosts* Lowell credited the "unrelated" method to John Gould Fletcher's poem "London Excursion," with its portrayal of a journey into and out of the city on a single day.[40] Bryher, however, in her appreciation of Lowell's poetry published in 1918, suggested that Fletcher's poem is dominated by the poet's personality, while Lowell's poem is "charged . . . with suggested personality" and has thus "snared the fluttering day itself."[41] Bryher's sensitive and enthusiastic account of Lowell's poetry makes much of how Lowell's "revolution" in verse is able to capture, in a semipsychoanalytic sense, aspects of modernity hitherto missing in contemporary writers: "For years I have grieved that poetry was inarticulate of the transient aspects of an hour, some effect of colour, some movement of wind or rain, actually forming an unconscious part of dream, yet apparently unrelated in any way to thought."[42] In some ways this comment resembles Virginia Woolf's later comments in "Modern Fiction" upon how contemporary novelists must try to capture the transient inner life of "the dark places of psychology."[43] Just as Woolf praised Joyce for avoiding the external materialism of Edwardian realist fiction, so Bryher praises "Spring Day" for "its escape from a mere photograph of actuality, in the union of colour with sound and the feeling of Spring, vivid with an intense, though merely suggested individuality . . . fluid with light."[44] Bryher links these transient nonphotographic images with the nature of the city as a subject matter in the poems "Spring Day" and the poetic sequence "Towns in Colour": "It has ever been a delight to wander about a city, noting the traffic, the noise, the street, that owns but three or four unalterable moods, yet daily makes them other with new delicacy of light, but none before Miss Lowell . . . have captured this sense I had unwillingly deemed too mutable, too fluid to be confined by any words."[45] The significant aspect of Bryher's insight is this stress upon the fluidity of Lowell's verse, a feature I have been arguing stems from the freedom of the many voices of polyphonic prose, and perhaps also from her gendered insights into flanerie in the city.[46]

"Towns in Colour" represents a fuller version of the imagistic city articulated in "Spring Day." This is a poem in five sections, each taking a facet of the city to present in a semiobjective fashion, without the presence of an observing protagonist as was found in "Spring Day." "Towns in Colour" is thus a kind of antiflâneur poetic series, with only the briefest of appearances of a protagonist in the poem. Lowell's urban focus is an eclectic one: a shop window in "Red Slippers," a public dining room in "Thompson's Lunch Room—Grand Central Station," "An Opera House," rain in "Afternoon Rain in State Street" and "An Aquarium." The emphasis upon color in the poems certainly suggests that these are, as Lowell claimed, poems devoted to a "purely pictorial effect, and with little or no reference to any other aspect of the places described."[47] I will concentrate upon the first poem, "Red Slippers," as it is the only poem in "Towns in Colour" to employ polyphonic prose. Even here, however, the pure pictorialism Lowell evinced is broadened by the many voices of polyphonic prose.

The poem revolves around a sharp visual contrast, between the red slippers on display in a shop window and both the "grey, windy sleet" of the city streets and the "white, monotonous block of shops" nearby. The vivacity of the slippers is emphasized by the manifold terms used to describe them: they are variously red, blood, claret, salmon, maroon, crimson, scarlet, vermilion, and rose. The slippers stand out as objects of visual pleasure and stimulation amid the monotonous whites, blacks and grays of the surrounding environment. They are said to "flood . . . the eyes of passers-by with dripping colour," with their visuality intruding in reflections upon cabs and trams, umbrellas and other shop windows. The poem concludes with Lowell contrasting the slippers with a peculiar display in another shop window of a "big lotus bud of cardboard" whose petals mechanically open to reveal a "wax doll, with staring bead eyes and flaxen hair." Pedestrians are said to ignore the slippers, for "[o]ne has often seen shoes, but whoever saw a cardboard lotus bud before?" This contrast between the artificiality of the flower doll and the red slippers suggests a form of resistance to the visual commodification of the window display; the poem rejects the more elaborate window display in favor of the merely mundane image of slippers. Lowell's poem can be read as an attempt to transform the everyday object perceived in the window into an instance redolent of aesthetic pleasure and replete with a colorful intensity that stands out against the gray metropolitan surroundings. The poem thus recalls Fredric Jameson's reading of modernism, where the visual pleasure one takes in colorful and sensual images such as those of abstract modernist paintings are designed to "restore at least a symbolic experience of libidinal gratification to a world drained of it"[48]—that is, an urban world of commodified objects displayed in shop windows.

As well as visual pleasure, however, the slippers also demonstrate the synesthetic qualities of polyphonic prose. The slippers "plunge the clangour of billions of vermilion trumpets into the crowd outside, and echo in faint rose over the pavement"; they also "snap" like "cracker-sparks of scarlet," and are said to scream their color into the street. These verbal qualities are matched in Lowell's familiar deployment of alliteration and assonance as poetic effects. This is brilliantly shown in a line such as "red slippers, myriadly multiplied in the mirror side of the window," where the aural echoing of the words captures the way in which the images of the slippers duplicate in the mirrored windows. There is a kind of euphoria in this poem, with the imagist drive to present a concrete object spilling over into a more active and "sensuous sense of seeing." As part of another resistance to the grayness of the streets or the shop window commodity, the poem is full of motion, with the slippers described by means of very many active verbs: "flooding" the eyes of pedestrians, "jamming" their reflections into passing cars, these very busy slippers also "plunge," "spout" and "swing" forth from their position in the shop window.

The vivacious life of this mundane object is never quite captured in the other poems in the "Towns in Colour" sequence. "Afternoon Rain in State Street," written in free verse, is an interesting attempt to describe the urban street as if it were a kind of cubist painting:

> The city is rigid with straight line and angles,
> A chequered table of blacks and greys.
> Oblong blocks of flatness
> Crawl by with low-geared engines,
> And pass to short upright squares
> Shrinking with distance.[49]

But the "many voices" of the city are seemingly lost here, as the lyric voice of the poet predominates over the polyphonic qualities of the pictured scene.

Can Grande's Castle

Lowell's major work in polyphonic prose is *Can Grande's Castle* (1918), composed of four lengthy narrative poems. S. Foster Damon called the volume the first "completely original" book by Lowell, and compared it to William Blake's prophetic book *America*.[50] The first poem, "Guns as Keys: And the Great Gate Swings," concerns American trade with Japan in the late nineteenth century, its theme being that of art versus commerce, a common enough modernist obsession. "Sea-Blue and Blood-Red" describes the life and death of the British naval admiral Lord Nelson, with some details of his sea battles and his love for Lady Hamilton, while "Hedge Island" is a faintly bizarre poem, ironically praising the British postal system while seeming to criticize England for being "trussed and knotted" in tradition and antiquity. The most successful poem is the last, "The Bronze Horses," which shifts among the cities of Rome, Constantinople, and Venice, following the location of the famous quadriga now located on the outside of St. Mark's Cathedral in Venice. These four horses harnessed to a chariot are a rare survival from the ancient world, and were placed outside the Hippodrome in Byzantium (Constantinople) before the fall of that city in 1204, when they were removed to be placed in the Venetian cathedral. The poem's shifting sense of time and place—from the ancient classical world of Rome to the medieval Byzantine Empire and Venice in the seventeenth century, and then up to the present of 1915—seems to suit the nonlinear narrative tendencies of polyphonic prose. Since narrative poetry can often appear monological, such as Robert Browning's dramatic monologues, reconciling the singular voice of most acts of narration with the many voices of polyphony is a difficult art. "The Bronze Horses" succeeds because of its leaps in time and space; there is no main narrative hampering the spread of multiple voices, only the central image of the equine sculpture. The horses link or relate the separate incidents but tell no singular story: polyphony here produces a text of polytopic and polychronic experiences.

Also of interest is the engagement with Venice and Constantinople, earlier than the more famous poems of Pound and Yeats about these cities. Before Yeats's "Sailing to Byzantium," Lowell writes of the city of "gold and alabaster," with "doors of embossed silver opening upon golden trees where jewelled birds sing clock-work notes" (*CGC,* 147) in the palace of the Emperor; she also notes the "raucous gongs" being beaten in the city. The watery architecture of Venice interests Lowell, as it did Pound, and as she writes of a "City of reflections" we are aware that the movement of her polyphonic prose is well-suited to the unique fluctuations of this city: "Floating, wavering city, shot through with the silver threads of water, woven with the green-gold of flowing water. . . . Strange city, belonging neither to earth nor water, where the slender spandrels of vines melt into the carvings of arched windows, and crabs ferry themselves through the moon-green water rippling over the steps of a decaying church" (*CGC,* 170–171). The poem concludes in wartime, with Venice being attacked from the air, and the bronze horses departing along the canal, as "Wars bite you with their little flames and pass away, but roses and oleanders strew their petals before your going, and you move like a constellation in a space of crimson stars" (*CGC,* 232). The horses symbolize an art that might endure the travails of war, for as Lowell suggests in her preface, these poems "all owe their existence to the war" though they are not strictly war poems (*CGC,* vii). Instead, they look back to previous times of war in order to try to make sense of the present.[51] Bryher, in her comments on *Can Grande's Castle,* pointed to the significance of how these polyphonic prose texts use history: "Is not the development peculiar to modernity an increased and impartial sense of the value of the past expressed by the vision of those who own the freshness and the thought of the future?"[52] Lowell's engagement with the past is an exercise that demonstrates a key feature of modernity, that entanglement of the new and the old that exercised many other modernists such as H.D. and Eliot.

The poems in *Can Grande's Castle* show both the pitfalls and pleasures of polyphonic prose. Some passages seem strained and artificial, existing somewhere between verse and florid prose. Other sections demonstrate that this liminal quality of polyphonic prose can produce effects of great intensity and interest. Always we are aware that what we are reading is not ordinary prose, and perhaps the nearest comparison is to sections of Joyce, especially in the more musically flavored passages—such as "Sirens"—of his *Ulysses.* Again, however, it is worth stressing that Lowell's experiments predate the first publication of parts of *Ulysses* in the *Little Review* in March 1918.

A description of Lady Hamilton's room in "Sea-Blue and Blood-Red" gives a characteristic flavor of Lowell's prose in this volume

> Blood-red on a night of stars, red like a wound, with lava scars. In the round wall-mirrors of her boudoir, is the blackness of the bay, the whiteness of a star, and bleeding redness of a mountain's core. Nothing more. All night long, in the mirrors, nothing more. Black water, red stain, and above, a star with its silver rain. (*CGC*, 5–6)

This passage works by its skillful use of internal rhyme ("stars" and "scars," "stain" and "rain"), its use of what Lowell calls "return," or the use of repeated phrases, in slightly altered contexts, such as "Nothing more." "Blood-red" is a phrase repeated throughout this poem, forming a premonition of the death of Nelson at the poem's close. Predominant here is the imagery of color, continuing the practice of "Towns in Colour," creating a visual kaleidoscope to parallel the multiple tonal colors formed by the pervasive alliteration and assonance of the passage ("Blood," "blackness," "bay," "boudoir," "bleeding").

Polyphonic prose is very much a synesthetic experience, trying not only to render sound and tone but to arrange visual elements of language in a painterly composition. As Lowell writes in her preface, it is an "orchestral form" unlike the "single and melodic" tone of ordinary vers libre. Sometimes the contrapuntal elements of the language interact like an orchestra to produce depth, color, and harmony; at other times the multiple elements clash and overwhelm one another. At their best they bear out Bryher's description of "Guns as Keys: And the Great Gate Swings": "Sound flinging words ahead, racing colour to re-gather them, history in pursuit of poetry to tangle it with blossom, the epic of modernity concentrated into thirty pages."[53] The multiple voices of modernity— history, urban life, warfare, or the avant-garde—collide and compete in the many sounds and tones of polyphonic prose. Lowell's unrelated method develops that openness to multiple voices that Bakhtin stressed was at the heart of novelistic polyphony. As noted by Bryher, it also has an ability to shift between these many voices, capturing the multiple flows of modernity in the city. That Lowell's work sometimes fails in its intentions, that its "unrelated beauty" sometimes remains rather *too* unrelated, should not detract from the determination to experiment with literary forms that she demonstrates and, more importantly, the many fascinating moments when polyphonic prose does articulate a significant version of the epic of modernity.

Notes

1. F. T. Marinetti, "The Founding and Manifesto of Futurism 1909," in *Futurist Manifestos,* ed. Umbro Apollonio (London: Thames and Hudson, 1973), 22. For a read-

ing of the nature of the avant-garde revolution proposed by Marinetti see Raymond Williams, *The Politics of Modernism: Against the New Conformists,* ed. Tony Pinkney (London: Verso, 1989), 52.

2. For further discussion of this see Andrew Thacker, "The Other Imagists: Amy Lowell and H.D.," *Women: A Cultural Review* 4, no. 1 (1993): 49–59.

3. Marinetti, "Manifesto," 22.

4. Mikhail Bakhtin, *Problems of Dostoevsky's Poetics,* trans. Caryl Emerson (Manchester: Manchester University Press, 1984), 6.

5. Ibid., 8.

6. For a detailed consideration of this aspect of Bakthin's work see Ken Hirschkop, *Mikhail Bakhtin: An Aesthetic for Democracy* (Oxford: Oxford University Press, 1999).

7. Julia Kristeva, "Word, Dialogue and Novel," in *The Kristeva Reader,* ed. Toril Moi (Oxford: Blackwell, 1986), 55.

8. See the section on "Discourse in Poetry and Discourse in the Novel" in Bakhtin, *The Dialogic Imagination: Four Essays,* trans. Caryl Emerson and Michael Holquist, ed. Michael Holquist (Austin: University of Texas Press, 1981), 275–300.

9. Pound also complained of the decline into the pianola in the article "Arnold Dolmetsch," in *Literary Essays of Ezra Pound,* ed. T. S. Eliot (London: Faber, 1954).

10. Florence Farr, *The Music of Speech, Containing the Words of Some Poets, Thinkers and Music-Makers Regarding the Practice of the Bardic Art Together with Fragments of Verse Set to Its Own Melody* (London: Elkin Matthews, 1909), 19.

11. Ibid., 5; 11.

12. William Butler Yeats, quoted in Noel Stock, *The Life of Ezra Pound* (Harmondsworth, England: Penguin, 1970), 92.

13. Pound, *Literary Essays,* 437.

14. Ezra Pound, "A Few Don'ts by an Imagiste" (1913) reprinted in *Imagist Poetry,* ed. Peter Jones (Harmondsworth, England: Penguin, 1972), 132.

15. For information on her friendship with the French-trained composer Carl Engel see Jean Gould, *Amy: The World of Amy Lowell and the Imagist Movement* (New York: Dodd, Mead, 1975), 84–91.

16. Lucas Carpenter, *John Gould Fletcher and Southern Modernism* (Lafayette: University of Arkansas Press, 1990), 115.

17. John Gould Fletcher, "Miss Lowell's Discovery: Polyphonic Prose," *Poetry* 6 (1915): 35.

18. John Gould Fletcher, *Life Is My Song* (New York: Farrar and Rinehart, 1937), 201.

19. For a brief overview of the rise of prose poetry in European modernism see Clive Scott, "The Prose Poem and Free Verse," in *Modernism: A Guide to European Literature 1890–1930,* ed. Malcolm Bradbury and James McFarlane (Harmondsworth, England: Penguin, 1976).

20. Amy Lowell, preface to *Sword Blades and Poppy Seeds* (London: Macmillan, 1914), x–xi.

21. Amy Lowell, "Some Musical Analogies in Modern Poetry," *Musical Quarterly,* January 1920; cited in S. Foster Damon, *Amy Lowell: A Chronicle With Extracts From Her Correspondence* (Boston: Houghton Mifflin, 1935), 471.

22. Lowell, "Some Musical Analogies," cited in Damon, *Amy Lowell: A Chronicle,* 471.

23. For an instance of such debates see T. S. Eliot's polemical rejection of vers libre as a form in "Reflections on *Vers Libre,*" *New Statesman,* 3 March 1917, 518–519.

24. Although both Lowell and Stein were in London at the same time in 1914 there is no evidence that they met or read each other's work; see Gould, *Amy*, 135. One contemporary who commented, negatively, upon the similar personalities of Stein and Lowell was Robert McAlmon in his *Being Geniuses Together 1920–1930* (1938); rev. ed. with additional chapters, ed. Kay Boyle (London: Michael Joseph, 1970), 203.

25. The setting of the poem seems to refer to Lowell's home in Brookline, a suburb of Boston.

26. Amy Lowell, "Spring Day," in *Some Imagist Poets 1916: An Annual Anthology,* ed. Amy Lowell (Boston: Houghton Mifflin, 1916), 82.

27. See Gertrude Stein, "Tender Buttons," in *Look at Me Now and Here I Am: Writings and Lectures 1909–45* (Harmondsworth, England: Penguin, 1971).

28. See Lowell, preface to *Can Grande's Castle* (Boston: Houghton Mifflin, 1918), xiii, for her admission that although "the typographical arrangement of this form is far from perfect" when polyphonic prose is read aloud any confusion in the audience disappears.

29. Lowell, "Spring Day," 84–85.

30. Lowell, preface to *Can Grande's Castle,* xiv.

31. This is a point made by Lowell in her *Tendencies in American Poetry* (Boston: Houghton Mifflin, 1917), 244.

32. T. S. Eliot, "London Letter," cited in Lyndall Gordon, *Eliot's Early Years* (Oxford: Oxford University Press, 1977), 108. It is interesting to note that Lowell's other contribution to the 1916 imagist anthology was a poem that tried to reproduce the "sound and movement" of a string quartet by the same composer.

33. See Ezra Pound, *Gaudier-Brzeska: A Memoir* (New York: New Directions, 1970), 90.

34. For further elaboration of this point see Thacker, "Amy Lowell and H.D.," 55.

35. Lowell, "Spring Day," 84.

36. Williams, *The Politics of Modernism,* 46.

37. Lowell, "Spring Day," 86.

38. Amy Lowell, preface to *Men, Women and Ghosts* (Boston: Houghton Mifflin, 1916), x–xi.

39. Ibid., xi.

40. John Gould Fletcher, "London Excursion," in *Some Imagist Poets: An Anthology,* ed. Amy Lowell (London: Constable, 1915).

41. Bryher, *Amy Lowell: A Critical Appreciation*, 2d ed. (London: Eyre and Spottiswoode, 1918), 32.

42. Ibid., 32.

43. Virginia Woolf, "Modern Fiction," in *The Crowded Dance of Modern Life: Selected Essays, Volume Two,* ed. Rachel Bowlby (Harmondsworth, England: Penguin, 1993), 10.

44. Bryher, *Amy Lowell,* 33.

45. Ibid.

46. For a recent overview of debates around modernist women writers and the flâneur see Deborah L. Parsons, *Streetwalking the City: Women, the City and Modernity* (Oxford: Oxford University Press, 2000).

47. Lowell, preface to *Men, Women and Ghosts,* x.

48. Fredric Jameson, *The Political Unconscious: Narrative as a Socially Symbolic Act* (London: Methuen, 1981), 63.

49. Amy Lowell, "Towns in Colour," in *Men, Women and Ghosts,* 358.

50. Damon, *Amy Lowell: A Chronicle*, 478. All subsequent page numbers for the poems in *Can Grande's Castle* are cited parenthetically in the text as *CGC*.
51. In some ways this theme recalls Yeats in his poems "Sailing to Byzantium" and "Byzantium," with their own sense of the mutability of the work of art.
52. Bryher, *Amy Lowell*, 37.
53. Ibid., 39.

Putting on the Voice of the Orient

GENDER AND SEXUALITY IN AMY LOWELL'S "ASIAN" POETRY

MARI YOSHIHARA

At the turn of the century, when the United States embarked upon full-fledged empire building in Asia and the Pacific Islands, the term *Asia* came to occupy an increasingly visible place in America's cultural vocabulary. The American engagement with Asia manifested in diverse cultural arenas ranging from material culture and visual arts to performing arts, creating a culture of American orientalism. For women in particular, orientalism offered adventure, freedom, and empowerment that were unavailable in other realms of sociopolitical life.[1] Orientalism also had a significant impact in American letters, particularly literary modernism. Like the modernists' use of dialect and the black vernacular, orientalism bolstered modernism's attempt to break from literary conventions and to invoke new representational forms. A woman such as Amy Lowell did not miss this opportunity for new forms of expression.

Orientalism in American literary modernism took two major forms. First was the translation of Asian texts into English. For literary modernism, the study and translation of foreign literary forms was an instrument for new aesthetics. Thus, while there already existed a corpus of English translations of Asian literature by the end of the nineteenth century, it was during the height of modernism in the 1910s and 1920s that the Anglo-American literary world saw a burgeoning of translations of Chinese and Japanese texts. The translations of Asian literature inspired another form of literary orientalism: creative works, especially poetry, by writers influenced by Asian forms and subject matters. As Cynthia Stamy argues, the deployment of Asian sources challenged traditional assumptions about poetic images and expanded both the scope and obscurity of poetic references.[2] Chinese notions and methods inspired the early modernist works of William Carlos Williams. Marianne Moore used Chinese poetry to resist the American habit of looking to Europe as a singular source of cultural tradition. Japanese forms like tanka and haiku inspired John Gould Fletcher. Thus, like French symbolism and Italian culture, orientalism was a constitutive element of literary modernism in the 1910s and 1920s.[3]

The brevity of Chinese and Japanese poetry and their use of images particularly inspired the imagists. Whereas Asian influences on Ezra Pound have been studied by many scholars, Amy Lowell's poetical exploration of Asia has not received much critical analysis.[4] Yet understanding the role of Asia in Lowell's poetry offers an insight into the cultural work of orientalism, particularly its politics of gender, in American literary modernism. This essay examines the different ways in which Lowell's translations and compositions engaged Asia. Lowell's "Asian" works expressed diverse, multi-layered functions of orientalism. On one level, her practice of translation reflected the hierarchical relations of knowledge and labor between her and her Asian subjects. Her relationship with her "native informant" on the one hand and her construction of classic Chinese poetry in her translations on the other together demonstrate the racialized and gendered notions that were at the base of her orientalism. On another level, her constructions of an exoticized and antiquated gender and sexuality in her own "Asian" poems allowed a form of racial masquerade for her and her readers, which offered the freedom and play of performative gender. At the same time, the gendered constructions of the East and the West, established through specific uses of language and form, also allowed Lowell to address and critique the masculinist vision of U.S. imperialism. These different, and seemingly contradictory, engagements with Asia in Lowell's work demonstrate how the gendered constructions of orientalism found their expressions in a complex mix of affect and power.

The Making of Amy Lowell's "Translations": *Fir-Flower Tablets*

The most important figure in nurturing Lowell's interest in Asia was her brother Percival, who visited Japan in 1883. After being appointed as foreign secretary and counselor in Korea, he spent ten years in Japan, rigorously studying Japanese culture, art, and history. His experience in Asia resulted in a series of books, including *The Soul of the Far East and Occult Japan*.[5] Percival's influence led Lowell to begin studying Japanese haiku and experimenting with its use in her own poems. Lowell was also strongly influenced by her friend Florence Ayscough, who introduced her to Chinese paintings and poetry in 1917. Ayscough, born and raised in China, became one of the most important sinologists of the period. Lowell studied Chinese poetry with Ayscough's help, and several years of intense transpacific correspondence between the two women resulted in their collaborative 1921 translation of Chinese poetry, *Fir-Flower Tablets*.[6]

The making of *Fir-Flower Tablets* shows the structures of knowledge and relations of labor involved in the creation of orientalism. Not knowing any Chinese, Lowell established a collaborative relationship with Ayscough, who worked with her Chinese mentor, Nung Chu. Lowell's preface presents her version of the "collaboration" process. She writes, "Let me state at the outset that I know no Chinese. My duty in Mrs. Ayscough's and my joint collaboration has been to turn her literal translations into poems as near to the spirit of the originals as it was my power to do. . . . The study of Chinese is so difficult that it is a life-work in itself, so is the study of poetry. A sinologue has no time to learn how to write poetry; a poet has no time to learn how to read Chinese. Since neither of us pretended to any knowledge of the other's craft, our association has been a continually augmenting pleasure" (v). Lowell thus justifies her lack of language skills by highlighting the mutually exclusive occupations of poetry and sinology and underscoring her authority as a poet. Yet, as Steven Bradbury demonstrates, in practice this relationship was less of "a continually augmenting pleasure" than a hierarchical division of labor, with power and decision-making authority concentrated at Lowell's end and labor-intensive tasks of literary translation placed upon Ayscough. Because Lowell refused to study the language but insisted on having multiple "approaches" to the original texts, Ayscough was burdened with the drudgery of producing the mountains of translations, glossaries, etymologies, and commentaries that Lowell demanded.[7]

Lowell's power and control over her "translations" was exercised even more forcefully in relation to the "native informant," Nung Chu. In response to Nung's suggestion that *Fir-Flower Tablets* include some poems by Chinese women, Lowell wrote Ayscough, "Be firm with your teacher, hold him strongly between your finger and your thumb, and keep him to classics. Never mind his chivalrous affection for the ladies. The ladies—and I hate to have to say so—are seldom worth bothering with."[8] The commentary reveals several dimensions of Lowell's orientalism. First, Lowell tried to protect her creative and interpretive authority by keeping the native informant in his place. The Chinese teacher was deployed solely for the mechanical details of "local knowledge" and was never entrusted with critical judgment about poetry, which was Lowell's province. While Lowell clarified the hierarchical relations between herself and Nung she did not hesitate to capitalize on his Chinese identity when it was convenient for her work. While anticipating the reviews of *Fir-Flower Tablets*, she asked Ayscough for a biographical account of Nung, instructing her to "make it as grand as possible—to show that we have a native Chinaman behind us."[9] In addition to such relations of labor, Lowell's insistence on focusing on the "classics" also typifies the orientalist construction of Asia as a timeless, utopian space removed from the reality of contemporary Asia. As a result, most of the poems in *Fir-Flower Tablets* are poems of the T'ang dynasty, with the greatest space devoted to Li T'ai-Po's poetry. Finally, her striking comment about "the ladies" exemplifies the gendered construction of her orientalism. While she was thus dismissive of the real women poets of China, her translations themselves actively construct women, gender, and sexuality in specific ways.

Many of the poems in *Fir-Flower Tablets* are narrated by women longing for their absent husbands. While poems about women's grief are common in classic Chinese poetry, Lowell's translations construct gender and sexuality in particular ways. The demarcation of gender relations as specifically foreign heightens the poems' exotic appeal. For example, in translating Li Po's famous poem, "Cha'ang Kan," Lowell stresses the foreignness of gender and sexuality:

> When the hair of your Unworthy One first began to cover her forehead,
> She picked flowers and played in front of the door.
> Then you, my Lover, came riding a bamboo horse.
> We ran round and round the bed, and tossed about the sweetmeats of
>   green plums.
> We both lived in the village of Ch'ang Kan.
> We were both very young, and knew neither jealousy nor suspicion. (28)

When we compare this first stanza with Pound's famous translation of the poem "The River-Merchant's Wife: A Letter," one sees the different effects:

> While my hair was still cut straight across my forehead
>   I played about the front gate, pulling flowers.
> You came by on bamboo stilts, playing horse,
> You walked about my seat, playing with blue plums.
> And we went on living the village of Chokan:
> Two small people, without dislike or suspicion.[10]

Whereas Pound simply translates the first-person pronoun as "I," Lowell starts the poem by using the term, "your Unworthy One," and accentuates the patriarchal relations whereby a woman is defined by her relation to her husband and is considered "unworthy."[11] While terms such as "Unworthy One" and "my Lord" are translations of Chinese words in actual use rather than Ayscough's or Lowell's creation, the choice of such translations exoticizes and antiquates women's roles in the eyes of American readers. Although the rest of the stanza depicts innocent, jovial scenes of childhood, Lowell uses "you, my Lover," in the first reference to the man, and prepares the reader for the remainder of the love poem. In contrast, Pound's translation simply refers to the object of narration as "you," and uses the word "dislike" where Lowell uses "jealousy." Consequently, from the outset, Lowell's translation bears a much more exoticized and sexualized tone.

    Lowell takes further measures to underscore the foreign locale in the third stanza:

> At fifteen, I stopped frowning.
> I wanted to be with you, as dust with its ashes.
> I often thought that you were the faithful man who clung to the bridge-
>   post,
> That I should never be obliged to ascend to the Looking-for-Husband
>   Ledge. (28)

The specific references in the last two lines emphasize the exotic setting. Ayscough's notes explain the legend behind the "bridge-post" reference: Wei Shêng, with a reputation for sincerity and reliability, had an engagement to meet a lady on a bridge. Although she did not come, he stood there in the rising flood clinging to the bridge post until the waves engulfed him. As for the "Looking-for-Husband Ledge," Ayscough explains the legend about a wife who went daily to the banks of the Yangze River to watch for her husband's return until she was turned to stone (190). Whether or not the readers actually referred to these notes as they read the poem, the translations such as the "man who clung to the bridge-post" and the "Looking-for-Husband Ledge" rendered the poetic narrative exotically appealing to the Western readers. The effect of Lowell's translation in underlining the Chinese setting is clear when we compare it to Pound's:

> At fifteen I stopped scowling,
> I desired my dust to be mingled with yours
> Forever and forever and forever.
> Why should I climb the look out?[12]

Pound does not bother with the specifics of the legend, and although the reference to climbing the "look out" beckons explanation, it does not create the same degree of foreignness as Lowell's more literal translation.

A comparison of Lowell's and Pound's ending of the poem further demonstrates the different ways in which the translations construct gender. Lowell's translation reads,

> It is the Eighth Month, the butterflies are yellow,
> Two are flying among the plants in the West garden;
> Seeing them, my heart is bitter with grief, they wound the heart of the
>   Unworthy One.
> The bloom of my face has faded, sitting with my sorrow.
> From early morning until late in the evening, you descend the Three
>   Serpent River.
> Prepare me first with a letter, bringing me the news of when you will
>   reach home.
> I will not go far on the road to meet you,
> I will go straight until I reach the Long Wind Sands. (29)

In contrast, Pound translates,

> The paired butterflies are already yellow with August
> Over the grass in the West garden;
> They hurt me. I grow older.
> If you are coming down through the narrows of the river Kiang,
> Please let me know beforehand,
> And I will come out to meet you
>   As far as Cho-fu-Sa.

Whereas Pound expresses the woman's grief with the simple sentences, "They hurt me. I grow older," Lowell expounds on the gender-specific meanings of her grief by again using the reference "Unworthy One," and making concrete the meaning of woman's aging by specifying, "The bloom of my face has faded, sitting with my sorrow." Finally, Lowell's mysterious last two lines would not make sense unless one read Ayscough's note about the Long Wind Sands, which imply "the end of the earth." (190) In contrast to Pound's phonetic transliteration, Lowell's literal translation of the place name and the final two sentences heighten the foreign quality of Lowell's translation. With these devices, Lowell effectively creates a vision of classic China through the foreignness of the woman's subjectivity and gender relations. This accentuation of alternative gender roles and sexuality is further evidenced in Lowell's own compositions.

Racial Masquerade and Performative Gender: *Pictures of the Floating World*

While working on *Fir-Flower Tablets*, Lowell also composed a number of her own poems, which were collected in *Can Grande's Castle* (1918) and *Pictures of the Floating World* (1919). It was in these two collections that the intersection of Lowell's orientalism and imagism produced the most distinct effect. Lowell's orientalism in both form and content allowed her to construct and perform alternative gender roles and sexuality through a type of racial masquerade.

Pictures of the Floating World, a collection of 174 short poems, represents Lowell's engagement with Asian art and poetry. The book's title, the translation of *ukiyo-e*, a genre of Japanese woodblock prints then enormously popular among Western artists, illustrates her attempt to capture Japanese aesthetics. The poems in the first section, "Lacquer Prints," depict Japanese subjects using the method of Japanese haiku, although they do not follow its strict syllabic rules.[13] Thus, Lowell's use of Japanese poems is, to a degree, conducted on both formalistic and content levels. On the other hand, the seven "Chinoiseries" are longer, and rather than following the Chinese poetic form, they simply evoke images and events derived from China. The rest of the collection, "Planes of Personality," consists of lyrical poems, "deriving from everywhere and nowhere as is the case with all poetry" (viii), a few of which explicitly refer to Japanese or Chinese themes.

The brevity and suggestiveness used in "Lacquer Prints" give the poems an exotic flavor and seemingly Japanese aesthetic. The exoticism rendered through the formal structure is sustained by various elements that mark the poems as Japanese. Some scenes are set in specific places, such as Kioto [*sic*], Yoshiwara, Uji River, Asama Yama, and Matsue. Some portray specific individuals, such as Hokusai (the famous Japanese woodblock artist) or the emperor. Many poems refer to flora and fauna that are used as markers of the Japanese setting, such as the maple, lotus, chrysanthemum, iris, camellia, and bamboo. Others make references to Japanese material life and social practices, such as lanterns, sliding doors, the New Year festival, processions of geisha, and a temple ceremony.

The exoticism furnished by these cultural clues is heightened by the poems' temporal setting. All fifty-nine poems that sketch Japan's miscellaneous scenes are set in Japan's historical past. As Lowell notes in her foreword, "Some of the subjects are purely imaginary, some are taken from legends or historical events, others owe their inception to the vivid, realistic colour-prints of the Japanese masters, but all alike are peculiar to one corner of the globe and, for the most part, to one epoch—the eighteenth century" (viii). Set in the social and cultural landscape of the past century—when Japan had closed its doors to foreign trade and distinct Japanese culture was peacefully in place—the poems embody the presumably pure, traditional Japanese aesthetics safe from the action, conflict, and instability of the "modern" society.

In these poems, the author, the narrator, and the reader all participate in a performance of alternative gender and sexuality through a form of racial masquerade. In the discursive context of orientalism, the qualities embodied in the Japanese characters in the poems—for example, faithfulness, self-restraint, patience—had specifically gendered and racialized meanings, and for white women to perform that role had both liberating and eroticizing effect. Like numerous productions of Giacomo Puccini's *Madame Butterfly* and other orientalist performances popular during this period, American women's performances of Asian women were signifiers of modern American womanhood. The freedom to cross racial lines and thereby performing a form of gender and sexuality distinct from their own—even if, or especially if, it was a temporary and fictive "play"—was an expression of the freedom and power of modern women. Such performances allowed both the producers and their audiences—such as Lowell and her readers—to engage and identify with Asian subjects, while masking the relations of power that was at the basis of such cultural appropriations.[14]

Many of the poems in the collection are written in the first person, and often include the second-person subject to whom the narrator speaks. As the settings are Japan or China of the past and the poetical structure is presumably Japanese or Chinese, the narrative "I" assumes the role of a Japanese or Chinese character even though Lowell's readers are aware of the author's real Western identity. Through identification and fantasy, the author, the narrator, and the reader all participate in a racial masquerade, which allows a performance of alternative gender and sexuality.

An important step in this performance is the donning of the Asian garb. For example, in the poem "Vicarious," the narrator's clothing is critical in her "Asian" performance:

When I stand under the willow-tree
Above the river,
In my straw-coloured silken garment
Embroidered with purple chrysanthemums,

> It is not at the bright water
> That I am gazing,
> But at your portrait,
> Which I have caused to be painted
> On my fan. (5)

The silken garment and the fan underscore both the authenticity and the performativity of the poem's orientalism. The title of the poem, "Vicarious," explicitly foregrounds the masquerade and performance the narrator engages in.

Once clothed as Japanese, the characters "do" things Japanese. Significantly, much of "acting Japanese" is done through the performance of "Japanese" gender relations and sexuality. For example, in both "By Messenger" and "A Lover," a Japanese character is sitting at night, composing a poem for the loved one. The gender of both the narrator and his/her lover is uncertain. If the narrator is assumed to be female, the poems create a highly "traditional" Japanese woman and gender/sexual dynamics—a woman longing for the absent lover, similar to the narrators in Li Po's poems. By assuming this Japanese womanhood, the narrator and the reader perform a gender role that is distinct from the ideals of modern women of America. On the other hand, if the narrator is assumed to be a Japanese male, the poems reinforce existing stereotypes of feminized, fragile, delicate Japanese men. In this scenario, the narrator and the reader would perform a form of masculinity that is quite distant from the one valued in the modern West yet also has a sensual appeal similar to the aestheticist fervor for Oscar Wilde.

Not all narrative voices are indeterminate of gender, however. "Road to the Yoshiwara" and "A Daimio's Oiran" portray the scenes from a red-light district in eighteenth-century Japan. Both poems evoke exoticism through the specifically sexualized setting. In "A Daimio's Oiran," the narrator is a courtesan waiting for the arrival of her samurai client:

> When I hear your runners shouting:
> "Get down! Get down!"
> Then I dress my hair
> With the little chrysanthemums. (21)

The racial masquerade allows the author, the narrator, and the reader to perform an exoticized female sexuality. The samurai status of the narrator's client implied by "your runners" demanding the people to honor him by getting down, the narrator's commodified sexuality indicated by the title "oiran" (courtesan), and her dressing of the hair with chrysanthemums all create a form of sexuality that is culturally foreign, falls outside the Western conventions of propriety, and is exotic and sensuous.

The politics and poetics of performance are most vividly represented in "Free Fantasia on Japanese Themes." Here, the narrator foregrounds the act of racial masquerade, making explicit her real Western identity. The poem opens and closes with the depiction of the room where the narrator sits with an open book. The passages at the beginning and the end of the poem, "And my heart is still and alert, / Passive with sunshine/ Avid of adventure" (105) and "I would anything/ Rather than this cold paper, / With, outside, the quiet sun on the sides of burgeoning branches, / And inside, only my books" (108) are juxtaposed against the middle section illustrating the imaginary Japanese settings and roles she plays. This frame is a familiar site from which to escape into the fantasy of "going native" in Japan. Even as the narrator immerses herself in her fantasy, she makes clear that this is an imaginary performance. Each stanza begins with the phrase "I would . . ."; each sentence is written in hypothetical past tense and sometimes further qualified with the word *perhaps*. In addition, the second stanza, where she sets herself up for the imaginary adventure, is filled with words that signify the object of fantasy as the Other:

> I would experience new emotions—
> Submit to strange enchantments—
> Bend to influences,
> Bizarre, exotic,
> Fresh with burgeoning. (105–106)

Once she foregrounds the "new," "strange," "bizarre," "exotic," "fresh" nature of the object of her fantasy, the narrator travels to one Japanese scene after another, dressed as a Japanese. First she would "climb a Sacred Mountain," struggling with other pilgrims up a steep path and prostrate herself before a painted shrine. Whereas here the "other pilgrims" are presumed to be the "real" Japanese among whom the narrator disguises her Western identity, in the next scene she sets up a fellow, supposedly Western, character to perform with her. The "you" in the following passages participates in the racial masquerade:

> I would recline upon a balcony
> In purple curving folds of silk,
> And my dress should be silvered with a pattern
> Of butterflies and swallows,
> And the black band of my *obi*
> Should flash with gold, circular threads,
> And glitter when I moved.
> I would lean against the railing
> While you sang to me of wars—
> Past, and to come—
> Sang and played the *samisen.*
> Perhaps I would beat a little hand drum
> In time to your singing;
> Perhaps I would only watch the play of light
> On the hilts of your two swords. (106–107)

As the narrator enacts the luxurious Japanese femininity by indulging in the glitter of the colorful kimono and obi, the "you" is made to join the performance of exotic sexuality by playing Japanese lyric music and the wearing swords. By playing the role of Japanese lovers, the narrator and her partner engage in performing an exoticized sexuality.

Racial masquerade in Lowell's "Asian" poetry allowed Lowell and her readers to cross the boundaries of Western gender and sexuality. In the cultural context where modernist identity and aesthetics were often expressed through performative self-fashioning and the donning of masks, the construction and performance of gender and sexuality of Japan's past offered a liberating tool for white women, such as Lowell and her readers, who had the power and freedom to play with such disguises.

Reframing the East-West Contact: "Guns as Keys: And the Great Gate Swings"

While Lowell's "translations" in *Fir-Flower Tablets* and her own "Asian" poems in *Pictures of the Floating World* constructed an exoticized gender relations and sexuality, the modes of Lowell's orientalism were not always consistent. The poem, "Guns as Keys: And the Great Gate Swings" in *Can Grande's Castle* shows Lowell's engagement with Asia that is distinct from her other "Asian" works. The poem's narrative voice is more self-referential and critical about the orientalism and U.S. imperial enterprise than that of *Pictures of the Floating World*.

"Guns as Keys" depicts the arrival of Commodore Matthew Perry's squadron in Japan and the consequences of United States–Japan contact. The poem consists of two parts and a postlude, each of which shows different formal and linguistic strategies. Part 1 stresses the contrast between the two worlds by alternating between "polyphonic prose" to represent the United States and "free verse" for Japanese scenes. This juxtaposition of form seems to reflect, at first glance, the orientalist binary that constructs the West as free and democratic and the East as more rigidly constrained. The language also shifts between the colloquial American speech and the subdued diction of the free verse representing the Japanese scenes. For example, in the opening scene, Perry's squadron is leaving the United States, while the Japanese live a bucolic, "premodern" life, unaware of the impending arrival of the foreign power:

> My! How she throws the water off from her bows, and how those
> paddle-wheels churn her along at the rate of seven good knots! You are
> a proud lady, Mrs. *Mississippi*, curtseying down Chesapeake Bay, all a-
> flutter with red white and blue ribbons.

> At Mishima in the Province of Kai,
> Three men are trying to measure a pine tree
> By the length of their outstretched arms.
> Trying to span the bole of a huge pine tree

By the spread of their lifted arms.
Attempting to compress its girth
Within the limit of their extended arms.
Beyond, Fuji,
Majestic, inevitable,
Wreathed over by wisps of cloud.
The clouds draw about the mountain,
But there are gaps.
The men reach about the pine tree,
But their hands break apart;
The rough bark escapes their hand-clasps;
The tree is unencircled.
Three men are trying to measure the stem of a gigantic pine tree,
With their arms,
At Mishima in the Province of Kai.[15]

As Richard Benvenuto notes, language and action in these stanzas function as an index to national characters. While the Americans, with daring enterprise, circle the globe with modern technologies such as "paddle-wheels," the Japanese are attempting a far more localized act of joining hands around a tree. Like the word "pine tree," the word "arms" is repeated four times, combined with the adjectives "outstretched," "lifted," "extended" in the first three and no adjective in the final one, suggesting that the arduous effort is destined to fail. The same description of the three men trying to measure a pine tree at both the beginning and the end of the stanza heightens the circularity and closure in the Japanese scene. Furthermore, the gaps in the clouds and the breaking apart of the men's "hand-clasps" symbolize the Japanese failure to complete the enclosure and anticipate the "opening" of Japan by Perry's arrival.[16]

Lowell further stresses the juxtaposition of the progress of the American frigate and the stasis of the Japanese landscape by the narrative structure of the poem's first section. The American scenes move progressively as Perry's ship *Mississippi* "noses her way through a wallowing sea; foots it, bit by bit, over the slanting wave slopes" (53). The ship circles the globe, starting from the Chesapeake Bay and stopping at the "stepping stones" of Madeira, Cape Town, Mauritius, and Singapore. On the other hand, the Japanese scenes depict miscellaneous images with no linear narrative: men hold hands to measure a tree, an "insect-seller" carries cicadas in the cage, a silk merchant is entertained by a geisha, and women visit Asakusa to gaze at peonies.

The contrast between the American and Japanese scenes is also gendered. The world aboard the *Mississippi* is a masculine one, and the sailors' robust, loud, and rough life is represented by their colloquial and plain dialogue:

Across the equator and panting down to Saint Helena, trailing
smoke like a mourning veil. Jamestown jetty, and all the officers in the
ship making at once for Longwood. Napoleon! Ah, tales—tales—with

nobody to tell them. A bronze eagle caged by floating woodwork. A heart burst with beating on a flat drop-curtain of sea and sky. Nothing now but pigs in a sty. Pigs rooting in the Emperor's bedroom. God be praised, we have a plumed smoking ship to take us away from this desolation.

    "Boney was a warrior
        Away-i-oh;
    Boney was a warrior,
        John François."

    "Oh, shut up, Jack, you make me sick. Those pigs are like worms eating a corpse. Bah!" (60–61)

In contrast to the language of machismo used in the American scenes, the free verse in the Japanese scenes is more delicate and feminine. Such language and style, combined with the depiction of women as part of the landscape, feminize the whole Japanese scene. For example,

    The ladies,
    Wistaria Blossom, Cloth-of-Silk, and Deep Snow,
    With their ten attendants,
    Are come to Asakusa
    To gaze at peonies.
    To admire crimson-carmine peonies,
    To stare in admiration at bomb-shaped, white and sulphur peonies,
    To caress with a soft finger
    Single, rose-flat peonies, Tight, incurved, red-edged peonies,
    Spin-wheel circle, amaranth peonies.
    To smell the acrid pungence of peony blossoms,
    And dream for months afterwards
    Of the temple garden at Asakusa,
    Where they walked together
    Looking at peonies. (61–62)

This description of the picturesque feminine is juxtaposed with the vulgar masculine world of the American squadron. Like the use of "pine tree" in the earlier stanza, the repetition of "peonies" not only stresses the Japanese locale and its feminine associations but also contrasts formalistically with the polyphonic prose of the American scene by giving the stanza a more versified structure and tone.

    The contrast between the cultures is made more explicit in the portrayal of gender and sexual relations. In one scene, Commodore Perry writes to his wife at his table aboard the *Mississippi*. The short passage, ending with the sentence, "Two years is a long time to be upon the sea," implies a marital relations where husband and wife are bonded by love and trust. In contrast, immediately after this passage, Lowell depicts a Japanese scene where a wealthy silk merchant is being entertained by a geisha at a teahouse (56–57). The portrayal of the commodified sexual relationship depicted in colorful detail and a highly sensuous language contrasts sharply with the brief and restrained passage about Perry's correspondence with his wife. The association between the merchant's extramarital sexual relations and his suspicious business presents Japan's impenetrable underworld in gendered and sexualized terms, contrasted with the practical, commercial trade to be initiated by the American power.

Although the carefully crafted contrast between the United States and Japan in the first section of the poem fits the orientalist binary drawn between the West and the East, Lowell's narrative is more complex than it appears. As the poem moves from one scene to another along Perry's progress en route to Japan, Lowell inserts a critical voice on American expansionism. These commentaries historicize Lowell's narrative and present a critical perspective on the American enterprise. For example, Lowell writes,

> The North-east trades have smoothed away into hot, blue doldrums.
> Paddle-wheels to the rescue. Thank God, we live in an age of inven-
> tion. What air there is, is dead ahead. The deck is a bed of cinders, we
> wear a smoke cloud like a funeral plume. Funeral—of whom? Of the
> little heathens inside the Gate? Wait! Wait! These monkey-men have
> got to trade, Uncle Sam has laid his plans with care, see those black
> guns sizzling there. "It's deuced hot," says a lieutenant, "I wish I could
> look in at a hop in Newport this evening." (57)

The representative speech—instead of third-person narrative—justifying American expansionism and the trade with the "heathen" "monkey-men" highlights Lowell's critical perspective on U.S. imperialism. While the reader is invited to identify with the "we" of the American scene, she is made to feel uncomfortable with that identification. Finally, Lowell showcases another American voice:

> Down, down, down, to the bottom of the map; but we must up
> again, high on the other side. America, sailing the seas of a planet to
> stock the shop counters at home. Commerce-raiding a nation; pulling
> apart the curtains of a temple and calling it trade. Magnificent
> mission! Every shop-till in every bye-street will bless you. Force the
> shut gate with the muzzles of your black cannon. Then wait —wait for
> fifty years—and see who has conquered. (63–64)

The remark about the historical changes to take place in the fifty years after Perry's opening of Japan locates the reader in her own time, when Japan itself has become an imperial power. By bringing the reader back to the present and reminding her of the conditions that followed Perry's expedition, Lowell critiques the masculinist visions of American expansionism.

Whereas part 1 of the poem heightened the contrast between the American and the Japanese scenes, part 2 foregrounds the merging of two cultures. Formalistically, part 2 is written entirely in polyphonic prose. The use of polyphonic prose for Japan signifies how Japan increasingly takes on the voice of the West after Perry's arrival. The Japanese lose their dignity and charm they represented in the previous part and now use the vulgar and masculine colloquial speech, which was an exclusively American language in part 1. Whereas Lowell's critical eye was directed primarily at American imperialists in part 1, it is now pointed to the Japanese as well. At the end of part 2, Lowell not only sheds a critical perspective on the Americans who forced themselves through Japan's closed gate but also on the Japanese who sold out to the West.

The formal structures and language used in "Guns as Keys" serve to both depict and problematize the contact between the United States and Japan. On the surface, the juxtaposition of the two nations seems to reproduce a binary between the feminine East and the masculine West. However, Lowell's strategic use of polyphonic prose also allowed her to expose the gendered construction of U.S.-Japan relations and to interject a critical perspective on American expansionism.

Lowell's modes of orientalism in her "Asian" works appear to be internally at odds. Her translations in *Fir-Flower Tablets* and her "Asian" poems in *Pictures of the Floating World* seem to be examples of an orientalist practice whereby Lowell constructs an exoticized and antiquated gender and sexuality for the Orient, a practice that is based on, and reinforces, the power relations between Lowell and her Asian subjects. On the other hand, "Guns as Keys: And the Great Gate Swings" presents a much more self-referential, critical look at American expansionism and its masculinist discourse.

These seeming contradictions in Lowell's engagements with Asia exemplify the multiple ideologies, expressions, and functions of orientalism, especially the gendered nature of the discourse. The gendered constructions of Asia reflected and shaped U.S. domestic racial and gender ideology on the one hand and the unequal power relations between the United States and Asia on the other. The gendered language functioned sometimes to endorse and at other times challenge U.S. imperialism, while constituting a mix of exoticism and fear, desire and threat, admiration and domination for the East as the racial Other.

White women were uniquely situated in America's orientalist discourse. On the one hand, orientalism as a masculinist discourse marginalized women while simultaneously using Western gender relations as an evidence of the superiority of Western civilization. Many of thus marginalized women saw themselves in alliance with the dominated peoples of Asia and voiced their anti-imperialist positions. On the other hand, U.S. imperial enterprise offered many white, middle- and upper-class women the opportunity to gain agency and power denied them in the conventions of their society. As imperial subjects, white women were situated in a position of superiority vis-à-vis the "natives."[17]

In this context, orientalism offered several things to American women such as Lowell. First, it provided new ideas, themes, and forms for expression, as we see in Lowell's "Asian" poetry. Secondly, as evidenced by the poet's status in the imagist movement and her relationship to her "native informant," orientalism bestowed women with authority and power, both in relation to American society and culture and to the Asian subjects. Finally, Lowell's racial masquerade and performance of alternative gender and sexuality illustrate that through orientalism women gained freedom from the conventions of Western gender and sexual relations, enabling them to engage in a play that enhanced their own identities as modern American women. Lowell's gendered constructions of Asia were both reflections and shapers of these mixed interests, as they were instruments of both affect and power.

Notes

1. For a broader discussion of women and American orientalism, see Mari Yoshihara, *Embracing the East: White Women and American Orientalism* (New York: Oxford University Press, 2003).
2. Cynthia Stamy, *Marianne Moore and China: Orientalism and a Writing of America* (Oxford: Oxford University Press, 1999), 24.
3. Zhaoming Qian, *Orientalism and Modernism: The Legacy of China in Pound and Williams* (Durham, N.C.: Duke University Press, 1995), 5.
4. Sample works on Pound's orientalism include Qian, *Orientalism and Modernism*; Beongcheon Yu, *The Great Circle: American Writers and the Orient* (Detroit: Wayne State University Press, 1983), chapter 10; and Earl Miner, *The Japanese Tradition in British and American Literature* (Princeton, N.J.: Princeton University Press, 1966), 108–112.
5. On Percival Lowell's life and work in Asia, see David Strauss, *Percival Lowell: The Culture and Science of a Boston Brahmin* (Cambridge, Mass.: Harvard University Press, 2001); and T. J. Jackson Lears, *No Place of Grace: Anti-Modernism and the Transformation of American Culture* (New York: Pantheon, 1981), 234–241.
6. Florence Ayscough and Amy Lowell, *Fir-Flower Tablets* (Boston: Houghton Mifflin, 1921). Hereafter, page numbers in the book are cited parenthetically in the text. On the process through which Ayscough and Lowell collaborated on the translation, see Harley Farnsworth MacNair, ed., *Florence Ayscough and Amy Lowell: Correspondence of a Friendship* (Chicago: University of Chicago Press, 1945); also see Lowell's preface to *Fir-Flower Tablets*.
7. Steven Bradbury, "Through the Open Door: American Translations of Chinese Poetry and the Translations of Empire" (Ph.D. diss., University of Hawaii, 1997), 129.
8. MacNair, *Florence Ayscough and Amy Lowell*, 104.
9. Ibid., 175.
10. Ezra Pound, *Personae: Collected Short Poems of Ezra Pound* (New York: New Directions, 1971), 130.
11. In her notes to an earlier poem, Ayscough explains that "[t]he term 'Unworthy One' is constantly used by wives and concubines in speaking of themselves to their husbands or to the men they love." See Ayscough and Lowell, *Fir-Flower Tablets,* 180.
12. Pound, *Personae,* 130.
13. Amy Lowell, *Pictures of the Floating World* (New York: Macmillan, 1919). Hereafter page numbers in the book are cited parenthetically in the text.
14. On gender politics of orientalist performances, see Yoshihara, *Embracing the East,*

chapter 3. On studies of various forms of cross-dressing, see, for example, Marjorie Garber, *Vested Interests: Cross-Dressing and Cultural Anxiety* (New York: Routledge, 1992); Eric Lott, *Love and Theft: Blackface Minstrelsy and the American Working-Class* (New York: Oxford University Press, 1993); Anne McClintock, *Imperial Leather: Race, Gender and Sexuality in the Colonial Contest* (New York: Routledge, 1995); Michael Rogin, *Blackface, White Noise: Jewish Immigrants in the Hollywood Melting Pot* (Berkeley and Los Angeles: University of California Press, 1996); Susan Gubar, *Racechanges: White Skin, Black Face in American Culture* (New York: Oxford University Press, 1997); Philip Deloria, *Playing Indian* (New Haven: Yale University Press, 1998); and Gayle Wald, *Crossing the Line: Racial Passing in Twentieth-Century U.S. Literature and Culture* (Durham, N.C.: Duke University Press, 2000).

15. Amy Lowell, "Guns as Keys: And the Great Gate Swings," in *Can Grande's Castle* (New York: Macmillan, 1918), 51–52. Subsequent page numbers for the poem are cited parenthetically in the text.
16. Richard Benvenuto, *Amy Lowell* (Boston: Twayne, 1985), 105.
17. Some of the recent scholarship on Western women and imperialism include McClintock, *Imperial Leather*; Kumari Jayawardena, *The White Woman's Other Burden: Western Women and South Asia during British Colonial Rule* (New York: Routledge, 1995); Gail Bederman, *Manliness and Civilization: A Cultural History of Gender and Race in the United States, 1880–1917* (Chicago: University of Chicago Press, 1995); Jenny Sharpe, *Allegories of Empire: The Figure of Woman in the Colonial Text* (Minneapolis: University of Minnesota Press, 1993); Rosemary Marangoly George, *The Politics of Home: Postcolonial Relocations and Twentieth-Century Fiction* (Berkeley and Los Angeles: University of California Press, 1999); Ann Stoler, "Rethinking Colonial Categories: European Communities and the Boundaries of Rule," *Comparative Studies in Society and History* 31, no. 1 (1989): 134–161; Ann Stoler, "Carnal Knowledge and Imperial Power: Gender, Race, and Morality in Colonial Asia," in *Gender at the Crossroads of Knowledge: Feminist Anthropology in the Postmodern Era,* ed. Micaela di Leonardo (Berkeley and Los Angeles: University of California Press, 1991), 51–101; Laura Donaldson, *Decolonizing Feminism: Race, Gender, and Empire-Building* (Chapel Hill: University of North Carolina Press, 1992); Vron Ware, *Beyond the Pale: White Women, Racism, and History* (New York: Verso, 1992); Nupur Chadhuri and Margaret Strobel, *Western Women and Imperialism: Complicity and Resistance* (Bloomington: Indiana University Press, 1992); and Laura Wexler, *Tender Violence: Domestic Visions in Age of U.S. Imperialism* (Chapel Hill: University of North Carolina Press, 2000).

Amy Lowell's Letters in the Network of Modernism

BONNIE KIME SCOTT

Amy Lowell has flickered repeatedly, if peripherally, on the screens of the new modernist studies, particularly as we have tuned in to questions of gender. Lowell's "feud" with Ezra Pound provides a precedent for resisting his version of modernism, and the mastery traditionally granted to the male makers of modernism. We now see gross sexism, instead of funny stories, in much that has been recorded about Lowell. The prime example is the bizarre incident when Pound ended Lowell's celebratory dinner for imagists by donning a small bath tub and proclaiming the new movement of "nagistes."[1] We also question the rhetoric and the priorities of the critics who were construing modernism through the 1970s. Take, for example, *The Pound Era,* where Hugh Kenner can be found patrolling the boundaries of masculine modernism against Lowell's incursion by air and sea. In this example, Kenner is concerned with both the familiar entry into imagism by Lowell, and her venture into another Pound preserve, Chinese translations:

> In a crystal cloud above Brookline, Mass., far-darting Apollo was preparing to smite with an illumination Amy Lowell, the "hippopoetess," to argue with whom, Carl Sandburg once remarked, was "like arguing with a big blue wave." The lady in whose company she received the revelation was to undergo seven years' nagging rather than argue.... [T]hus Amy, on 21 October 1902, had suddenly, aged 28, sat down and "with infinite agitation" written her first poem. "It loosed a bolt in my brain and I found out where my true function lay." In 1913, concurrent with the arrival of the January *Poetry,* another bolt was loosed: "Why, I too am an *Imagiste.*" She hied her twice from Massachusetts to the Imagist headquarters in London, crossing like a big blue wave or like Daisy Miller, in 1913 to join the movement and in 1914 (with maroon-clad chauffeur and matching auto) to appropriate it since she had not been properly accepted.[2]

Kenner borrows the "hippopoetess" from Pound, and likes Sandburg's "big blue wave" analogy enough to use it twice—both semiotic selections betraying visceral disgust at Lowell's formidable female force.[3] Kenner's mock-heroic mode accesses traditions of misogyny reaching back to Alexander Pope's "Rape of the Lock." There is also a hint of the "scribbling woman" conjured up from Pope to Nathaniel Hawthorne, when Kenner finds that Lowell "dashed off" her latest work on impulse, her only strategy being imitation and appropriation of Pound's genius.

In contrast to these multigenerational male antics over Lowell are the letters she received from D. H. Lawrence, made accessible through publication in 1985.[4] One finds here that Lawrence—always an odd fit to modernism—clearly related positively and comfortably to Lowell. He shared with her a mutual appreciation of nature and like her made generous use of natural images—questionable behavior to the hard-edged, urban, canonical modernists. Lowell and Lawrence exchanged publications on a regular basis, and in their letters they list the poems that they admire most, sometimes noting what does not work so well. The letters also reveal a mutual interest in the ways their transatlantic cultures connect, weighing various representations of America, in particular. This is an area of particular interest, as it relates to the renewed interest in modernist geographies. I will argue that the correspondence was just as important to Lawrence, personally and artistically, as it was to Lowell.

The gradual emergence of Amy Lowell can be detected in *The Gender of Modernism,* a "critical anthology" published in 1990, for which I served as general editor. The work offered sections on twenty-six modernist authors, all but five of them female, each prefaced by an introduction from the scholar who organized the section. For each author we offered a set of gender-sensitive, difficult-to-access primary texts. Lowell did not have a section of her own, but she figured in the Lawrence and H.D. sections, and accordingly made it into "A Tangled Mesh of Modernists," a chart that summarized the networking of the authors recentered in this recuperative work. For the section on H.D., Susan Stanford Friedman selected several letters from H.D. to Lowell. Though Friedman commented upon ways that H.D. maintained her own opinions in the exchange, the letters themselves give evidence of community among a set of poets who no longer felt attuned to Pound's doctrine and methods. Even such random appearances of Lowell as these complicated our understanding of modernist politics, including its gendered dimensions, its vast web of connections, and the ways its various practitioners can be grouped and regrouped, as well as recentered for increased understanding.

The present volume comes at a good time to reconsider not just this poet and producer of modernism, but also the approaches that have evolved with feminist cultural studies over the last two decades. As an alternative to hierarchical accounts that seek to proclaim who "makes" a literary movement, or what genius's poetry deserves to sit at the top, feminist scholarship, in collaboration with cultural studies, delights in tracing networks and connections, some of which traverse the categories and boundaries previously used to conceptualize modernist literature, and indeed a large array of cultural formations. One way of characterizing an author or promoter of modernism is to analyze the specific array of intellectual and personal connections they maintained. How do these connect or reconfigure gender, race, or class? What genres, geographies, and occupations are involved? In an intriguing article that engages the twentieth century preoccupation with boundaries, Paul Lauter suggests that it was the "boundary-dissolving qualities" of Lowell that were threatening to her contemporaries, occasioning a surprising "degree of vituperative comment" that may have been an effort to control such violations.[5] Among the traversals that interest Lauter are Lowell's violation of the boundary between poet and promoter, and her violation of cultural taboos on corporeality, which we have also seen in Kenner's grossly sexist metaphors.

Lowell also presents terrific material for the theoretical turn toward performance studies, which consider performance basic to the constitution of identity, rather than a stigma denoting artificiality. The first step in this direction was to see Lowell among lesbian writers, expressing her sexuality with an erotic imagery of flowers and a throwing off of garments.[6] At another angle, Melissa Bradshaw sees Lowell as a performer in commodity culture, and identifies both Pound and Lowell as outstanding commodifiers.[7] Related to this, Lowell can join a set of women writers who took their careers on the road as lecturers, deliberately promoting not just their own work, but their cultural preferences; Emma Goldman and Rebecca West shared in this sisterhood. Lowell can also be grouped with the set of wealthy women who, with greatly varying lifestyles, visibility, and levels of involvement, dedicated their resources to the making of modernism. Lowell, Bryher, Nancy Cunard and Harriet Shaw Weaver (among others) pose vexing problems concerning class privilege, and the potential to manipulate selection and production.[8] But it is time to assert their foundational importance.

Strategic Communications with Women

It is well known that poetic inspiration was provided to Lowell by the Italian actress Eleonora Duse, whom she met in 1902, and Ada Dwyer Russell, who became the love of her life after their meeting in 1912. But at almost every stage of Amy Lowell's development, she had female intimates to learn alongside; they contributed to her thinking, and expedited her publications and performances.[9] Her mother and sister were her first collaborators, with Mrs. Lowell arranging for the publication of *Dream Drops, or Stories from Fairy Land, by a Dreamer,* for benefit of a charity. Some of Lowell's pieces extended her sister Bessie's bedtime stories, Mrs. Lowell added a story of her own, and she filled out the volume with translations from Mme. Sophie Rostopchine, Comtesse de Ségur.[10] Although Lowell is frequently portrayed as a lonely child, she formed lasting alliances with childhood friends. She and Bessie Ward exchanged their poems for mutual critique, agreeing that any thought of publication should await the distant future. They studied the romantics together, including Lowell's lifelong favorite, John Keats.[11] Lowell's early female network may have helped in placing her first published poetry with the *Atlantic Monthly* in 1910, as her childhood friend Mary Cabot had married the journal's editor, Ellery Sedgwick. Another friend, Florence Ayscough (a sinologist who was born in Shanghai, raised in America, and returned to China after marriage) collaborated on *Fir-Flower Tablets* (1921). This back-and-forth collaboration, lasting from 1917 to 1921, depended upon Ayscough's detailed prose translations of original Chinese characters, and her rechecking of Lowell's poetic version. The project produced a significant correspondence (published in 1945) that reveals both the careful nature of the collaboration and Lowell's efforts to outshine Pound's similar Chinese project.[12] Poignantly, Ayscough dedicated the volume of letters to Russell, "great friend of two great friends," reinforcing our sense of the Lowell network.

Along a more professional line were Lowell's correspondences with Harriet Monroe, editor of *Poetry*, and Margaret Anderson, editor of the *Little Review*. Monroe provided Lowell's first modernist outlet for her poetry, both public and private discussion of the values of the New Poetry, and a model for its promotion. Accounts of Lowell's dealings with Monroe tend to emphasize her demands rather than the women's common interests;[13] Her letters to Monroe do regularly angle for appearances as the featured poet for an issue, but Lowell was prepared to wait for the honor, and respects Monroe's priorities, for example in focusing upon Carl Sandburg.[14] Lowell was a defender of Monroe to other modernists; she criticized Richard Aldington for harshly rejecting a set of Monroe's own poems, though her letter is decidedly patronizing in tone.[15] She should be credited with bolstering this important journal and influencing its generous treatment of rhythm and cadence.

Lowell posed tensions for Monroe. Alice Corbin Henderson, a poet as well as Monroe's collaborating editor, was no fan of Lowell, and it is likely that Monroe had to do considerable juggling to keep them both satisfied. Lowell crafted confiding letters to both Monroe and Anderson concerning her contentions with Pound. They were also receiving Pound's version of things, and strove to balance their options with both poet-promoters, cutting off neither, and indeed resisting the commanding nature Monroe detected in both. Lowell's gloomy predictions about Pound's future productivity, contained in this correspondence, do not serve her well today, given his resistance to fading away.

The Lowell-Monroe correspondence reveals a great deal about the goals and problems of editing *Poetry*. Sharing an interest in developments in American poetry, Lowell runs some of her ideas about the origins of imagism past Monroe. Their correspondence might start on the problems of finding space and adequate compensation for longer poems, and end with a discussion of the relative merits of these two forms. Monroe provided space for the first of Lowell's Chinese translations, as well as an article by her loyal collaborator, Florence Ayscough. Letters preparatory to the publication discuss short lines, the function of cadences, and the root concepts of Chinese characters.[16] Monroe continued her discussion of cadences, begun with Lowell, in presenting her ideas on the "Rhythms of English Verse," a chapter in her *Poets and Their Art*: "Free verse has been called by Amy Lowell 'cadence verse,' but all poetry is cadence verse in this sense, that all poetry has a double rhythm, an overlay of sweeping cadences on the smaller patterns of time-unit bars.[17]

Monroe's assessment of Lowell in *Poets and Their Art* denies her the designation of genius and firmly situates her in the autocratic tradition of her ancestors—a line that has been followed by successive interpreters, including another friend, the eventual editor of her complete collected poetry, Louis Untermeyer. But Monroe hedges on the genius designation, granting Lowell genius as an organizer of "herself as well as the world" and noting the limitations of genius, unaided by the sober persistence that marked Lowell's character. Monroe testifies that Lowell's letters gave her a tremendous boost when the journal was just beginning. As evidence, she quotes from an early letter in her autobiography, *A Poet's Life*: "You cannot think how much I have the welfare of your magazine at heart. The more I see of them in New York—editors and their papers—the more I realize that *Poetry* has a field all to itself, and one which I believe of immense importance."[18] Lowell leads off Monroe's list of "lifelong friendships," and again the heart is critical. Monroe again quotes Lowell, "'*Poetry* is my mother,' and Chicago 'my adopted city,' 'the city of my heart.'"[19]

Lowell's relationship to *Little Review* editor Margaret Anderson appears from letters to have been of equal intellectual interest, with less tension over business. Their common endeavors began in the spring of 1914, with Lowell's offer to write a "London Letter" for the *Little Review* during her second planned visit with the imagists. Lowell was able to get going with her promotion of new poetry when Anderson published Lowell's critique of contemporary American writing, "Miss Columbia: An Old Fashioned Girl" in June, 1914. Anderson wrote a glowing review to Lowell's second volume of poetry, *Sword Blades and Poppy Seeds,* in December 1914. But, as Holly Baggett has argued, Anderson's view of her journal was that it should permit "conversation" among various points of view, and the December 1914 number offered critical as well as supportive articles on imagism and vers libre.[20] She may also have doubted Lowell's capacity for conversation.

Anderson's breezy account of their first meeting, which occurred in Chicago in January 1915, is a model of negotiation, avoiding domination by either of the contenders in the Pound-Lowell fracas. Anderson reports, "Her first words were congenial to me. I've had a fight with Ezra Pound."[21] But Anderson does not accept Lowell's offer of financial support, contingent on becoming director of poetry for the journal, despite assurances that Lowell would not "dictate." Lowell's choice of the term *direct* is hardly compatible with the more democratic ideology she was bringing to her imagist associates. Anderson's resolution is wise and spirited without being egotistical or defensive: "No clairvoyance was needed to know that Amy Lowell would dictate, uniquely, and majestically, any adventure in which she had a part."[22]

Lowell and Anderson had serious discussions in their letters, touching on the difference between love and lust, and the uses of violence in literary tests—discussions that carry over into Lowell's exchanges with D. H. Lawrence. While she could support the erotic imagination of Lawrence, Lowell stopped far short of Anderson's promotion of James Joyce. Anderson's interests also included anarchism and involved strong support of Emma Goldman—an aspect of Anderson that lies outside usual modernist boundaries. In *My Thirty Years' War*, Anderson humorously recalls a conversation with Goldman in which her illustration, drawn from Lowell's 1916 poem "Malmaison," failed. Goldman's objection was that "the working man hasn't enough leisure to be interested in black swans."[23] Probing the possibility of lesbian acknowledgment between Lowell and Anderson, Baggett finds in their correspondence "a brief semblance of intimate comradeship," citing in particular Lowell's references to a white hyacinth given to Lowell by Anderson, as reminiscent of a Lowell poem she particularly liked, "Vernal Equinox" (1915).[24]

Lowell's capacity to network productively with women poets is nowhere more evident than in her introduction of Bryher to Bryher's future partner, H.D. It was through Lowell's writings that Bryher first encountered H.D.'s poetry, and Lowell happily gave her a letter of introduction to her friend. On first meeting Bryher, H.D. confides her impression to Lowell of a "very, very simple—an underdeveloped, lonely child" who is "very queer" about her wealth, something that "could make no difference to *you*."[25] The contact with Bryher did have its rewards. In 1918, Bryher published a pamphlet describing the themes and techniques of Lowell's poems to date, book by book, in rapturous tones: "I had stumbled into a freshness of vision denied so long that it had become a myth." More practically, the pamphlet seems aimed at securing Lowell a wider audience in Britain. It opens with Bryher's confession that America had seemed to her "unknown, unworthy of exploration, a Polar waste lit, at best, with the sparse and mediocre echoes of English writers of a forgotten age."[26] Lowell functioned for Bryher, as she later would for Lawrence, as a geographer of American literary terrain. We should also credit Lowell with the networking that would put Bryher in a position to sustain modernism along her own lines. Though the connection to H.D. has long been acknowledged, only recently has her influence on modernist film studies in the journal *Close-up* received adequate attention.

Imagist Connections and Disconnections

A discussion of Lowell's networking with imagist poets begins with her own eager reception of the poetry of H.D., published in the January 1913 issue of Monroe's *Poetry*, and Lowell's instant sense of affiliation with the French *imagiste* movement. Her introduction to Pound, and through him to other imagists, came from Monroe as well. Lowell secured her imagist credentials when Pound selected one of her poems for his collection *Des Imagistes*. Their letters, however, reveal somewhat of a disconnect. Correspondence about her poem for *Des Imagistes,* "In a Garden" (1913), is confused. It is not clear that she gave permission for its inclusion prior to seeing it advertised. Dismissing as too late any question of removing her poem, Pound moved quickly to new schemes for funding journals where he could expand his own influence. Though at his urging Lowell did sponsor *Poetry* and the *Little Review* for significant periods of time, she never fit neatly with his plans for her money.[27] In the interval between her first and second visits to London, Pound offered Lowell the editorship of the *Egoist* in return for her investment of funds.[28] Financed elsewhere, he quickly proposed a new quarterly, with staffs on both sides of the Atlantic, French content, and perhaps even contacts in Vienna and Florence. Additional schemes would follow, even after Pound and Lowell went their separate ways.[29]

It is unclear whether Lowell fomented or merely facilitated the mass defection that took imagists from Pound and allied them with her following her second visit to London in summer 1914. In April 1914, she sought and received Pound's permission to "astigmatize" him in verse. Her resulting poem, "Astigmatism" (1914) strains at the term *friend*, making it clear that Pound has a very different way of operating with other poets, and even with living things. Though she credits him with crafting a fine walking cane, her poem casts doubt on his use of it, as he slashes to bits first one poet-flower after another because they are not the rose he is seeking.

Despite the well-known insults dealt her at dinners dominated by Pound and his cronies, Amy Lowell gained her first real sense of poetic community from her English visits. She enjoyed reading and critiquing poetry with other members of the group. She began long-term correspondences with the recently wed H.D. and Richard Aldington, with D. H. Lawrence and his wife Frieda, and with John Gould Fletcher. Democracy, with equal representation of a set of six of seven poets, and a group discussion of what would be included in proposed anthologies, were the political planks Lowell articulated. She found a responsive group eager to escape Pound's dictatorship. Pound rejected this proposed democracy in the arts, and in his letters made numerous suggestions to keep the term *Imagiste* off the cover of their anthology. As he was ready to give up the imagist title and theory altogether, H.D. worries in one letter to Lowell that Pound "is making [imagism] ridiculous" in his writing for *T.P.'s Weekly* and *Blast*. She complains that she and Aldington "can't go watching him like two keepers."[30] In suggesting the alternate title *The Six*, she plays repeatedly upon a group practice: "We have talked it over—all of us here—and we think it a good title." H.D.'s sense of identity resolves to "We would all be individuals without being *isme* and we would in addition, be a group!" There is a firmer postscript, apparently dictated by Aldington, reiterating the position that "*in no event can we now appear under the direct title Imagiste.*"[31] Lowell collected more opinions. With the help of Fletcher, she found evidence that it was T. E. Hulme, not

Pound, who originated the imagist idea. This returned the term to collective access. The eventual title, *Some Imagist Poets,* was probably more Lowell's will than that of the majority, but their collaboration stood. Somewhat the autocrat, she still maintained a space for discussion—and the network that enabled it.

In the years that followed, Lowell conducted a great deal of business correspondence with her confederate imagists: placing poetry (hers and theirs) in little magazines, and journals with wider circulation, and with reputable publishing houses such as Boston-based Houghton Mifflin. She secured positive reviews in conspicuous places, saw to publication in the years 1915–1917 the three anthologies titled *Some Imagist Poets,* and painstakingly shared the resulting royalties, and sometimes a bit more, with her struggling confederates. The distribution of royalties seems to have provided a welcome excuse for communicating, and through this mode of business, Lowell escaped some of the patronizing that can come with being a patron outright. The letters to H.D. and Aldington are particularly interesting for their handling of the schism with Pound, for the decisions the group of three made about the anthologies, and for moments of intimacy and mediation.[32] When it comes to epistolary form, Lowell offers no competition to Pound as an avant-garde stylist. She is methodical about letters received and business contracted. Occasionally she grows expansive in discussing specific poems or poetic forms, in assessing cultural effects of war, or in offering a frank difference of opinion; she typically closes in a mannerly fashion, reinforcing friendship with sincerity and, occasionally, a hint of jocularity. Her correspondents were not blindly loyal to Lowell. At times they expressed doubts about her poetry and the very lectures she used to spread their reputations. They worried that they were not always enhanced by her agency.[33]

The Lawrence Correspondence

There are many connections between the H.D./Aldington letters and Lowell's correspondence with D. H. Lawrence. This probably originates in the experience of community she derived from first meeting the Lawrences at a dinner in her London rooms—an occasion shared with the Aldingtons. E. Claire Healey and Keith Cushman present this evening as an irresistible contrast to the dinner with Pound, less than two weeks earlier, that ended in his "nagiste" exhibition.[34]

Healey and Cushman avoid the temptation to exaggerate the quality or importance of the Lawrence-Lowell correspondence they have edited. They suggest early in their introduction that "[s]elf-interest was part of the relationship for both writers. Lawrence realized the value of having an influential, wealthy friend at the center of the new poetry in the United States. . . . It was a personal coup for Lowell to be able to enlist Lawrence under the banner of her version of Imagism." The editors then lead us on with a modest promise of documenting a friendship: "It was not self-interest that kept the correspondence going. Instead the letters were generated primarily out of a bona fide, enduring (though not deep) friendship."[35] In their final assessment of the quality of the correspondence, Lowell bears responsibility for mediocrity: "The literary talk contained in the letters is not consistently of a high order, even at the beginning. When it comes to literature, Lowell writes almost exclusively about politics and the literary market-place."[36] In short, they sell Lowell short. Not only did Lowell write more often, and eagerly anticipate the arrival of Lawrence's next letter, but on important themes, such as American diversity, she often emerged with the more interesting statements. She also stood to gain from a change in literary studies.

Interest in the literary marketplace has certainly increased—as one of the border crossings of the new modernist studies—since Healey and Cushman wrote their introduction, and the pervasiveness of literary politics has become both accepted and embraced as important. Indeed, in her correspondence with Lawrence, Lowell comes across as a very deft marketer of his work and her own opinions when, for instance, within a half a page she thanks him for his new volume of poetry, titled *Touch and Go* and notes that she will review it favorably for the *New York Times*, but that on the side she intends to disagree with his preface to his *New Poems*, and suggests that she set up the periodical serialization of his forthcoming novel *Women in Love* with the *Dial*. There are reasons beyond commercial interest for feeling that Healey and Cushman fail to do justice to Lowell's letters to Lawrence. While friendship is extended in many of Lowell's correspondences, this exchange has a rare quality of give and take. It allows further explanations, following upon the expression of frank opinions. It is more in the democratic spirit that Lowell claimed for her imagist endeavors, but failed to convey in her exchanges with Monroe or Anderson. Lawrence and Lowell get to serious and sometimes controversial subjects, including fidelity to the artist's self, the experience of war and its impact on poetry, puritanism, and the trajectory of American versus European culture. Clearly Lawrence liked a number of Lowell's poems; he frequently shared his reasons for his preferences, as did she in return when receiving a new set of his poems. She willingly became his promoter at *Poetry* and with publishers such as Ben Huebsch, and she advised him on the advisability of his plans to lecture and live in specific sections of America. As with the other contributors to her *Some Imagist Poets* series, she was painstaking in sending Lawrence his share in the royalties, always coupling such missives with personal news, and once famously sending on a used typewriter. It was as a poet, a friend, and a facilitator, rather than a patron, that she was rewarded his dedication of *New Poems* to her in 1918.

Lawrence rightfully worries about his own "impertinence," which takes several forms in a letter dated 18 November 1914. His letter reacts to Lowell's recently published collection *Sword Blades and Poppy Seeds* and a single poem, "The Bombardment," which had appeared recently in a war issue of *Poetry*. Based on his own grim endurance of war on the home front, Lawrence takes issue with her representation of war in "Bombardment." He was "quite cross with [her] for writing about bohemian glass and stalks of flame, when the thing is so ugly and bitter to the soul."[37] Lowell's metaphors of fireworks and broken glass ornaments, however trivial or decorative they may seem to Lawrence, invite a long series of observations on war—the Lawrences' problems finding housing, Frieda Lawrence's concern for her family in Germany, and the induction of friends into the military. Lawrence volunteers, "The spirit of militarism is essentially destructive, destroying the individual and the constructive social being. It is *bad*. How Aldington will stand it I don't know. But I can tell that the glamour is getting hold of him: the 'now we're all men together' business, the kind of love that was between Achilles & Patroclus."[38] One relieving aspect of this correspondence is that Lawrence spares Lowell the military metaphors that pervade so many accounts of her manner,[39] sharing with her instead ideals of constructive being. Indeed, just such ideals characterize her wishes for her correspondents— particularly the Lawrences and the Aldingtons.

The same Lawrence letter of November 1914 makes the dubious claim that Lawrence knows the essential Amy Lowell better than she does, and that she should revise her poetry accordingly. Lawrence situates her firmly in Anglo-Saxon, Puritan traditions:

> Why don't you always be yourself. Why go to France or anywhere else for your inspiration. If it doesn't come out of your own heart, real Amy Lowell, it is no good, however many colours it may have. I wish one saw more of your genuine strong, sound self in this book, full of common-sense & kindness and the restrained, almost bitter, Puritan passion. Why do you deny the bitterness in your nature, when you write poetry? Why do you take a pose? It causes you always to shirk your issues, and find a banal resolution at the end. So your romances are spoiled. When you are full of your own strong gusto of things, real old English strong gusto it is, like those tulips, then I like you very much. But you shouldn't compare the sun to the yolk of an egg, except playfully. And you shouldn't spoil your story-poems with a sort of vulgar, artificial "flourish of ink."[40]

There is a lot to respond to here, and Lowell takes her time (Lawrence is typically kept waiting for her letters). Lawrence's comments include specific critiques of images, such as the unfortunate egg, that Lowell might use to improve her writing. This is the very sort of help she had been looking for when she first sought out imagist colleagues in London. As he recommends, she did keep working on narrative poetry with increasingly good results, joining Robert Frost (whom she admired and publicized) in a distinctly American genre. Lawrence's effort to find sources of "passion" for her work, though probably misdirected, speaks to something she was seeking in her poetry. In 1919, having received his *New Poems,* she would write, "You always manage to get tremendous feeling into your poems, and really a passion and emotion which fills me with envy and admiration."[41] But there were other aspects of the letter that she stored away for a retort.

More than a year after receiving this letter, Lowell mentions the publication of her new critical study, *Six French Poets*. She refrains from sending this book to him, explaining, "I remember your wrestling with me last year was because of my French pose. You see it is not a pose, it is a reality, and if you do come to New York, you will see why it is a reality. You will realize that America is now more Continental than British. The immigration that has been going on for years is having an effect, and even we who are of pure Anglo-Saxon ancestry cannot help being affected by it."[42] Later she would defend her Chinese poetry as being "a perfectly authentic side of my nature."[43] Lowell thus refuses to be defined in terms of the old English gusto that Lawrence finds in tulips, arrayed as tunic-clad squadrons of antique soldiers in a walled garden. But this is just the first of several exchanges in which Lowell resists Lawrence's essentializing, and moves toward more options for identity, found on a global scale. Far from embracing the old English aspects of her heritage, Lowell admits to the youth and crudity of her country, but argues that this is compensated by its being "sincere, and vital, and open-minded."[44] Unlike England, America doesn't let authors rest on past achievements. Such thought probably grounds Lowell's own indomitable work ethic, and her repeated tackling of new genres (an aspect of her much admired by Harriet Monroe).

In another gesture against essentialism, Lowell offered a sustained theme on American regional diversity in her letters. Both she and Lawrence make transatlantic cultural connections and test assumptions generated from the other side of the water, and the discussion is useful to both parties. It serves Lowell's role as the provider of an American matrix for imagism and other forms of new poetry. It serves Lawrence as he seeks to visit the United States and then eventually does. Both Lowell and Lawrence may have been warming up for the books on American literary traditions that they would write; neither is entirely consistent in emphasis throughout this exchange.

Lowell argues that there are many Americas, varying by region. She resists the narrow impressions that may have been conveyed to Lawrence by H.D., Pound, or Aldington: "Hilda was only a school-girl—a misunderstood and out of place school-girl—who mistook her own environment for the country at large, and Richard is merely prejudiced, and with no real grounds for the prejudice. He apparently gets his feeling about America from Ezra Pound and Hilda."[45] Lowell would have liked to see H.D. return to the United States—a possibility that briefly seemed imminent.

In 1919, when Lawrence begins seriously consulting Lowell about making a lecture tour in the United States, she was less encouraging, particularly when it comes to a visit to her native New England. She was likely much more comfortable to have Lawrence arrive by envelope, rather than in person. Lowell did occasionally put visitors up in her home, Sevenels, or found them a place to stay in Boston and invited them out for dinner. But there is more than reluctance as a hostess here. She was consistent in predicting an uncongenial reception of Lawrence by New Englanders, due to his (she claimed undeserved) reputation for *The Rainbow* and his marriage to a German woman. "New England is far more puritanical than Old England," she once wrote. "It is the most puritanical corner of this country."[46]

Lawrence's arrival in New Mexico in 1923 elicited one of Lowell's most sustained commentaries on America—one that offers a muted criticism of his growing primitivism. In it, Lowell resists both reducing America to one of its aspects, and turning back to what is "old" in culture. While she expresses interest in his "impressions of the Indians" published in the *Dial,* she limits her curiosity to the artistic, and not the ethnological aspects of "the colour of the Pueblo Indians, their dances, their songs. . . . I do not want to go back to the primitive; I have not the slightest desire to lose what civilization has gained."[47] Concerned that he may not be "in love with my country people," she offers the prospect of variety:

> America is so vast that one section of it is very unlike another, as you will discover when you come East, and I do believe that alien nations such as the Indians and the Peons give a colour and picturesqueness to life in New Mexico and Arizona which, of course, we entirely lack on the Atlantic Coast. New York is unique, unlike anywhere in the world, I believe. Boston is much like England; mentally, extremely so. Even its scenery does not differ very greatly from English scenery. As I look out of my window where I am writing, I see my little sunken garden flanked with clipped trees on both sides, and over the greenhouse, past the shaven hedge, a road bordered by elm trees, a wide country road. I have been many times struck, in looking at just that view, with its resemblance to a garden corner, and road beyond, I once saw in Liverpool.[48]

They both play with the notion of a visit; Lowell writes, "My library is paneled with English oak, so when you come to see me, you will probably find yourself in the uninteresting surroundings of complete familiarity,"[49] and Lawrence hopes that he and his wife can "pay you a little visit, if you feel equal to visitors. While the flowers still last in your garden."[50]

As shown in the American exchanges, Lawrence and Lowell connect over rural landscapes and gardens. Early on, Lawrence sends descriptions of Cornwall that elicit Lowell's high praise: "I do not know anybody that writes abut the English countryside as you do, and I had rather read what you say about it than look at it, which is a high tribute."[51] She adds her own brief description of Dublin, New Hampshire: "You would like this place, it is all hills, and rushing brooks, and clear, placid lakes."[52] When he suggests that she buy a pot of fuchsias with one of his royalty checks, she refuses, but responds, "The bond between us is intensified by your picking fuchsias, as they are one of my favourite flowers. I shall never forget how they used to hang over the walls of the house in Devonshire when I passed a Summer there years ago."[53] They both set enormous importance upon the sense of place in their writing. This sort of glue sustains the entire correspondence, even as it provides essential imagery to the poetry they like best by one another.

Like many of the commentators on Lawrence's alliance to imagism, Lowell assumes in her early letters that Lawrence is disinterested in theory. She passes very lightly over the prefaces she is writing for *Some Imagist Poets*: "I know you are not so much interested in the technical side of verse as we are; indeed technique is only a means to an end, and the reason one talks about it is because other people do not seem to understand it. The fundamentals of poetry do not change, it is the mode of expression that differs."[54] Lawrence may actually endeavor to become more theoretical in response. One of his interpretations of America (and quite a departure from his earlier advice about her puritanism) makes America the natural source for imagism:

> It is very surprising to me, now I have come to understand you Americans a little, to realise how much older you are than us, how much further you and your art are really, developed, outstripping us by far in decadence and non-emotional aestheticism, how much beyond us you are in the last stages of human apprehension of the physico-sensational world, apprehension of things non-human, not conceptual. We still see with concepts. But you, in the last stages of return, have gone beyond tragedy and emotion, even beyond irony, and have come to the pure mechanical stage of physical apprehension, the human unit almost lost, the primary elemental forces, kinetic, dynamic-prismatic, tonic, the great, massive, active, inorganic world, elemental, never softened by life, that hard universe of Matter and Force where life is not yet known, come to pass again. It is strange and wonderful. I find it only in you & H.D., in English: in your "Bath," and the fire of the lacquer musicstand, & Acquarium, & some Stravinsky, and here & there in Roxbury Garden which, to my mind, is not quite chemical and crystollographical enough. Of course, it seems to me this is a real *cul de sac* of art. You can't get any further than
> "Streaks of green & yellow iridescence
> Silver shiftings
> Rings veering out of rings
> Silver-gold— Grey-green opaqueness sliding down"[55]

Lowell wasn't sure that Lawrence had got Walt Whitman right in a 1921 article. "I doubt whether you will quite get America until you see it. It is so different from any other country, but it seems to me the only country left reasonably alive just now."[56] When Lawrence's *Studies in Classic American Literature* came out, Lowell greeted it "with a great deal of interest, and not a little divergence of view." She returned to familiar themes, writing, "The Puritans were not so puritanical as they have been represented, but it takes some time to know that. Neither is any corner of America America; until you have seen the whole of it you cannot be said to have seen it all. But of course, you dear prejudiced soul, you will never believe that. If you will come to me without fail the next time you are in this region, I can show you something you have not yet seen."[57]

It was her last letter to Lawrence. Their cultural conversation, with its transatlantic effort to connect, is of enduring interest. More generally, Lowell's letters demonstrate that a firm, unapologetic attachment of modernist poetry to America and Americans, studied with sensitivity to their regional and cultural differences, was a major contribution, one that today still awaits adequate appreciation.

Notes

1. E. Claire Healey gives a fairly comprehensive account of the various dinners and performances involved in Lowell's 1914 sojourn among the imagists; see Healey, "Amy Lowell Visits London," *New England Quarterly* 46 (1973): 450. Healey also recounts Ford Madox Ford's hostile reaction to Lowell at this same dinner, where he gave his own dismissive speech on imagism. Ford objected to Lowell's money, and other people's quest for it. He pictures Lowell insultingly, as a glutton. The tale of Pound's bathtub is taken from John Gould Fletcher's biography, *Life is My Song: the Autobiography of John Gould Fletcher* (New York: Farrar and Rinehart, 1937). The dialog includes references to a bather in Lowell's "In a Garden" which appeared in Pound's collection *Des Imagistes* (1914). Lowell's designated biographer and friend, S. Foster Damon, considers Ford's speech at the dinner and his subsequent article the real affront; see Damon, *Amy Lowell: A Chronicle with Extracts from Her Correspondence* (Boston: Houghton Mifflin, 1935), 233. He is more vague about Pound, who in his version "was sufficiently elated to improvise some sort of juggling with one of the waiters' trays" (233).

2. Hugh Kenner, *The Pound Era* (Berkeley and Los Angeles: University of California Press, 1971), 291–292.

3. Pound quipped, "And poor dear Amy. It is only a month ago that I heard someone manifestly NOT an enemy refer to the 'Hippopoetess' (a native amurkn [*sic*] joke, I should say)." Ezra Pound to Margaret Anderson, 20 August 1917, in *Pound/The Little Review: The Letters of Ezra Pound to Margaret Anderson: The Little Review Correspondence,* ed. Thomas L. Scott and Melvin J. Friedman (New York: New Directions, 1988), 116. Kenner, in *The Pound Era,* 553, extended his disgust of modernist feminine forms to Virginia Woolf, characterizing her mind as "treacly."

4. This correspondence was published as *The Letters of D. H. Lawrence and Amy Lowell 1914–1925,* ed. E. Claire Healey and Keith Cushman (Santa Barbara: Black Sparrow Press, 1985). As the editors note in their introduction, Aldous Huxley had omitted any letters to Amy Lowell from his 1932 edition of Lawrence's letters and Henry T. Moore included only four in his two-volume 1962 edition (10). S. Foster Damon did make thorough use of Lawrence's letters in his pioneer 1935 study and acknowledges their importance; see Damon, *Amy Lowell: A Chronicle,* xviii. For my first summary of the Lawrence-Lowell exchange, see Bonnie Kime Scott, "D. H. Lawrence," in *The Gender of Modernism,* ed. Bonnie Kime Scott (Bloomington: Indiana University Press, 1990), 218–219.

5. Paul Lauter, "Amy Lowell and Cultural Borders," in this volume and in *Speaking*

the Other Self: American Women Writers, ed. Jeanne Campbell Reesman (Athens: University Georgia Press, 1997), 291, 288.

6. See Gillian Hanscombe and Virginia L. Smyers *Writing for Their Lives: The Modernist Women, 1920–1940* (London: Women's Press, 1987); and Andrew Thacker, "Amy Lowell and H.D.: The Other Imagists," *Women: A Cultural Review* 4, no. 1 (1993): 54–56. My favorite throwing off of garments comes as Lowell greets Sappho in her (1925) poem "The Sisters."

7. Harriet Monroe was perhaps the first to draw comparisons between the two, considering both "born autocrats." She explains their quarrel as follows: "Two captains, each accustomed to command, could not get on together in the same boat." See Monroe, *A Poet's Life* (New York: Macmillan, 1938), 276–277.

8. Melissa Bradshaw observes that while Lowell may have brought poetry to the middle classes on the lecture circuit, she "increasingly demanded the right to issue polemicisms without being contradicted" and avoided having question-and-answer sessions after her performances. See Bradshaw, "Outselling the Modernisms of Men: Amy Lowell and the Art of Self-Commodification," *Victorian Poetry* 38 (2000): 155–156.

9. Hanscombe and Smyers, *Writing for Their Lives*, provides a fine introduction to this way of viewing Lowell.

10. Damon, *Amy Lowell: A Chronicle,* 73–75.

11. Ibid., 150.

12. Florence Ayscough and Amy Lowell, *Florence Ayscough and Amy Lowell: Correspondence of a Friendship,* ed. Harley Farnsworth MacNair (Chicago: University of Chicago Press, 1945). In her reminiscences Ayscough recalled another friend who "struck up a very intense intimacy with Amy" (15). The letters document Lowell's presentation of her ideas on cadences and Chinese characters to Harriet Monroe, and her plot to "knock a hole in" Pound's Chinese writings (43), which having come through a Japanese source translated by Ernest Fenollosa, were less reliable. Lowell shared the *Poetry* magazine payment for poems with Ayscough. Ayscough's closely coached article, "Written Pictures," appeared in *Poetry* 13 (1918): 268–272.

13. See, for example Philip L. Gerber's "Dear Harriet . . . Dear Amy," *Journal of Modern Literature* 5 (1976): 233, in which he characterizes their relationship as "a decade of professional sparring." According to Gerber, "their advancement to a 'Dear Harriet, Dear Amy' basis only just managed to mask the antagonisms pouring through their hundreds of letters." Lowell can be experienced as both extremely demanding and sorely needing of affection (rather than antagonistic) in a letter that complained at length of Monroe's omission of her name in a report on the Poetry Club, of which Lowell was president. See Damon, *Amy Lowell: A Chronicle,* 359.

14. A 1917 letter opens humorously: "You are a wretched, miserable, low side-stepper. The idea of kicking me out of the November issue and then putting it up to me that it is for Sandburg. Just as if I could ever get in Sandburg's way, the dear boy! Of course, give him November, and of course, give Alice Henderson the rest of November, and I perfectly understand about December, and give me the lead in January. But do you realize that I have not had the lead since August 1916?" Amy Lowell to Harriet Monroe, 10 October 1917, bMS Lowell 19 (909), Houghton Library, Harvard University.

15. Lowell wrote, "Harriet is a poor woman, with hardly enough money to live upon, on the wrong side of middle age. She is lonely and exceedingly unattractive. Her one

consolation in life is to believe herself talented. It is frightfully pathetic, and is a subject in which Balzac or Maupassant would have revelled. Would it hurt you, who are young, vigorous, and have a future before you, to have done what we call 'letting her down easy'; and would it have done any serious harm to those artistic principles in which you believe?" Amy Lowell to Richard Aldington, 20 May 1915, bMS Lowell 19.1 (15–16), Amy Lowell Collection, Houghton Library, Harvard University.

16. It is interesting to compare Lowell's discussions with Monroe with an account of these discussions that Lowell wrote at the same time in a letter to Ayscough. She reports that Monroe "wrote and suggested that we should not write the poems in short lines, and I wrote back and sounded as learned as if I really knew something. I told her what was perfectly true, that to anyone who had studied cadence it must be evident that lines are not determined arbitrarily but by the very lilt of the cadence itself. I then went on to discourse about the roots of the [Chinese] characters being the things which give overtones to the poems in the same way that adjectives do with us." Amy Lowell to Florence Ayscough, 28 June 1918, in *Florence Ayscough and Amy Lowell: Correspondence of a Friendship,* 37.

17. Harriet Monroe, *Poets and Their Art* (New York: Macmillan, 1932), 320.

18. Monroe, *A Poet's Life,* 278.

19. Ibid., 400.

20. Holly Baggett, "Aloof from Natural Laws: Margaret C. Anderson and the *Little Review*, 1914–1929" (Ph.D. diss., University of Delaware, 1992), 135–136.

21. Margaret Anderson, *My Thirty Years' War* (1930; reprint Westport, Conn.: Greenwood Press, 1971), 61.

22. Ibid.

23. Ibid., 126.

24. Baggett, "Aloof," 147–149.

25. H.D., quoted in Richard Aldington and H.D., *Richard Aldington and H.D.: The Early Years in Letters,* ed. Caroline Zilborrg (Bloomington: Indiana University Press, 1991), 139–140, n. 152.

26. Bryher, *Amy Lowell: A Critical Appreciation,* 2d ed. (London: Eyre and Spottiswoode, 1918), 7–8.

27. Lowell tended to collect payment for her poems, on principle, though she was also an active patron of little magazines. She withdrew support from the *Little Review* when she thought it was featuring Pound and Wyndham Lewis excessively.

28. Pound wrote, "The paper made enough in the first six months to pay for the next three. It is assured up to June. That is, I think, fairly good when one considers what it usually takes to get a paper started. I think they have been timid. I think it would have paid better to pay an occasional 'selling' contributor than to trust too much to voluntary work. With any sort of business management the thing ought to pay its expenses, or at least to cost so little that it would be worth the fun. A clever manager could make it a property (perhaps)." Ezra Pound to Amy Lowell, 23 February 1914, in *The Letters of Ezra Pound, 1907–1941,* ed. D. D. Paige (New York: Harcourt, Brace, 1950), 33.

29. Pound told Margaret Anderson that he had offered one more deal as his price for participating in the anthology—"a yearly prize for poetry judged by Yeats, Ford, Pound—she could even be on the committee" the competitive advantage being that "we could have bust the British academic committee (called British Academy) to smithereens, and she could have been something over here (which she wanted to be)

rather than being driven back to Hylo Kennels"; Ezra Pound to Margaret Anderson, 20 August 1917, in *Pound/The Little Review*, 116. He encouraged Anderson to accept a funding/editing package from Lowell in 1922. By then his tone had become crass and his attitude toward Lowell distant. Pound warned Anderson that Lowell couldn't write "for the mondaine [*sic*] London clientele" (22 November, 1917), but was willing to grant her a distinct American section for which he would not be responsible, feeling "right glad to see her milked of her money, mashed into moonshine, at the mercy of monitors"; Ezra Pound to Margaret Anderson, 25 January 1918, in *The Letters of Ezra Pound to Margaret Anderson,* 163. Unsurprisingly, Anderson felt warded off.

30. H.D. to Amy Lowell, 17 December 1914, cited in Susan Stratford Friedman, "H.D.," in Scott, ed., *The Gender of Modernism,* 134.

31. Ibid., 134–135.

32. Caroline Zilborrg, editor of Richard Aldington's correspondence with H.D., is firmly convinced that Aldington was "always closer" to Amy Lowell than was H.D., citing instances in which he "even confided" in her: see Aldington and H.D., *The Early Years,* 25. Jayne Marek, in *Women Editing Modernism: "Little" Magazines and Literary History* (Lexington: University of Kentucky Press, 1995), 107, suggests that H.D. relied on Lowell to convey criticisms of Aldington's poetry indirectly back to him.

33. Their letters reveal that neither Aldington nor H.D. was fully confident in Lowell's role as a promoter. Aldington remarks, patronizingly, "Amy's lecture is dreadful, but I am very touched by it—the poor old thing was really trying to please me and to help me. It isn't her fault that she can't see how very foolish she is." Richard Aldington to H.D., in *The Early Years,* 151. Having expressed to him fear that Lowell will cheapen her reputation as a poet, Aldington reassures H.D. that Lowell can do no harm.

34. Healey and Cushman, eds., Introduction to *Letters of D. H. Lawrence and Amy Lowell,* 7–8.

35. Ibid., 11.

36. Ibid., 15.

37. D. H. Lawrence to Amy Lowell, 18 November 1914, in *Letters of D. H. Lawrence and Amy Lowell,* 27.

38. D. H. Lawrence to Amy Lowell, 23 August 1916, in *Letters of D. H. Lawrence and Amy Lowell,* 45–46.

39. Philip L. Gerber and C. David Heymann take particular delight in creating a militant and explosive Lowell. See Gerber, "Dear Harriet . . . Dear Amy," 239, and Heyman, *American Aristocracy: The Lives and Times of James Russell, Amy, and Robert Lowell* (New York: Dodd, Mead, 1980), 214.

40. D. H. Lawrence to Amy Lowell, 18 November 1914, in *Letters of D. H. Lawrence and Amy Lowell,* 27.

41. Amy Lowell to D. H. Lawrence, 17 February 1919, in *Letters of D. H. Lawrence and Amy Lowell,* 71. Difficulty in expressing emotion was a weakness others—including Monroe—found in her work. We have better access to Lowell's emotional expression, read within lesbian traditions, today.

42. Amy Lowell to D. H. Lawrence, 15 December 1915 in *Letters of D. H. Lawrence and Amy Lowell,* 36.

43. Amy Lowell to D. H. Lawrence, 22 August 1917, in *Letters of D. H. Lawrence and Amy Lowell,* 54.

44. Amy Lowell to D. H. Lawrence, 1 February 1916, in *Letters of D. H. Lawrence and Amy Lowell,* 39.

45. Ibid., 39.

46. Amy Lowell to D. H. Lawrence, 10 June 1919, in *Letters of D. H. Lawrence and Amy Lowell,* 76.

47. Amy Lowell to D. H. Lawrence, 6 April 1923, in *Letters of D. H. Lawrence and Amy Lowell,* 113.

48. Ibid., 113–114.

49. Ibid., 114.

50. D. H. Lawrence to Amy Lowell, 21 April 1923, in *Letters of D. H. Lawrence and Amy Lowell,* 115.

51. Amy Lowell to D. H. Lawrence, 5 August 1916, in *Letters of D. H. Lawrence and Amy Lowell,* 44–45.

52. Ibid., 45.

53. Amy Lowell to D. H. Lawrence, 6 July 1921, in *Letters of D. H. Lawrence and Amy Lowell,* 97.

54. Amy Lowell to D. H. Lawrence, 1 February 1916, in *Letters of D. H. Lawrence and Amy Lowell,* 39.

55. D. H. Lawrence to Amy Lowell, 14 November 1916, in *Letters of D. H. Lawrence and Amy Lowell,* 49.

56. Amy Lowell to D. H. Lawrence, 1 November 1916, in *Letters of D. H. Lawrence and Amy Lowell,* 102.

57. Amy Lowell to D. H. Lawrence, 31 December 1924, in *Letters of D. H. Lawrence and Amy Lowell,* 124.

Amy Lowell, *Some Imagist Poets*, and the Context of the New Poetry

JAYNE E. MAREK

Poet-as-publisher Amy Lowell is probably best known in current literary history for her work in bringing out the three anthologies *Some Imagist Poets* from 1915 to1917. As the chief American representative of imagism, Lowell worked hard to establish a context in which modern poetry could find popular acceptance as well as a place in the literary canon. Through her activities, she made sure that imagism would go into the history books. In the United States, free from the stringencies of wartime England, Lowell was able to travel freely for speaking engagements, arrange the production of various books of poetry, and publish vigorous defenses of imagism and free verse in many periodicals. She permanently changed public attitudes toward contemporary poetry during a crucial time in its development through her deliberately chosen combination of tactics. Her success in establishing this unusual new form of free verse in the United States was exemplary: in the aggregate, the three-volume series served as one of the most important markers of literary modernism in English.

The idea for the series *Some Imagist Poets* came to Lowell as a result of the movement's brief history. Imagism had arisen 1908–1909 among a group of young poets surrounding T. E. Hulme, whose philosophical and aesthetic theories led to the idea of the "image" that was picked up by Ezra Pound upon his arrival in London; Pound printed poems by Hulme in his *Ripostes* (1912) as evidence of a "school of images." Pound began sending poems by himself and by Richard Aldington to *Poetry* magazine in Chicago, and late in 1912 declared that the poetry being written by H.D. was *imagiste*. Under that designation, three of her poems appeared in *Poetry* in January 1913, where Lowell read them, recognized that H.D.'s work represented a new effect, and decided that she too was an imagist in spirit. In March, *Poetry* printed two statements, "Imagisme" under the signature of F. S. Flint (but purportedly written by Pound) and "A Few Don'ts by an Imagiste," by Pound. By mid–1913, Lowell had traveled to England to meet imagist poets, and was invited to appear in the poetry collection edited anonymously by Pound, *Des Imagistes* (1914). She was dissatisfied, however, that Aldington's and Pound's poems occupied several pages while she, among others, had only one page. The makeup of the anthology was also confusing, as it lacked a preface that might have explained the presence of eleven poets, not all of whom could be considered "imagistes" according to the standards of March 1913. *Des Imagistes* received a spate of uncomprehending reviews in the United States, and imagism was left at a standstill.[1]

Lowell, always a promoter of the arts, saw the need to launch imagism in a fresh way. During a visit to England in the summer of 1914, she proposed to subsidize a series of anthologies of imagist poetry that would be selected and edited cooperatively by the contributors, a proposal she may have had in mind before she sailed. H.D. and Aldington endorsed the idea in July. Other imagist alumni were interested, but Pound was upset and tried to subvert Lowell's plan.[2] Notwithstanding, Lowell managed to assemble a manuscript despite the momentous events of August 1914, and began trying to place the book with a publisher when she returned in September.

As the sole contributor with the freedom, the funds, and the drive to see the books through, Lowell worked virtually by herself to bring the anthologies to print. She was the locus of the other imagists' correspondence about which poems to include; she placed the volumes; and she finalized the organization of selected poems, assembled the typescripts, consolidated the prefaces for the 1915 and 1916 volumes, read proofs, and stood firm in favor of preserving the poems' exact spacing and lineation despite printers' urge to standardize.

The fact that Lowell had to work largely alone impelled and encouraged her to find creative means of promotion. The combination of Lowell's public appearances and her behind-the-scenes energy on behalf of numerous publications comprise an extensive, and critically undervalued, contribution to the success of *Some Imagist Poets* and, more broadly, to the instantiation of literary modernism. Only a person deeply committed to cultivating the growth of poetry would have taken on such a range of activities, and only a person with exceptional skills of persuasion and communication could have earned the substantive results that Lowell achieved.

Proposing the Serial Anthologies

As a single gesture in the history of modernist literature, the proposal for three volumes of *Some Imagist Poets* has been treated as Lowell's attempt to take imagism away from Pound, a claim that simplifies the climate at that time. The poet's extensive literary activities, momentum generated by other publications, Pound's movement to vorticism, and Lowell's experience with placing her first two books of poetry all suggest that Lowell's offer arose from her self-confidence and awareness of several ways in which a better market for poetry might be fostered. In a letter to Pound, 7 April 1914, Lowell said she thought it "necessary to create a public which shall no longer be bound by the Victorian tradition. That can be done . . . if one can only get an ear." She also mentioned investigating sales potential for a possible magazine collaboration.[3] When her ideas for cooperative publication turned toward an anthology, Lowell made sure to invite Pound to contribute, despite the other imagists' growing impatience with Pound's autocratic manner. The fact that Lowell's initiative irritated Pound was a by-product, not a fundamental aim, of her proposal.

By July 1914, Lowell had modified her ideas about modern aesthetics in response to Robert Frost's blank verse, the vorticist magazine *Blast,* the Ballet Russe's innovations, and F. S. Flint's deep knowledge of French poetry.[4] London's *Poetry Review* had been featuring articles about new poets and dramatic readings since 1912, and, in Lowell's own backyard, *Boston Evening Transcript* poetry editor William Stanley Braithwaite had in 1913 begun producing his serial *Anthologies of Magazine Verse,* which may have helped inspire Lowell's proposal. Lowell had already realized that serial anthologies could create the effect of a literary review;[5] if she could not take editorial direction of a literary review, which she had been seeking to do, perhaps she could exercise her ideas through a sequence of books.

In its early form, the anthology was intended to include poems by Aldington, H.D., John Gould Fletcher, Flint, Ford Madox Hueffer (later Ford Madox Ford), D. H. Lawrence, and Lowell. Placing the first *Some Imagist Poets* required imagination and persistence to overcome American publishers' resistance to new poetry in any form, particularly an eccentric form such as imagism. Lowell shopped the manuscript to several publishing houses, beginning with Macmillan, which was America's foremost poetry publisher and which had accepted her second book (*Sword Blades and Poppy Seed,* 1914). Lowell assumed the company would see the imagist anthologies as an opportunity to add the energy of a talked-about movement to its list. Unfortunately, Macmillan was wary of Hueffer's contribution, the long poem "On Heaven," due to its title and topic; Lowell noted in a letter to Fletcher of 25 November 1914 that all the publishers objected to that poem.[6] Late in 1914, also, Pound took issue with an advertisement for *Sword Blades and Poppy Seed* that called Lowell the "foremost member of the Imagists."[7] He wrote to Macmillan threatening litigation, and, despite an exchange of letters between Lowell and Pound in which Lowell disarmingly apologized for the "mistake," Macmillan refused the volume.

Lowell then decided to approach Ferris Greenslet at Houghton Mifflin, the firm that had published Lowell's first book (*A Dome of Many-Coloured Glass,* 1912). Greenslet turned out to be just the right connection at the time. He was instrumental in the production of the imagist anthologies and represented a balance between businesslike conservatism and literary innovation. Lowell's discussions with him led not only to acceptance of the imagist anthology but also to Greenslet's initiation of a new poetry series, starting with Fletcher's *Irradia-*

tions, for which Lowell had the manuscript. Lowell reported to Fletcher on 27 November 1914 that the idea for the new series came to Greenslet as a result of Lowell's comments about the state of poetry publishing. This series of books was meant to foster interest in contemporary innovations and to support and build on the imagist anthology. This success showed Lowell that her personal enthusiasm could be highly influential and that, if she explained her ideas well, her audience would find value and excitement in the New Poetry. She used this knowledge to great effect in her later speaking engagements.

Greenslet had one condition for accepting the imagist anthology: deletion of Hueffer's "On Heaven." By this point, Lowell had had time to think over Hueffer's participation in the new anthology. She no doubt recalled their earlier argument over literary principles and probably concluded that Hueffer, like his friend Pound, might prove difficult to work with.[8] In fact, Hueffer was not part of the group of poets making mutual criticisms and decisions about this manuscript (a letter from H.D. on 23 November 1914 suggested collusion between Pound and "Ford Hueffer" against the other poets).[9] Lowell indicated to Aldington that she was unwilling to fight for "On Heaven" because publishers considered it sacrilegious and it threatened the success of the anthology.[10] To Fletcher, Lowell was more blunt: "The publishers shy away from Hueffer's 'Heaven' like a plague and what I am going to succeed in doing I cannot imagine," she complained on 25 November 1914. However, two days later she had apparently made up her mind: "I think the only chance of publishing in a first class house is this one. I think it is better to sacrifice one poem than to have to take the book to a [smaller] firm like Boni's." In reply to Lowell's letters, Aldington indicated that he did not really care about the matter, despite the name recognition that Hueffer's contribution might entail, and suggested on 13 January 1915 that Lowell write to Hueffer directly if she truly wanted him in the book.[11] Flint and Fletcher were also satisfied to leave the decision to Lowell. Fletcher called the piece "a very fine thing" but admitted that Lowell was "probably right" in her doubts. Furthermore, Fletcher agreed that it was "much more important, if the group is going to carry any weight at all, for its anthology to be published by a good firm, than for it to go out looking for trouble."[12] Lowell's excision of "On Heaven" removed Hueffer entirely and focused the anthology more precisely on imagist form. Evidently this suited Lowell, since she used Hueffer as an example of outworn poetics in her lecture to the Round Table Club in April 1915, shortly before *Some Imagist Poets* was to appear.[13] Hueffer, on his part, tried to persuade Aldington to leave the group and then, in a review of the book in July 1915, claimed that he had led the imagists but had been repudiated.

Finalizing the book's title presented another difficulty. Mindful of Pound's threats to Macmillan, Lowell reconsidered her initial impulse to build on the name that had appeared in print on several occasions. Greenslet wanted the "mercantile value" of the imagist name and, according to Lowell in a letter to Fletcher of 25 January 1915, felt that a change would be "the greatest mistake in the world." The ensuing correspondence among the imagists in early 1915 suggests that they wanted their project to show its independence of spirit, both from Pound and from other contemporary movements. As possible alternative titles for the anthology, H.D. suggested *The Six*; Aldington *Some Twentieth-Century Poets*; and Fletcher *The Allies, The Independents, The Vitalists,* and even (inappropriately) *The Young American Club*. Greenslet proposed *The Quintessentialists*. Flint did not want a pretentious name and called Pound a "late comer" to imagism, or so he claimed on 24 January 1915: "Perhaps you had better stick to the old title of Some Imagists or whatever it was. Never mind about Ezra. He no more invented Imagism than he invented the moon."[14] On 7 December, Aldington reported that he had told Pound the anthology would use the title "Some [Imagist] Poems," which Pound had supposedly suggested when he had first heard of Lowell's project (another of Pound's suggestions was *"Vers Libre* or something of that sort"[15]). Aldington remained undecided, however, writing to Lowell on 13 January 1915 that the group was eager for the anthology to appear, and "though we really don't want the Imagiste title we won't stand in the way." Fletcher had had a stronger opinion, writing on 11 January, "I think it is time to drop the title Imagism which Ezra has so covered with mud. . . . At the same time, I still think that to abandon the anthology would be a thousand-fold shame now, because to do so would be equivalent to letting Ezra think that we were dead and done for." Despite these discussions, the title *Some Imagiste Poets* was used in the book contract Lowell received on 4 January 1915, a misspelling Lowell corrected by dropping the *e* in *Imagiste* when she sent typographical corrections later that winter. Clearly her initial concept of the book and its title was maintained during preparations, at least between herself and Greenslet, who together finalized the title. As a result, the 1915 anthology and a special *Egoist* issue in May of that year built on imagism's name recognition, which, though fragile and volatile, was drawing attention.

A third matter of importance involved composing the volume's introductory statement, needed to explain its differences from *Des Imagistes* and to distinguish imagist practice amid the welter of other poetic experiments (and criticisms thereof). The preface to *Some Imagist Poets* represented a compromise. Other imagists contributed ideas—H.D. had suggested to Lowell on 17 December 1914 that the preface include a disclaimer about the title so as to avoid irritating Pound—but the final version seems to have been written by Aldington and modified by Lowell in small but significant ways. A letter to Greenslet accompanied "the altered preface," which Lowell had "changed very slightly" to excise mention of Pound and to present a statement that was "as dignified and as little provocative as possible."[16] Lowell also noted, on 28 January 1915, that "they [my poets] will all object at first and come round in the end." Lowell wanted the preface, first, to provide more than a simple reprise of imagist dicta that had appeared earlier and, second, to modulate strong opinions from the imagists who were still annoyed with Pound—Fletcher, for example, had suggested writing a combative "manifesto" titled "Against Poundism" as a preface (11 January 1915). Lowell's better sense prevailed; after all, she would be the chief liaison with Houghton Mifflin if Pound decided to raise a fuss.

The 1915 preface is clearer and better focused than Flint's "Imagisme" and Pound's "A Few Don'ts." An opening reference to *Des Imagistes* stresses that those former contributors have taken "different paths" and that the "wider scope" of the present volume allows adding two new poets. Lowell edited this paragraph to avoid mentioning Pound directly and to establish a judicious and self-assured tone. The preface mentions a mutual editorial committee and states that the poets had "absolute freedom" to choose their own selections, a misrepresentation of their critical exchanges that suggests democratic agreement. Imagist principles are restated, with the notable additions of "freedom in the choice of subject," the importance of "hard and clear" poetic quality, and an essential "concentration." After brief mention of musical cadence and prosodic precedents, the preface concludes by stating the goal of showing "mutual artistic sympathy" through publishing books "for a short term of years, until we have made a place for ourselves and our principles such as we desire."[17]

Emphasizing the volume's democratic makeup and imagism's integrity as a movement was all the more important to Lowell since she was paying for production of the anthologies. Although the practice was not uncommon—Fletcher, Lowell, and Pound had all subsidized their early books—Lowell wanted to avoid accusations that poetic success had been bought or "compromised."[18] Her financial support shows that she was deeply committed to the business aspects of encouraging the New Poetry. In fact, her proposal to subsidize the imagist anthologies and to track and distribute royalties brought painstaking detail work that she had not fully anticipated (she was still remitting anthology receipts to D. H. Lawrence in 1923 when the last copies of the editions left Houghton Mifflin's offices).

Lowell had come away from her meetings with Greenslet with some notable accomplishments. In addition to a three-year agreement to publish *Some Imagist Poets,* there was the new series of modern poetry books. Greenslet and Lowell's initiatives poised Houghton Mifflin to catch the rising tide of interest in poetry both traditional and new in England and America. Lowell's success in putting *Some Imagist Poets* into print demonstrates her personal style and drive to extend the appeal of imagist poetry, despite the confusion that had arisen over its names and aims. She knew that introducing new work would require more ambitious strategies in order to set imagism properly in the public awareness. Printing the anthologies would be only a first step.

The Context of *Some Imagist Poets*—1915 and After

The imagists' discussions about the aims and contents of their anthologies continued after the successful appearance of *Some Imagist Poets* in April of 1915. Despite early negative comments, the book began to garner positive reviews by summer—including, in a burst of mischievous enthusiasm, Lowell and Fletcher's review under the pseudonym George Lane in the May issue of the *Little Review*.[19] Then came the special imagist number of the *Egoist* on 1 May 1915, compiled by Aldington. Although she had hoped to gain additional advertising spin from the *Egoist*, Lowell was dismayed by the issue. There was, first, Dora Marsden's philosophical article, which everyone agreed was problematic but could not be omitted due to Marsden's friendship with *Egoist* editor Harriet Weaver. Another problem, to Lowell's mind, was the fact that laudatory comments had been removed from Fletcher's article about her; the milder tone of this article and, especially, the judicious criticisms of Harold Monro's assessment of imagism created an altogether too negative impression for Lowell's tastes. She paid for all the issues of the *Egoist* that had been sent to her but did not distribute them. In this respect, Lowell's drive for positive recognition overcame her interest in "democratic" decision making and the more restrained critical proclivities of Aldington, H.D., and Flint, who did not mind Monro's comments as Lowell did and were, according to Flint on 31 May 1915, not "over-anxious to 'boost' anyone."

One must remember that it was Lowell who endured the unexpected outcry about imagism in public earlier in 1915. She was on the firing line when poetry societies took issue with imagism's unconventionality, as, for instance, at the March meeting of the Poetry Society of America when her brief reading caused a storm of response, the first of waves of contentious criticisms that Lowell withstood as she gave a series of lectures about the New Poetry.[20] Lowell's subsequent sensitivity to the stated and implied criticisms about imagism in the special issue of the *Egoist* is understandable. Nevertheless, her suppression of that paper in America led to some impatience among other imagists and may have helped provoke discussion about changing the roster of contributors for the 1916 volume.

Aldington may have wanted to prove that imagism was catching on despite the criticisms (a letter of 8 July 1915 noted increased subscriptions to the *Egoist* after the imagist issue), and on 8 September 1915 he surprised Lowell by suggesting the next anthology include more writers, such as Clara Shanafelt and Marianne Moore. On 24 September 1915 Fletcher also mentioned names, including T. S. Eliot and Wallace Stevens. Lowell mulled over the idea of adding contributors to the 1916 volume of *Some Imagist Poets*, and even suggested Jean Untermeyer as a possible contributor, but finally concluded in a letter to Fletcher of 11 October 1915 that it would be best for the group to remain as it was so the imagists could develop in their own ways. Lowell's comment to Fletcher that she wanted to show variation in her submissions for the next anthology suggests that she thought the six poets would provide enough freshness to the upcoming volumes through their individual approaches.

These exchanges intimate that, behind the facade of mutual agreement fostered by the anthologies' prefaces and Lowell's public lectures, Lowell's attitude toward the anthologies was complicated by hidden pressures. Despite wanting to preserve the volumes' original spirit of sharing critiques and discussing choices, Lowell resented Aldington's dislike of her "polyphonic prose" pieces; Lowell also liked maintaining as much control as possible over her valuable position as coordinator of the anthology in the United States, which brought her visibility and credibility as poet and critic. Despite wanting to encourage individual development and experimentation, Lowell wanted the anthologies to be fairly consistent in order to build marketing momentum and establish a clear sense of imagism in the public mind. From a promotional standpoint, considering that the public was still reacting to the first volume of *Some Imagist Poets*, it would be confusing as well as unnecessary to introduce new poets or a new rubric (Lowell resisted Greenslet's suggestion that the anthology's title be changed in 1916 because Houghton Mifflin's sales representatives wanted to avoid confusion). While it would have benefited Lowell's purposes to show that imagism was gaining adherents, she wanted to avoid the feeling of miscellany that she perceived in Pound's *Des Imagistes,* and she certainly did not want the added bookkeeping that would accompany an expansion of contributors. The other poets probably did not understand how much effort Lowell expended in accounting for six divisions of royalties, a task complicated by the fact that Houghton Mifflin's payment notices did not separate receipts for the anthologies from receipts for Lowell's own books.[21]

Lowell's personal investment in the series *Some Imagist Poets* was greater than that of the other imagists, and her work in production and promotion more demanding. When one considers the pressures Lowell felt from these efforts, her speaking engagements, and the continuing disputes about imagism, one may detect in the preface for the 1916 anthology a particular tone that belies the fiction of democratic editorship and suggests the stories behind the scenes. Although one of Lowell's letters to H.D., on 12 January 1916, indicates that Fletcher had written a draft of the preface, certain aspects of the contents, tone, and aesthetic dicta display Lowell's editorial hand.[22] For one thing, she added a note of thanks to Harriet Monroe after Monroe's irate response to not being thanked in the 1915 volume, but had neglected to tell the others; this series of actions irritated H.D.[23] Lowell also inadvertently omitted Flint's dedication to Aldington of the poem "Easter," for which she apologized on 10 May 1916.[24] Perhaps most notable is the preface's extensive explanation of poetic purpose. Imagism is characterized as "a clear presentation of whatever the author wishes to convey. Now he may wish to convey a mood of indecision, in which case the poem should be indecisive; he may wish to bring before his reader the constantly shifting and changing lights over a landscape, or the varying attitudes of mind of a person under strong emotion, then [sic] his poem must shift and change to present this clearly"; in part, this effect may be achieved through the manipulation of poetic cadence and sensed through reading poetry aloud.[25] These points depart from earlier, more limited definitions of imagism, such as those espoused by Aldington in correspondence with Lowell as a reason for omitting her experiments in polyphonic prose.

The preface, in fact, sounds very like the introductory statements in

Lowell's *Sword Blades and Poppy Seed* and *Men, Women and Ghosts* (1916), which discussed Lowell's flexible new mode of writing (polyphonic prose), musical cadence, and the antecedents of vers libre in a similar tone. The transcribed sections of Lowell's speeches in S. Foster Damon's biography of her show many affinities with the preface to *Some Imagist Poets* 1916, and remind one of Lowell's dedication to reading poetry aloud in her talks. The emphasis in this particular preface fits in more directly with Lowell's aims than with those of the imagists in England. Lowell's efforts were rewarded with the continuing success of both anthologies and a growing reputation as a pundit of contemporary poetry.

Lowell enjoyed her position of authority and took exhaustive pains over the appearance and promotion of the books she helped produce. Her persistent attention to details proved essential to fulfilling the agreement to produce the imagist anthologies. It took considerable determination to place *Some Imagist Poets* with a publisher and then to keep the series going for three years despite the disruptions of war and the fluctuations in group members' concerns. Lowell's ability to respond quickly to critics and audiences in the United States was the key factor in maintaining imagism as a viable commodity amid the confusing variety of the poetry renaissance.[26]

As involved as Lowell was in the controversy and public interest generated by the serial anthologies, she probably worried more than the others about how and whether to continue. Certainly, had Lowell stopped her subsidy or her preparations for publication, the anthologies could not have gone on, for the English writers lacked funds and were less able to concentrate on literary matters, especially at such a distance. One of Lowell's letters to Aldington, on 15 December 1915, hinted at the strain she felt even at that early date: "Sometimes I wish I had never undertaken the Anthology . . . because I feel the weight of responsibility as the go-between—between the poets on one side, and the publishers and the public on the other—so much." In a letter from Lowell to Fletcher on 11 October 1916, she noted that she did not "believe there is much point in having another" anthology because "the moment for its usefulness has gone by," especially since other anthologies had appeared and Lowell found H.D.'s "narrow tenets" restrictive. Lowell thought it time for the poets to branch out. "But still," she wrote, "you know my sense of honour, and I said I would do it for three years, and I will." She also felt certain that Aldington and H.D. wanted the book to appear and might "feel it a good deal if we abandon this year's 'Anthology.'" While Lowell empathized with her friends' financial and emotional stress, she felt, well before 1917, that changes in writing styles and life situations meant the anthologies should end, and suggested as much to H.D. on 13 October 1916. By the following summer, H.D., in a letter to Lowell on 10 August, acknowledged the wisdom of discontinuing the books; the anthologies had achieved their purposes, and it was becoming increasingly difficult to collect and critique the contributions in a timely way. Even so, Lowell noted to Fletcher on 11 October 1916 that the failure of the magazine *Others* suggested the need to do a good job on the 1917 collection of *Some Imagist Poets*. The United States' entry into World War I was the final factor that led to a lackluster sales debut for the third and final volume, which appeared without a preface and thus hinted that the imagists' project had waned. In hindsight, one notices that the 1917 volume nevertheless contains some of the most significant poetry of that period in the careers of Aldington, H.D., Lawrence, and Lowell.

Overall, the anthologies' success validated Lowell's multipartite approach to marketing this peculiar new poetry in the United States and helped to establish Lowell as an influential poet and critic. Her public identity had been transformed in direct response to the critical debates—in her private correspondence and public talks—occasioned by *Some Imagist Poets*. Lowell actively sought to write a new chapter in literary history by bringing out the imagist anthologies in a context of popular discussion, even dissent. She shaped this context through her extensive series of lectures and writings meant to bring new poetic works to the attention of the public and to establish these experiments as legitimate and progressive. Lowell's solution to the poetic competition of the times was admirable: in her lectures, she built up a line of development from traditional poets and ended by using examples of imagism. She learned to anticipate audiences' questions and forestall much hostile reaction by disarming her listeners with frankness and humor. At the same time, Lowell was acutely aware of the kinds of public comment that she herself attracted as the cigar-smoking, independent scion of the redoubtable Lowell line. She managed to use her personal attributes and the mythology of "being a Lowell" as leverage in order to re-create her public image as dramatic poet and knowledgeable critic. She reconfigured herself even as she pushed for acceptance of the new in poetry.

Throughout, Lowell maintained a steady eye on the goal of promotion and education, which she firmly believed helped to disseminate knowledge about poetry in general as well as to assist the sale of books. A long letter from Lowell to Greenslet, written some years after the last anthology appeared, demonstrates the extent to which Lowell believed in the efficacy of a multifaceted approach to promotion: "Nobody in their senses ever supposed that advertising affected directly more than a handful of a book's sale, but it does have an enormous indirect effect. It makes the title of a book known and, in the case of a well established author, it announces to his public that another volume of his is ready," Lowell stated on 28 June 1922. She made it clear that she felt she was "making history" in her poetry and critical work, and urged Greenslet to have Houghton Mifflin add more modern poets to its publishing list, which she saw as lacking. "This failure on your part in the matter of important poets cuts directly into me and has to be obviated by advertising," Lowell added, noting that poetry cannot be marketed as fiction is, that it must be advertised directly to people who already like it—"hence the stress which I feel sure should be laid upon advertisements in papers and magazines" and on bookstore consignments, which could encourage sales by relieving bookstores of having to purchase outright.

"I know quite well that I am no great asset to you except in the matter of a quasi-fame, which we will hope will become a real fame some day," Lowell continued. "It is, however, impossible for me not to be aware that my reputation is already considerable. Part of it is legend, no doubt, but part of it is honest achievement. My books have never sold as well as they should, considering the legend, which shows partly of how little value a legend is. . . . Remember . . . that you have not only an author in me, but an extremely good advertiser. My lectures have been worth more to you than all the advertising in the papers or efforts of salesmen."

This language of the commodity market was the language Lowell needed to use with publishers in order to get the New Poetry into print. More than any other individual, Lowell made sure that imagism, free verse, and other aspects of modern poetry would be accepted as valid across the spectrum of public awareness, from the arbiters of "high culture" such as universities and libraries to the fora of "low culture" such as newspaper articles and advertisements. Lowell's energetic promotion of poetry on both commercial and aesthetic grounds is particularly significant because the flux between high and low culture helped bring about literary modernism. Fine art, of course, had long been considered set apart from considerations of marketing and commercialism, yet the poetic renaissance begun in *Poetry* magazine and thoroughly promoted by Lowell explicitly participated in "a system of exchange" that tied "commercial mass culture" to a modernism that needed to establish itself as "art" and, in so doing, supposedly shunned the popular and the material.[27] Prior efforts to promote imagism had not had the benefit of Lowell's prolonged and well-directed methods.

Lowell's championship of the New Poetry showed an initiative that not only promoted her own career but also demonstrated the persistence of the nineteenth-century social-service impulse to help others and to "educate the public." Lowell knew that her activities compounded the imagist poets' mutual success with enhanced reputations for the future and better financial prospects in the short term. As a patron and a leader among collaborators, Lowell made astute decisions to allay some of the potential fallout that could have come from her subsidy of the books. She thought it important to forestall accusations that she had bought her way into the literati, both because she wanted to gain credibility as a poet and critic and because she wanted imagism to gain a solid foothold in the poetry renaissance. Through her series of public lectures given over a number of years, she added a dramatic overlay to her public persona, significantly raised circulation figures for her books, and promoted other publications as well.

The subtext of discussion about the title for the series *Some Imagist Poets* demonstrates that, whatever the label, the imagist poets had wanted to continue developing their work, and that Lowell's suggestion for collaborative independence had suited both the poets' intentions and the nurturing of poetry in general. Along with the serial anthologies, these poets published articles, translations, reviews, and their own books; several provided volumes for the Poets' Translation Series of the Egoist Press. Lowell herself busily developed her own poetic and critical writing, producing more books of poetry and the influential critical works *Six French Poets* (1915) and *Tendencies in Modern American Poetry* (1917). Imagism may have stalled in 1914 less as a result of disputes with Pound than from the multiple interests that the writers wanted to pursue. It is a testimony to Lowell's sense of commitment that she was able to coordinate these busy writers' efforts enough to produce the 1915–1917 imagist anthologies and set the movement permanently in the public awareness. The fact that Lowell was able to make a lasting difference in the climate of reception for modern poetry is all the more striking since her activities deliberately leaped the fence surrounding academic elitism.

The times seem to have demanded this particular combination of advantages in order to launch a new understanding of poetic possibilities and to establish the careers of important new writers. Lowell was energized by the demands of her commitment to the imagist program, which included the anthologies and other promotional articles and publications. Her sponsorship made more of subsidized publishing than had seemed possible before, as she worked to create relative commercial viability for little-known poetry out of thin air. The anthologies helped to place and sell other volumes of the poets' works and shape the huge market for anthologies later dominated by such best-selling collections as Harriet Monroe and Alice Corbin Henderson's *The New Poetry* and Louis Untermeyer's volumes. Lowell's various publishing-related activities established the place imagism now holds in the modernist literary canon. More important, Lowell was instrumental in fostering the flowering of literary modernism that occurred after the war and the knowledgeable reception of poetic innovation that continues to this day.

Notes

1. See Claire Hoertz Badaracco, *Trading Words: Poetry, Typography, and Illustrated Books in the Modern Literary Economy* (Baltimore: Johns Hopkins University Press, 1995), 52; Stanley K. Coffman Jr., *Imagism: A Chapter for the History of Modern Poetry* (Norman: University of Oklahoma Press, 1951), 21; S. Foster Damon, *Amy Lowell: A Chronicle with Extracts from Her Correspondence* (Boston: Houghton Mifflin, 1935), 224; Edmund S. De Chasca, *John Gould Fletcher and Imagism* (Columbia: University of Missouri Press, 1978), 89; and Glenn Hughes, *Imagism and the Imagists: A Study in Modern Poetry* (Palo Alto, Calif.: Stanford University Press, 1931), 34.
2. Damon, *Amy Lowell: A Chronicle,* 238–239.
3. Amy Lowell to Ezra Pound, 7 April 1914. Amy Lowell Papers, bMS Lowell 19.1 (1027). Houghton Library, Harvard University. All unpublished correspondence cited in this article is housed in this library and used by permission of the Houghton Library, Harvard University. Unpublished letters by Amy Lowell are printed and made available by permission of the Trustees under the Will of Amy Lowell.
4. Damon, *Amy Lowell: A Chronicle,* 211, 232–235, 246–247.

5. De Chasca, *John Gould Fletcher,* 51.

6. Amy Lowell to John Gould Fletcher, 25 November 1914. Amy Lowell Papers, bMS Lowell 19.1 (478)

7. Damon, *Amy Lowell: A Chronicle,* 272–274; Jean Gould, *Amy: The World of Amy Lowell and the Imagist Movement* (New York: Dodd, Mead, 1975), 141.

8. Damon, *Amy Lowell: A Chronicle,* 232.

9. Hilda Aldington [H.D.] to Amy Lowell, 23 November 1914. Amy Lowell Papers, bMS Lowell 19 (8). Unpublished letters to Amy Lowell by H.D. (Hilda Doolittle), from *Unpublished Letters,* copyright © 2003 by The Schaffner Family Foundation. Used by permission of New Directions Publishing Corporation.

10. Amy Lowell to Richard Aldington, 25 November 1914. Amy Lowell Papers, bMS Lowell 19.1 (16).

11. Richard Aldington to Amy Lowell, 13 January 1915. Amy Lowell Papers, bMS 19 (9). Unpublished letters by Richard Aldington © The Estate of Richard Aldington. Used by permission of Rosica Colin Limited, London.

12. John Gould Fletcher to Amy Lowell, 30 November 1914. Amy Lowell Papers, bMS Lowell 19 (431). Unpublished letters by John Gould Fletcher used by permission of Ethel C. Simpson, Head, Archives and Manuscripts, Special Collections, University of Arkansas Libraries, Fayetteville.

13. Damon, *Amy Lowell: A Chronicle,* 299.

14. F. S. Flint to Amy Lowell, 24 January 1915. Amy Lowell Papers, bMS Lowell 19 (432). Unpublished letters by F. S. Flint used by permission of Oliver Flint.

15. Richard Aldington to Ezra Pound, in *The Selected Letters of Ezra Pound 1907–1941,* ed. D. D. Paige (New York: New Directions, 1971), 39.

16. Amy Lowell to Ferris Greenslet, 28 January 1915. Houghton Mifflin Papers, bMSAm 1925 (1142).

17. [Amy Lowell], "Preface," *Some Imagist Poets* (Boston: Houghton Mifflin, 1915), viii.

18. Badaracco, *Trading Words,* 55.

19. Amy Lowell to Margaret Anderson, 23 April 1915. Amy Lowell Papers, bMS Lowell 19.1 (32).

20. Damon, *Amy Lowell: A Chronicle,* 292–294.

21. Amy Lowell to Ferris Greenslet, 1 February 1921. Houghton Mifflin Papers, bMSAm 1925 (1142).

22. Amy Lowell to Hilda Aldington [H.D.], 12 January 1916. Amy Lowell Papers, bMS Lowell 19.1 (15).

23. Cyrena N. Pondrom, ed., "Selected Letters from H.D. to F. S. Flint: A Commentary on the Imagist Period," *Contemporary Literature* 10, no. 4 (1969): 566.

24. Amy Lowell to F. S. Flint, 10 May 1916. Amy Lowell Papers, bMS Lowell 19.1 (479).

25. [Amy Lowell], "Preface," *Some Imagist Poets,* vol. 2 (Boston: Houghton Mifflin, 1916), v–vi, viii–x.

26. Badaracco, *Trading Words,* 35.

27. See Melissa Bradshaw, "Outselling the Modernisms of Men: Amy Lowell and the Art of Self-Commodification," *Victorian Poetry* 38, no. 1 (2000): 166; and Maria DiBattista and Lucy McDiarmid, eds., *High and Low Moderns: Literature and Culture 1889–1939* (New York: Oxford University Press, 1996), 3.

Remembering Amy Lowell

Embodiment, Obesity, and the Construction of a Persona

MELISSA BRADSHAW

You said, I think, "300 pounds and a charmer." . . . Poor Amy, poor Amy. It is all very distressing and my Arm Chair has never been the same since she bounced with glee over some witticism. No upholsterer can do anything with it, the springs still do such funny things.
—Ezra Pound to Alice Corbin Henderson, 5 May 1916

Amy Lowell was fat. She was also rich, headstrong, opinionated, self-promoting, cigar-smoking, and lesbian. But mostly, she was fat. These observations should seem out of place in a serious, scholarly essay. After all, this is not a tabloid article or a gossip column, and what Lowell looked like should be far less important than what she wrote, where it was published, its influence, and the place it occupies in modernist poetry. And yet her body and her personality find their way into much of what has been written about Lowell in a way that those of her thinner contemporaries do not. In fact, the scholar who attempts to research and write about Lowell must sift through an inordinate amount of demeaning and irrelevant commentary about her person in order to find information about her work. The result of this insistent emphasis on the body of a long-dead poet is the construction of an Amy Lowell who present-day readers understand primarily as a joke—an obnoxious woman who bought her way into a literary movement—rather than as an artist and critic who played a key role in developing and promoting a modernist poetics.

What do we really know about Amy Lowell? And how much of what we think we know is colored by homophobia and misogyny? Lowell herself left behind few clues as to how she felt about her size; obviously, we cannot understand

FIGURE 1. Amy Lowell in the garden of her home, Sevenels, 1922.

the way she experienced her subjectivity, nor can we presume that hyper-scrutinized textual representations of her body offer insights into her lived embodiment. What we have access to is a culturally disseminated "body," a multiply rendered Amy Lowell whose dimensions can never be stable, can never, of course, be "objectively" presented. In this essay I pull from the ubiquitous references to Lowell's body and examine the "bodies" they collectively produce, and, unfailingly, pathologize.

The disruptive power of Lowell's body is perhaps most clearly seen in the controversies surrounding her poetic depictions of the nude female body. The most notorious of these was her reading of her poem "Spring Day" (1915) at a crowded meeting of the Poetry Society of America. In the poem's first section she describes someone taking a bath:

> The day is fresh-washed and fair, and there is a smell of tulips and
> narcissus in the air. . . . Little spots of sunshine lie on the surface of the
> water and dance, dance, and their reflections wobble deliciously over
> the ceiling; a stir of my finger sets them whirring, reeling. I move a
> foot, and the planes of light in the water jar. I lie back and laugh, and
> let the green-white water, the sun-flawed beryl water, flow over me.
> The day is almost too bright to bear, the green water covers me from
> the too bright day. I will lie here awhile and play with the water and the
> sun spots.[1]

Margaret Widdemer, present that evening, reported that "as the vivid picture continued there was a suppressed snicker which rose to a roomful of undisguised laughter."[2] As biographer Jean Gould tells the story, when Lowell finished reading there was an immense uproar, with people leaping to their feet and "roaring denunciations." The event made the news the next day and for years after this reference to "Amy's bathtub" surfaced in newspaper features about her. Gould attributes the audience's response, in part, to this being Lowell's first public reading: the society "probably expected her to be a sylphlike, frail, nerve-wracked, intense creature instead of the amazonian chieftain who rose majestically to read. . . . Perhaps because of her very bulk the effect of it was almost as shocking as if she had actually appeared in her bathtub in public."[3] According to Widdemer, "she was going too far in her implicit demand that her personality be forgotten. It was inexcusable; it was rude."[4] In other words, the audience could not listen to a poem about bathing and forget that a fat woman was reading it—they could not hear it as anything but autobiographical confession.

Perhaps in drawing attention to the corporeal reality of bodies—smooth skin in places that never see the light of day, feet that stir the water, body parts that stick up from the water—Lowell affronted squeamish listeners with reminders of their own embodiment. But more specifically, of course, her reading of this poem draws attention to the corporeal reality of her *own* body. And, as the symbolic "smell of . . . narcissus in the air" suggests, her poetic persona, soaking leisurely in the tub, "play[ing] with the water and the sun spots," is not ashamed of her nakedness. She is quite possibly enthralled by it. This is what the audience cannot forget; this is what brings on first snickers, then anger, for fat women do not get to love their bodies, they do not get to be narcissistic.

From the early nineteenth century on, a cluster of cultural anxieties surround the corpulent female body. As Eve Kosofsky Sedgwick and Michael Moon explain, with the rise of industrialism, the bourgeois body, particularly the corpulent female bourgeois body, came to symbolize an increasingly ambivalent response to economic accumulation and excess. "Visible on the one hand . . . as a disruptive *embolism* in the flow of economic circulation, the fat female body functions on the other hand more durably . . . as its very *emblem*."[5] In the years surrounding World War I, the shape of this emblematic body changed, while the economics of exploitive accumulation remained constant, and in what Sedgwick terms an "extravagantly sublimatory semiotic reassignment" the slender female body came to represent not poverty, as it had previously, but upper-class refinement and sophistication: "not her bodily opulence but her bodily meagerness comes to be the guarantee of the woman of substance" as "the fleshy female body is catastrophically declassed."[6] Eventually this body was not only declassed, but villainized. Hillel Schwartz connects the same World War I propaganda campaigns that placed reminders that "Food is sacred. To waste it is sinful," and "Do Not Help the Hun At Meal Time" on railroad cars and inside telephone bills and gum wrappers, to an abrupt cultural targeting of the obese body as the ultimate in wastefulness.[7] Whereas fat had previously connoted sloppiness, feebleness, even gluttony, it now took on a more sinister cast: to be overweight was to be selfish. One social commentator even suggested that "it may become a serious question as to whether a patriot should be permitted in times of stress to carry excess body-weight, for the expense of carrying it around calls for calories that other people need."[8]

In Lowell's lifetime, which straddles exactly twenty-five years in the nineteenth century and twenty-five years in the twentieth, this shifting perception of obesity is further complicated by a move in medical discourse during the nineteenth century from naturalizing inconsistencies to pathologizing them. Rosemarie Garland Thomson attributes this change to the anonymity imposed on bodies by a culture-wide movement away from farms and extended families into modern cities, a movement that "saturated the entire social fabric, producing and reinforcing the concept of an unmarked, normative, leveled body as the dominant subject of democracy. . . . [T]he notion of progress and the ideology of improvement . . . implemented the ascendance of this new image of a malleable, regularized body whose attainment was both an individual and national obligation."[9] According to Schwartz, as this regularized body became leaner and more spare toward the end of the nineteenth century and into the twentieth, aberrant bodies that carried extra weight were medically, and in turn, popularly, classified as either exogenous or endogenous. In cases of exogenous obesity, primarily afflicting males, the weight was said to be the result of overeating, while the endogenous fat body, usually that of a woman, suffered from glandular malfunctions *within* as the body failed to properly assimilate any food and instead turned it into excess fat, even if she restricted her intake. These medical diagnoses, of course, are rooted in long-standing cultural connotations of men as active, women as passive. As fat lost its status as a marker of vigor, robustness, and happy prosperity, fat men lost their benign jolliness and became monsters or gluttons—literally, symbols of conspicuous consumption. Fat women, however, became patients, disfigured from within, hapless victims of inadequate metabolic systems. "Where fat men inspire or terrify," Schwartz notes, "fat women draw the camphor of sympathy and disgust—sympathy because they cannot help themselves; disgust because they are sexually ambiguous, emotionally sloppy."[10] Further, while the fat man's condition is seen as fixable—he can diet, he can take exercise—the fat woman's is seen as irreparable and tragic.

Lowell's body carries an entirely different set of cultural signifiers than her mother's would have a generation earlier. While her mother might be described as plump or bosomy, Lowell's similar body, at just over five feet tall, weighing between 200 and 250 pounds, reads as monstrous, crippled by a glandular disorder. In the discourses surrounding her, her frequently invoked body operates both as a text onto which cultural anxieties are projected and as a site of resistance to these shifts in meaning that, increasingly, signal the impossibility of "correctly" inhabiting a woman's body.

The tendency toward invoking and describing Lowell's body when she is spoken of first becomes apparent in memoirs and letters of her contemporaries.

Many of these references are relatively innocuous, such as this quick dig from Edna St. Vincent Millay, in a 1920 letter to Jessie Rittenhouse: "I went out to Cincinnati in February and gave a lecture and reading from my own published and unpublished poems before the Ohio Valley Poetry Society. (Last year they had Amy [Lowell]; wherefore I deduce the system as being: one year a fat girl, next year a thin girl)."[11] But other references to Lowell's size are less benign, as her corpulence functions as a metaphor for her personality, a way of displacing onto her body anxiety about Lowell's outspokenness, ambition, even her vast wealth and the homoeroticism of her poetry. In the memoirs of *Chicago Tribune* literary editor Fanny Butcher, Lowell appears as "the grand panjandrum of free verse . . . so fat that she literally waddled."[12] Ford Madox Hueffer called her "a monstrously fat, monstrously moneyed, disagreeably intelligent coward," while according to Ezra Pound, William Carlos Williams referred to her in frustration "as 'that tub of guts.'"[13] When her third hernia operation in as many years kept Lowell from writing to D. H. Lawrence for a few months, he explained her silence to his agent by supposing that she was busy "trying to keep afloat on the gas of her own importance: hard work, considering her bulk."[14]

It has often, and incorrectly, been attributed to Pound, but it was the poet Witter Bynner who nicknamed Lowell "the Hippopoetess," sharing the joke with his friends in the American Poetry Society's New York and Chicago chapters. According to Gould, Hippopoetess soon became an "unshakable label" in literary and gossip columns.[15] Pound may not have originated the title, but he found it delightful and passed the epithet on in a letter to Margaret Anderson.[16] Almost ten years after Lowell's death he invoked the nickname again in a letter of encouragement to a young poet named Mary Barnard; suggesting that she model her verse after that of Elinor Wylie, he assured her that she needn't "worry about *lightness*. You ain't an Amy Lowell. Shall the gazelle mimic the hippo."[17] Pound even references Lowell's body in his "Canto LXXVII," which remembers a dinner party in London celebrating the initiation of the Pound//Wyndham Lewis/Henri Gaudier-Brzeska journal *Blast*: "Well, Campari is gone since that day / with Dieudonné and with Voisin / And Gaudier's eye on the telluric mass of Miss Lowell."[18]

Lowell's contemporaries' catty asides, of course, bespeak much more than revulsion at her size: her body is repeatedly characterized as voracious, engulfing, and out of control, but so, too, is her personality, her poetry, her public speaking style, her home, even her dinner parties. Everything she does, says, touches becomes imbued with images of consumption, gluttony, and sloppiness as her bodily excess becomes a metaphor through which her entire person is interpreted. Between her wealth, her family name, her commercial popularity, her gender, her sexuality, her prolific writing output, and her overbearing personality, it isn't hard to imagine why Lowell might have been perceived as overwhelming and threatening. And her body, of course, provides an easy target for a bundle of societally condoned hatreds: sexism, homophobia, misogyny, and a rapidly escalating intolerance of obesity.

When Pound repeatedly ridicules Lowell's poetry as "emotional slither," "mushy technique," and "general floppiness," he never only objects to an excessively verbose writing style. His overstated repugnance at what he describes as the irritating sentimentality, fluidity, and mushiness of her poetry suggest as well a fear of her soft, fleshy, fluid, female body. Her softness is a menace to his virility. That this derision extends into his critique of other American poets—John Gould Fletcher, Edgar Lee Masters, and even H.D.—testifies to the power of Lowell's style (body?) to leak, spill over, contaminate, render effeminate, for when Pound marks these poets "fluid, fruity" and "facile" he does so by listing them alongside Lowell.[19] To Marianne Moore he writes, "Thank God, I think you can be trusted not to pour out flood (in the manner of dear Amy and poor Masters)"; to Margaret Anderson he laments that "(H.D.) has also (under I suppose the flow-contamination of Amy and Fletcher,) let loose dilution and repetitions." And perhaps most graphically, in a letter to Alice Corbin Henderson he mourns a purer imagism "before it went to hell with Amy's gush and Fletcher's squibbs, fluid diarrhoea in the first case and a diarrhoea of bent nails and carpet tacks in the second."[20]

Pound's equation of Lowell's verbosity with fluidity is as well an equation of her fatness with fluidity. Schwartz notes that women's bodies have long been conceived of in terms of fluids, especially those associated with the major bodily changes marked by menarche, childbirth, and menopause. As soon as fat began to be conceived of pejoratively it too was linked with fluids and excretions in women.[21] Verbal incontinence, incontinence of the flesh, incontinence of the bowels: all imply a lack of control, all are shameful and frightening to Pound, the consummate editor. He cannot control Amy Lowell; he cannot pare either her words or her body down to a more manageable size. Unlike H.D. or T. S. Eliot, she rejects his editorial control. And to the impoverished Pound, increasingly preoccupied with usury, Lowell's fiscal liquidity would perhaps have been her greatest threat. Her seemingly endless riches gave her a very real power over him: ultimately, it *was* within her reach to buy herself a literary movement, as many detractors have charged. That what is at issue for Pound is not Lowell's talent, but her unmalleability and her unwillingness to follow his lead, emerges in a 1918 letter he writes to Margaret Anderson, "IF (which is unlikely) she ever wanted to return to the true church, and live like an honest woman, something might be arranged."[22]

A threatening, rapacious Lowell appears even in an ostensibly appreciative essay by John Gould Fletcher. Indulging in metaphors of feasting and unregulated, uncontrollable growth, he imagines her artistic development in bacchanalian terms, writing, "She had talent . . . but it was a talent that had lain fallow, neglected, a plant that had been pruned and lopped to a stunted and desiccated shape. The imagists, with Pound at the head, poured out for her all their headiest goblets of poetry distilled from the Anglo-Saxon, the Greek, the Chinese. . . . So that which was in Amy Lowell grew monstrously, and became an enormous tree, overshadowing the landscape. At thirty-eight she was set headlong on that course of endless experimentation, restless and omnivorous adaptation of other poets, unlimited—and, alas, often inchoate and disordered—creation which only ended on the day of her death."[23] In Fletcher's metaphor modern poetry becomes an ambrosial wine distilled by the more educated Pound, Richard Aldington, and H.D. from classical forms and meters. Once introduced into Lowell's ravenous system, it sets off uncontrollable growth within her: she grows monstrously, she overshadows the landscape, and, always, she threatens to engulf those around her. Imagism makes her strong and heedless, adapting and devouring not only foreign literary traditions but also the work of her contemporaries, as she grows in power without actually gaining in wisdom. Ferris Greenslet engages a similar metaphor when he describes Lowell's introduction to imagism: "she grasped the basic idea with great force, and . . . ate it alive." So too does Van Wyck Brooks in characterizing her as a perpetual child "among her objets d'art . . . a Gargantuan child with the reach of a Khan or a brigand; and she pillaged books—she tore the entrails out of them." [24]

This tendency to read Lowell's life through her body is not solely an indulgence of her contemporaries and detractors. When C. David Heymann claims in his 1981 biography that Lowell's "egotism, though infinitely elastic, was a fragile skin enclosing a giant inferiority complex," and that "at any moment the skin might burst," his hostile metaphor discursively constructs the shape of Lowell's body. Even more disturbing, his word choice seems to be a graphic allusion to the health problems she struggled with for the last decade of her life—burst blood vessels in her eyes, a heart attack, an umbilical hernia for which she was operated on four times in three years (as the stitches repeatedly burst), and finally, the stroke that killed her.[25]

Though they readily indulge in metaphors of corpulence and excess, Lowell's biographers usually stop just short of calling her a glutton. Whether they are writing in the 1920s or, most recently, in the 1990s, they are quick to label her obesity a symptom of a glandular disorder, that, as one puts it, "made the heavy body seem more swollen and the short frame more stunted than it really was," pointing to her "thin" extremities as evidence of her normality.[26] S. Foster Damon rails at an incompetent medical profession that tried to regulate Lowell's weight through diet: "Medical science in those days knew nothing of glandular troubles and the like; the fact that her hands, feet, and head were perfectly normal did not affect the doctors' opinion that the whole trouble lay in her food."[27] Gould similarly laments that although "her hands and feet were small and her ankles slim . . . she was built more like a freighter than a clipper ship."[28] Even contemporary critical writings follow up their inevitable disclosure of Lowell's size with a qualifying phrase emphasizing that she suffered from a glandular disorder.

Attributing weight gain solely to metabolism, however, was a relatively brief medical and cultural phenomenon at the turn of the century, quickly eclipsed by the success of restricted calorie diets in the teens and twenties, which shifted the culprit in female obesity from glandular malfunctions to eating patterns. By

1925 a journalist could claim that "reducing has become a national fanaticism, a frenzy. . . . People now converse in pounds, ounces, and calories."[29] Still, the perception of fat women as invalids lingered, and it is not completely out of keeping with the times in which they wrote for Damon, Clement Wood, and Horace Gregory, writing in the twenties, thirties, and fifties, to characterize Lowell as suffering from glandular troubles. But that such descriptions persist as recently as Cheryl Walker's chapter on Lowell's poetic personas in her 1991 book *Masks Outrageous and Austere*, or even more recently, in Mary E. Galvin's 1999 *Queer Poetics*,[30] during a cultural moment when obesity is rarely attributed to glands and, in fact, an entire multi-billion-dollar industry revolves around female weight loss through exercise and altered eating habits, is perplexing, suggesting a continued pathologization of female fat as an internal weakness, as the ever-present, insidious threat of the fundamentally unstable female body. It suggests, as well, a *need* to characterize Lowell as ill, as a victim of her own body.

The indomitable imagist leader who emerges in biographies and critical memoirs, however, bears little resemblance to the anemic, easily fatigued, listless, endogenously fat woman. Lowell certainly does not diet like a woman afflicted with a glandular imbalance. Such a woman would have followed a strict, regulated meal plan, supplemented by thyroid drugs, designed both to jump-start her slow metabolism and ward off the accumulation of fat.[31] Instead, one attempt at reduction involved Lowell and a few companions journeying down the Nile on a small boat, called a dahabeah, where it was thought that a combination of hot sun, physical exertion, and a diet of asparagus and tomatoes would cause her to lose weight. Although the diet was unsuccessful, she looked back on this trip as a physical and mental challenge that taught her leadership skills. In fact, in a particularly vociferous letter from abroad, she bragged to her father that she had learned to be "glad I am an American, and was brought up like a boy."[32] Another ill-fated reducing plan had Lowell taking gondolier lessons in Venice. These fleeting attempts at weight loss more closely resemble those plans marketed to men, which promised adventure, physical prowess, and self-control, than those designed for women, which stressed cautious regulation of both food and stimuli.

There is a short period of her life, however, from just after her mother's death until after her father's, when Amy Lowell does seem to have been sickly, ailing, and nervous. In her letters from Egypt she sounds every bit the inveterate wealthy American tourist, efficiently ticking off a long list of must-see sights, snapping five albums worth of pictures, and bullying her native guides, in one instance even wresting control of the dahabeah from its reluctant captain and pulling it on foot up a series of cataracts. At the end of her time in Egypt she gradually brought her travels to a close by spending several weeks each in Italy, France, and England. But the pluck and audacity Lowell demonstrated abroad quickly dissipated upon her return to the United States: instead of arriving home strong, refreshed and ready to resume her newly acquired responsibilities as mistress of the family mansion Sevenels, she came back suffering from "nervous

FIGURE 2. Amy Lowell as a debutante, 1891. Biographer Jean Gould describes Lowell at this age as having "the soul of a sylph and the body of a hippopotamus."

prostration," her constitution "undermined" by the rigors of "banting" and the extreme acidity of her tomato and asparagus diet. For the next seven years, biographers tell us, Lowell suffered from nervous prostration. She was sent to live first in California, then in Devonshire, England, locations with moderate climates "where the excitements of sightseeing would be impossible."[33] The regimen of rest, quiet, and a milk- and cream-based diet prescribed by Lowell's doctors suggests that her treatment was a variation of Silas Weir Mitchell's popular rest cure.

This episode, as well as sporadic adolescent journal entries in which she bemoans her size and worries that she will never find love, suggest that—like many young woman at the turn of the century—Lowell felt stifled by the pressure of societal strictures as to what a woman should be and how a woman's life should be lived. But in their eagerness to paint a suffering Lowell, her biographers and memoirists emotionally freeze her here in her early twenties, not allowing for her maturing into a strong-minded, independent woman, not accounting for the shift halfway through her life, when a still fat, still emotionally unattached Lowell launched a highly public, highly prolific career. Even as they describe her rise to prominence as a popular public lecturer, a best-selling author, a notoriously convention-flaunting single woman, inside, they insist, she still cringed at her weight, still mourned the loss of "real" love in her life.

Glenn Richard Ruihley's critical reconsideration of Lowell, for example, creates a tragic heroine from the first paragraph, as he insists she "never recovered from the emotional denials of her youth."[34] Gould, writing in the 1970s and aiming for a popular as well as a literary audience, is particularly relentless in victimizing her, referring to her weight as a handicap, a physical deformity, and imagining her despair in excruciatingly melodramatic detail. Discussing Lowell as a debutante, she writes, "Amy had the soul of a sylph and the body of a hippopotamus. How she envied those skinny girls who were always chosen [to dance] first. She must often have pictured herself swaying like a slender reed, as they did, in the arms of some handsome boy during the waltz. . . . At least her ankles were slim [and] her feet small."[35] She claims that Lowell "filled her days and nights with activities to forget the headaches, the attacks of nerves, the depressions that subconsciously seethed beneath the surface."[36] Richard Benvenuto blames Lowell's neurasthenia directly on her humiliation at being fat, but Ruihley makes just the opposite claim, "posit[ing] an emotional causation for her lifelong glandular imbalance." He roots her emotional distress, and subsequent weight problem, in a visit she took as an eight-year-old to a Medieval torture museum in Nuremberg, after which she was afraid of the dark for many years.[37] It is striking that these biographers consistently gloss over the rigid social strictures governing marriageable young women in late Victorian America as a possible factor in Lowell's unhappiness. In her case, such pressures can only have been exacerbated by being an heiress and the last unmarried daughter of one of Boston's most prominent families. Nor do they take into consideration that, left alone to care for her aging parents after her siblings' departure from the family home, she nursed her mother (who had been an invalid since before Amy's birth) through a long final illness, and, at twenty-one, was expected to keep house for a demanding, conservative father.

Lowell's biographers uniformly cite seven years as the duration of her neurasthenia, dating her illness from 1898, when she suffered a nervous breakdown upon her return from Egypt, until around 1905–1906, when she completed extensive renovations on Sevenels. But her bout with nervous prostration appears to have been much briefer than this, ending, not coincidentally, with her father's death in 1900. Significantly, though Lowell's biographers fail to mention it, her oldest brother, Percival, also suffered from neurasthenia during this period. Reluctant to join his father in managing the family cotton mills, he spent a decade in Japan, serving as a diplomat and writing several books. This was followed by his founding an astronomy observatory in Arizona. Returning to his father's Brookline estate in 1897, he immediately fell ill, remaining in bed until 1901. Even though Percival Lowell was past forty at the time of his illness, T. J. Jackson Lears suggests that the poet's brother's protracted bed rest was a passive rebellion against his father's impossibly strident standards of productivity and "autonomous Western manhood."[38] Similarly, Amy Lowell's nervous breakdown may be read as her only means of protesting a life she did not choose or want: as soon as she had a modicum of control over her life, she exercised it.

Shortly after Augustus Lowell's death, Percival recovered and returned to Arizona; Amy bought the family home from her siblings. She immediately refurbished the mansion to reflect her passions, tearing down two parlors to create an enormous library that would become the center of her kingdom, the site of amateur theatricals, and later, of her after-dinner literary salon. As was expected of her, she assumed the civic duties of an upper-class Boston woman, joining the Brookline Education Society, the Women's Education Association, and the Women's Municipal League, quickly taking leadership positions in each of these organizations. But when she redefined her civic responsibilities to include speaking out at meetings and traveling to rural communities to give lectures about building functional libraries, she broke new ground, becoming the first female Lowell ever to speak in public. And in 1902, inspired by a performance of the actress Eleonora Duse, she wrote her first poem and decided that she would train herself to be a poet.

As even this brief account of Lowell's journey from a troubled early adulthood to a productive, mature adult life demonstrates, narratives of Lowell's life might just as easily stress the vigor and stamina with which she met physical and emotional challenges as the despair and hopelessness she endured along the way. What the ubiquitous biographical portrayals of a suffering Lowell seem to have in common is an *investment* in presenting her as ill, as burdened by a diseased body. It seems that her biographers share a fear that the life of a fat woman, let alone a powerful, ambitious, aggressive one, does not make for compelling reading and that they must justify their projects by rendering her a tragic semi-invalid. By insisting on her helplessness, on her utter lack of control over her body, they can present Lowell as a sympathetic subject, normal in every way except her size.

Placed at the center of biographical narratives of her life, Lowell's body becomes both her curse and her salvation. On the one hand, it purportedly keeps her from marriage, the ostensible goal of all young women, and even from a career in acting, which they explain she had a natural talent for and which would have been her likely career choice had she not been so overweight, even though such a career would have been an outrageous, unheard-of, act of rebellion for a Lowell. Her uncontainable body, then, made it so that she could neither comply with nor rebel against her destiny as an upper-class woman. On the other hand, her biographers claim, it proved a boon by forcing her to be more cerebral, to seek refuge in building a reputation as a poet. Ruihley puts this in particularly melodramatic terms: "the tragic fate which had immobilized Amy Lowell in giving her a clownish human form unveiled the beauty and life of things with the same movement while setting her irrevocably beyond their pale."[39] A slender Amy Lowell, he implies, would not have become a poet.

War correspondent and reporter Elizabeth Sergeant, beginning an essay on Lowell by discussing her "large and unwieldy body," refers to her fatness as "a kind of fleshly discomfort that no woman could bear in youth without suffering self-consciousness, and the sense of a lost paradise."[40] Biographers emphatically attribute the loss of this paradise—presumably, the heteronormative pattern of courtship, marriage, and children—solely to her weight. While Ruihley characterizes her size as "the quietus to her hope to be loved," John Gould Fletcher departs from euphemism entirely when he bluntly states that "if she had not been unfortunately too fat from young womanhood on, she would undoubtedly have attracted *many* men, for her *face* was regally handsome and her manner charming."[41] In these instances, Lowell's weight becomes a handy scapegoat for her spinsterhood, allowing biographers to avoid considering why she may have chosen to remain unmarried, or to even consider this a decision at all.

Anxious to avoid reading her life as a conscious departure from contemporary mainstream values, biographers construct it as a failed attempt to live by heterosexual mores. For example, Lowell's surprised entry in her adolescent journal that she loves a boy named Paul Hamlin ("How long I have loved him I don't know, but I must have loved him for some time") is often cited as evidence of her inherent "straightness" and as part of a slowly dawning, anguished understanding that, because of her looks, she will never be loved by a man: "I shall be an old maid, nobody could love me I know. Why, if I were somebody-els [*sic*], I should hate myself. I am doomed."[42] Choosing to focus on this and a few other entries about young men, however, is a conscious decision on the part of biographers to heterosexualize the teenaged Lowell. For while it is true that she despaired of ever finding love, only a few entries express dismay at not being able to find male love, and, in fact, her occasional attempts to foster friendships with boys usually ended in frustration on Lowell's part because they could not understand her sarcasm and, consequently, she found them dull. Entry after entry, however, chronicles her intense, passionate, unrequited love for several female friends. In these entries, Lowell tries to imagine how a life devoted to loving women might unfold and what it might look like. Unable to quite conceptualize this, she instead wishes to be a man: "I can imagine falling in love with a woman, but not with a man, I should *like* to be a man, and fall in love with a woman."[43] In one particularly anguished entry, routinely ignored by biographers, Lowell clearly articulates her desire for women, her despair at ever being allowed to fulfill her desires, and her suspicion that others might feel similarly:

> Nobody could ever love me I know. I am but a contemptible being, but I want love, love. I know I am making a fool of myself but shurely (sic) there are others who have such thoughts. . . . If I were a man I'd ask [her friend, Patty Storrow] to be my wife. But I am a woman. I can only ask her to love me and and I cannot do that. . . . Men I could not love. My ideal is too high. But I want, need, yearn, for the love of a strong, tender woman.
>
> Oh God! Bless her and help me! Amen![44]

Other entries confirm that Lowell's desires are sexual as well as emotional, as in a humorous entry where she reports having read a book that defines a "pretty girl" as someone who "you don't mind drinking out of her glass when she is done with it." Her "idea of a loveable girl is, one you could love is: you would like to have her kiss you."[45] That Lowell understands her desires are not socially acceptable is reflected in several defensive entries, such as one from her fifteenth year, where she exclaims, "I have a fondness for pretty girls. But it is nowhere a 'crack' as yet and I don't think it ever will be" and in a hesitancy to finish especially transgressive thoughts, such as her wish that a friend would find out about her love for her "and, and you know the rest," or her confusion over a crush on a male actor playing a female lead in one of Harvard University's Hasty Pudding theatricals: "He (she) had such a sweet face. . . . If there were such a thing as, as, oh well you understand."[46]

By insisting on Lowell's painful adolescence as only the beginning of a lifetime of misery and loneliness rather than reading it as part of a difficult, but necessary process of understanding and accepting her lesbianism, biographers deny her any agency, any control over her life. I use this willful misreading of Lowell's journals as only one example of a larger narrative pattern of writing her as a tragic misfit.

In order to temper the threat posed by so unconventional a subject, her biographers seem compelled to gender her absolutely: hers must be a flawed, but unquestionable heterosexually oriented femininity. Lowell's size, however, makes this difficult, as fat female bodies evade easy classification, destabilize categories, invite paradox. They are at once pathetic and threatening, weak and overpowering. Overwhelmingly feminine, with their exaggerated secondary sex characteristics, they are, at the same time, perceived as disconcertingly masculine in their bulk. In a culture that holds up hyperbolically youthful, hipless, slender bodies as the standard for femininity and sexual desirability—as the inverse to the robust, virile male body ideal—the body of a fat woman challenges this corporeal binary, and is therefore excluded from acceptable definitions of "feminine" and even "female." In fact, an unapologetic fat woman who does not actively mold herself to popular conceptions of femininity risks being read not only as masculine, but as a de facto lesbian. Because as sites at which gender binaries are contested, these "unnatural" bodies contain as well the threat of an aberrant sexuality.

Clearly, Lowell's biographers are aware of these damning stereotypes. In explaining her decade-long fight with a repeatedly rupturing umbilical hernia, Horace Gregory explains that hernias are normally male afflictions, and that Lowell bore hers with "masculine fortitude." Thereafter, however, "renewed signs of thoroughly feminine weakness marked her responses to a sometimes hostile world: she wept more easily—and adverse reviews of her books caused tears to flow as well as violent anger."[47] Lowell's childhood friend Elizabeth Ward Perkins describes her as "virile and uncompromising in thought, yet with a woman's concrete dependence on affection."[48] Editor and critic Alfred Kreymborg tells us that when he met her "she seemed an intensely feminine person . . . and I decided . . . that her abnormal ambition and industry had obscured her true character. The role she played was masculine, valiant, combative—and the inner-being, private, lonely, susceptible to human fragility."[49] Even as a child, Gregory explains, Lowell was both "full of tomboy mannerisms and quivering, delicate girlish sensibilities."[50] And Louis Untermeyer notes that although Lowell was "more masculine than most males, she could also be the most charming feminine persuader."[51] In fact, Untermeyer is so concerned with Lowell's femininity that he even claims that her trademark cigars "instead of seeming a rakish masculine affectation . . . merely accentuated her *essential* femininity."[52] Because Lowell is not "feminine" in her response to illness, much less in her speech, her thoughts, her ambition, or most importantly, her insistence on the validity of her opinions, she must therefore be feminized by the disclosure of a "true," weaker, "quivering" side, a part of her that needs affection, is manipulative, and, being lonely, cries easily.

Each new biography laments Lowell's critical neglect, promising to reintroduce her once and for all, and yet, in creating a nonthreatening Amy Lowell—victimized by ill health, trapped in an unwieldy body, forced to channel her loneliness and frustration into her work—they do not offer a compelling reason *to* reread her. To tell the story of Amy Lowell's life is to tell the story of a prolific and influential literary modernist, a powerful woman who achieved her personal and professional goals without capitulating to heteronormative ideals of how a woman should act, what she should want, and what she should look like. To read that life as a failure, or worse yet, to turn that life into a joke, that body into a punchline, is facile and misogynist.

Paradoxically, even as biographers and memoirists focus obsessively on Lowell's obesity, they simultaneously attempt to draw attention away from it by emphasizing what they perceive as the *good* parts. Damon tells us that "It was a commonplace remark in Boston that if Amy Lowell had been beautiful, she would have been a great actress. . . . On the lecture platform, without scenery, costumes, or even gestures, she could make the public forget her size, and follow the drama solely from her voice."[53] This is a common refrain in descriptions of Lowell, as friends and acquaintances, however inadvertently, erase the totality of Lowell's body by focusing on inoffensive extremities, such as fingers, ankles, and feet. For example, in the introduction to Lowell's collected poems, Untermeyer grossly overstates his case as he tries to characterize Lowell as petite and feminine: "She was forty when I first met her. I was prepared for the monstrous distribution of flesh—although a short woman, she weighed well over two hundred pounds—for the cigars with which she affronted genteel society. . . . What I was not prepared for was the extraordinary delicacy as well as the dignity of the woman. . . . The disproportionate bulk was forgotten the moment she spoke, for the voice, half prim, half peremptory, drew attention to the tiny mouth, to the fastidiously fine features, the almost transparent porcelain skin the quizzical but not unkind eyes. I noticed also the incongruously small hands and little

FIGURE 3. Amy Lowell, 1916. This portrait, rare because it shows the poet in a low-cut evening gown rather than in one of her trademark severe, high-collared suits, is by Boston's renowned Bachrach Photography Studio.

ankles."[54] He catalogs Lowell's features again in his autobiography—"the marvelous neatness, the fine hands and delicate ankles, the small mobile mouth"— this time summing her up, and, rather reluctantly, pronouncing her attractive: "One saw a woman who was not only intelligent but—there is no other word for it—pretty."[55] His wife, Jean Starr Untermeyer, expresses the same sentiment: "Admittedly, she was far too stout for a short woman, but there was never a hint of that slovenliness that often goes with excess weight. . . . After one or two meetings, one forgot all about Amy's unusual proportions. [She] impressed by her intelligence and vigor; she charmed by her wit and gaiety."[56] Supposedly complimentary, these descriptions constitute an act of erasure, of *refusing* to acknowledge her as a fat woman. Further, as Gregory implies, such descriptions are contingent on Lowell presenting herself as nonthreatening, for as we have seen, her contemporaries seldom forgot her size when it served their purposes. He observes, *"whenever she took pains to be charming,* it was noticed that her features were small and delicate, that her hands and feet were gracefully turned, that the eyes behind the pince-nez had a certain brilliance that spoke intelligence and rejected platitudes."[57] Lowell's body, then, serves as a pawn: if she behaves well, is not too opinionated or too demanding, her peers will overlook it, but if she oversteps the boundaries of gentility, they will not see anything else.

Missing from the ubiquitous descriptions of Lowell's body is any sense of joy it may have given her, any sense that she believed in its integrity, in the rightness of her embodiment. After her disastrous reducing experience on the Nile, Lowell resolutely avoided losing weight ever again, refusing to modify her eating habits, take diet pills (which at the time commonly contained strychnine and arsenic), or undergo any experimental cures. When one doctor suggested operating on her thyroid to cure her "imbalance" Lowell refused because she feared it would interfere with her thinking process.[58] Such resistance to changing her body—and, of course, valorizing her intellect over her looks—was just as anomalous in turn-of-the-century American culture as it is today. But Lowell ate, and proudly served her guests, rich, several-course meals, even demanding a roast beef sandwich as soon as she woke from the anesthesia after one of her hernia operations. In a letter to Eleanor Robson Belmont she justifies having single-handedly finished a box of chocolates by explaining "only when I recollect how short is life, how fleeting, do I reflect that it makes very little difference whether a skeleton was once fat or thin. This consoles me greatly and I eat on, unmoved and unmoving."[59]

Perhaps this candid comment holds the key to how Lowell's body might be productively read: as the prism through which she experienced and understood the world, as the locus of her subjectivity. This reading, though obvious, even reductive, has profound implications: in this letter we see a woman asserting, without shame or guilt, the pleasure she takes in eating. In describing her experience, in relishing the pleasure she takes in physicality, *she* controls the interpretation of her body. The instance of Lowell's controversial public reading of the poem "Spring Day" with which I began this essay serves as another example of this. The mouth that eats an entire box of chocolates and the body that soaks leisurely in the bathtub, splendid in its nakedness, both avow the materiality of her experience and the erotic pleasures associated with that. Margaret Widdemer's assertion that in her reading Lowell "implicit[ly] demand[ed] that her personality be forgotten," that she tried for an abstraction but failed, is a misreading. I would argue that Lowell willfully draws attention to her corporeality, that she implicitly demands that her personality, or rather, her body, *not* be forgotten. The very act of constructing a cerebral exercise around the wholly temporal experience of bathing constitutes an act of defiance on Lowell's part, an insistence on *not* choosing between visibility as a sensual, material being, and recognition as an active, creative intellect.

Notes

Special thanks to the Houghton Library, Harvard University, for permission to reproduce photos of Amy Lowell.

1. Amy Lowell, "Spring Day," in *The Complete Poetical Works of Amy Lowell* (Boston: Houghton Mifflin, 1955), 145.
2. Margaret Widdemer, "The Legend of Amy Lowell," *Texas Quarterly* 2 (1963): 193–200.
3. Jean Gould, *Amy: The World of Amy Lowell and the Imagist Movement* (New York: Dodd, Mead, 1975), 174.
4. Widdemer, "Legend," 196.
5. Eve Kosofsky Sedwick and Michael Moon, "Divinity: A Dossier, A Performance Piece, A Little Understood Emotion," in *Tendencies* (Durham, N.C.: Duke University Press, 1993), 217, 218; emphasis in the original.
6. Ibid., 233.
7. Hillel Schwartz, *Never Satisfied: A Cultural History of Diets, Fantasies, and Fat* (New York: Free Press, 1986), 140–141.
8. Anonymous, quoted in Schwartz, *Never Satisfied,* 142.
9. Rosemarie Garland Thomson, "Introduction: From Wonder to Error—A Genealogy of Freak Discourse in Modernity," in *Freakery: Cultural Spectacles of the Extraordinary Body,* ed. Rosemarie Garland Thomson (New York: New York University Press, 1996), 12.
10. Schwartz, *Never Satisfied,* 18.
11. Edna St. Vincent Millay to Jessie Rittenhouse, n.d. (1920), quoted in Nancy Milford, *Savage Beauty: The Life of Edna St. Vincent Millay* (New York: Random House, 2001), 181.
12. Fanny Butcher, quoted in Gould, *Amy,* 231.
13. Ford Madox Hueffer, "Henri Gaudier: The Story of a Low Tea-shop," *The English Review,* October 1919, 297; Ezra Pound to Alice Corbin Henderson, 5 May 1916, in *The Letters of Ezra Pound to Alice Corbin Henderson,* ed. Ira B. Nadel (Austin: University of Texas Press, 1993), 137.
14. D. H. Lawrence, quoted in E. Claire Healey and Keith Cushman, introduction to *The Letters of D. H. Lawrence and Amy Lowell 1914–1925,* ed. E. Claire Healey and Keith Cushman (Santa Barbara: Black Sparrow Press, 1985), 13.
15. Gould, *Amy,* 231.
16. Pound wrote, "And poor dear Amy. It is only a month ago that I heard someone manifestly NOT an enemy refer to the "Hippopoetess." Ezra Pound to Margaret Anderson, 20 August 1917, in *Pound/The Little Review: The Letters of Ezra Pound to Margaret Anderson: The Little Review Correspondence,* ed. Thomas L. Scott and Melvin J. Friedman (New York: New Directions, 1988), 116.

17. *Selected Letters of Ezra Pound: 1907–1941,* ed. D. D. Paige (New York: New Directions, 1971), 346.

18. Ezra Pound, *The Cantos of Ezra Pound (1–95)* (New York: New Directions, 1926), 47.

19. Ezra Pound, quoted in Richard Aldington, *Life for Life's Sake: A Book of Reminiscences* (New York: Viking, 1941), 137.

20. Ezra Pound to Marianne Moore, 16 December 1918, in *Selected Letters,* 204; Ezra Pound to Margaret Anderson, 17 July 1917, in *Pound/The Little Review,* 92; Ezra Pound to Alice Corbin Henderson, in *The Letters of Ezra Pound to Alice Corbin Henderson,* 206.

21. Schwartz, *Never Satisfied,* 18.

22. Ezra Pound to Margaret Anderson, 25 January 1918, in *Pound/The Little Review,* 178.

23. John Gould Fletcher, *Selected Essays of John Gould Fletcher,* ed. Lucas Carpenter (Fayetteville: University of Arkansas Press, 1989), 211.

24. Ferris Greenslet, *The Lowells and Their Seven Worlds* (Boston: Houghton Mifflin, 1946), 384; Van Wyck Brooks, *New England: Summer 1865–1915* (New York: E. P. Dutton, 1940), 537.

25. C. David Heymann, *American Aristocracy: The Lives and Times of James Russell, Amy, and Robert Lowell* (New York: Dodd, Mead, 1980), 239.

26. Louis Untermeyer, "Storm Center in Brookline," in *From Another World* (New York: Harcourt, Brace, 1939), 102.

27. S. Foster Damon, *Amy Lowell: A Chronicle with Extracts from Her Correspondence* (Boston: Houghton Mifflin, 1935), 121.

28. Gould, *Amy,* 38.

29. Schwartz, *Never Satisfied,* 183.

30. Cheryl Walker, *Masks Outrageous and Austere* (Bloomington: Indiana University Press, 1991); Mary E. Galvin, *Queer Poetics: Five Modernist Women Writers* (Westport, Conn.: Praeger, 1999).

31. Schwartz, *Never Satisfied,* 136–140.

32. Amy Lowell, quoted in Damon, *Amy Lowell: A Chronicle,* 133.

33. Ibid., 138.

34. Glenn Richard Ruihley, *The Thorn of a Rose: Amy Lowell Reconsidered* (Hamden, Conn.: Archon, 1975), 18.

35. Gould, *Amy,* 45–46.

36. Ibid., 81.

37. Richard Benvenuto, *Amy Lowell* (Boston: Twayne, 1985), 5; Ruihley, *The Thorn,* 43.

38. T. J. Jackson Lears, *No Place of Grace* (New York: Pantheon, 1981), 235.

39. Ruihley, *The Thorn,* 30.

40. Elizabeth Shepley Sergeant, *Fire under the Andes* (Port Washington, N.Y.: Kennikat Press, 1966), 11.

41. Ruihley, *The Thorn,* 20; John Gould Fletcher, *Selected Letters,* ed. Leighton Rudolph (Fayetteville: University of Arkansas Press, 1996), 207.

42. Amy Lowell, quoted in Gould, *Amy,* 43.

43. Amy Lowell, Daily Journals, 1889–1890, Houghton Library, Harvard University bMS Lowell 10 6.25, 6 January 1889. Publication by permission of the Houghton Library, Harvard University. Unpublished journal entries by Amy Lowell are printed and made available by permission of the Trustees under the Will of Amy Lowell.

44. Ibid., 26 January 1890.

45. Ibid., 25 November 1889.
46. Ibid., 13 May 1889, 26 January 1890, 1 April 1889.
47. Horace Gregory, *Amy Lowell: Portrait of the Poet in Her Time* (New York: Thomas Nelson and Sons, 1958), 160.
48. Elizabeth Ward Perkins, "Amy Lowell of New England," *Scribner's Magazine* 82 (1927): 329.
49. Alfred Kreymbourg, *Our Singing Strength* (New York: Coward-McCann, 1925), 354.
50. Horace Gregory and Marya Zaturenska, *A History of American Poetry 1900–1940* (New York: Harcourt, Brace , 1942), 185.
51. Louis Untermeyer, "Storm Center in Brookline," 102.
52. Louis Untermeyer, "A Memoir," in *The Complete Poetical Works of Amy Lowell* (Boston: Houghton Mifflin, 1955), xxii; emphasis added.
53. Damon, *Amy Lowell: A Chronicle,* 393.
54. Untermeyer, "A Memoir," xxii.
55. Untermeyer, "Storm Center in Brookline," 102.
56. Jean Starr Untermeyer, *Private Collection* (New York: Alfred A. Knopf, 1965), 87.
57. Gregory, *Amy Lowell: Portrait,* 76; emphasis added.
58. Ibid, 39.
59. Eleanor Robson Belmont, *The Fabric of Memory* (New York: Farrar, Straus and Cudahy, 1957), 197.

Amy Lowell

BODY AND SOU-ELL

JANE MARCUS

The extra syllable in this essay's title—elongating the *l*'s in Lowell, vulgar as it may sound to you—is a tribute to the project of restoring Amy Lowell's size and stature as a public figure to American, and, more particularly, New England, life in the twentieth century. Can we say "Amy Lowell" in the same breath as we say "Eleanor Roosevelt"? Yes, I say—with practice. I want the *l* at the end to bounce back and rob the Harvard University name Lowell of its primary reference to Robert, the poet in the family who is currently more revered, and to roll backward over the graves of all the dead and famous Lowells before Amy. But I do not neglect her body. It was because of her body that Amy Lowell had soul—soul in the sense of rhythm. We could concede a little soul to cousin James, the poet and professor, Virginia Woolf's godfather, whose gift of a "posset dish" included a poem wishing the child a certain tenderness to "vein through" her father's wit. Tenderness is not a virtue in the tart Virginia Woolf we know. And the wit seems sharper than her father's. Only in Woolf's early letters to Violet Dickinson do we see Amy Lowell's kind of tenderness is erotic in a way.

Roll the extra "l" on the tongue until it washes the writer out of her house, called Sevenels for its seven Lowells, and into the world. The sound of the word *sou-ell*, as I use it here, lengthens itself across the class and race borders I was crossing and recrossing when I first read the poems of Amy Lowell. Now when I read them, they still echo with the rhythm and blues of black clubs in Roxbury where I first read them in the little books I carried on streetcars from high school and Harvard, my version of being "on the road," the poems and the music making a lovely map of mixed messages and (my) roads (certainly) taken that led me out of Boston Irish Catholic ethnicity.

It amuses me to think that others can't hear the soul in my private Boston marriage of Lowell's poems with the blues. What I hear in "Lilacs" (1925) is not only Walt Whitman writing as a woman or the song of my own particular patriotism of place. I hear Gertrude Stein trying to hear an American voice in the black voices of the sung text of her *Four Saints in Three Acts*. "Lilacs" is about being transplanted to American soil and *taking*. It is about hybridity and hope, about finding a voice. "Lilacs" is Lowell's claim that her hybrid poetry of free verse and formal orientalism is the voice of the Great American Poet:

> Lilacs,
> False blue,
> White,
> Purple,
> Colour of lilac,
> Heart-leaves of lilac all over New England,
> Roots of lilac under all the soil of New England,
> Lilac in me because I am New England,
> Because my roots are in it,
> Because my leaves are of it,
> Because my flowers are for it,
> Because it is my country
> And I speak to it of itself
> And sing of it with my own voice
> Since certainly it is mine.[1]

Surely, for Gertrude Stein, the lines "Because it is my country / And I speak to it of itself / And I sing of it with my own voice / Since certainly it is mine" in Lowell's "Lilacs" must have had a certain resonance, not only with her Cambridge years, but with the insistent claim to power of the public poet's place in the person of a woman, announcing an idiosyncrasy and an originality born of the lilac's transplanted hybrid strength as

> a very decent flower,
> A reticent flower, A curiously clear-cut candid flower,
> . . . .
> brighter than apples,
> Sweeter than tulips. (72)

It is easy to think of the hybrid American woman writer's voice and its rhythms as sounding like false blue/false black.

Lowell's lines, "Lilacs in dooryards / Holding quiet conversations with an early moon" (69) refer directly to Whitman's "When lilacs last in the dooryard bloom'd," but she is not writing an elegy to a dead friend nor rewriting that elegy as T. S. Eliot is in *The Waste Land*'s Bloomian revision of Whitman's classic "thought of him I love." Both male fantasies of founding fatherhood, the Whitman/Eliot line poems declare themselves a national poetry. Lowell's lilacs lack the sentimentality and personal mix of "memory and desire" of the static "new" worlds of the male poets caught in a present seen through mourners' eyes. Lowell's lilacs root in the soil of New England, hybrids from the east, naturalizing the towns and beaches and coastlines to mark the woman poet's territory; her lilacs out of a living land assert the primacy of the local, New England's primacy as the heart of the nation and the poet's primacy "because my roots are in it." In "Lilacs," Amy Lowell declares herself the primary poetic voice of her nation and her region. No apologies: "And I speak to it of itself/And sing of it with my own voice/Since certainly it is mine." Certainly it is not Eliot or Whitman's. The voice calls out to the future, not the past.

Less openly feminist or Sapphic in its claim for a voice than other poems of Amy Lowell—though of course the purple palette of the poem invokes both a lesbian and a New England spinster's presence—"Lilacs" claims the right and the duty of the hybrid (female, black, and here specifically Asian) to speak to America of itself, to sing of it with one's own voice. This poem was the anthem that led me out of a cultural backwater. It gave me a homeland where I lived, replacing the lost Ireland of family legend. Playing under the lilacs as a child, I remember making sandwiches of the blossoms between the bitter heart-shaped leaves, taste and smell contradicting each other as the real Amy in Lowell contradicts the fictional Amy of *Little Women*, our model for the female artist. When I said "I am New England" at sixteen, I cast off centuries of superstition and soggy religion and some, but not all, fear and trembling, guilt and shame. New England culture is often called constricting. Compared to the ruder calvinisms of Irish Catholicism, it was liberating. In Lowell's world, the local church becomes a "strange meeting-house" or the mast of a "tea-clipper" "just back from Canton."

The voyage of the clipper ships from China to Boston traces a cultural heritage for America that deliberately bypasses the dead land of Europe and all its cultural baggage. The bloody battlefields of Whitman's Civil War and Eliot's Great War scenes from which the poet rises as a preacher are not present in "Lilacs." Nor is Whitman's exceptionalist America. Lowell claims a contrary past for the American poet, a direct route to New England with the ancient beauties of Asian cultures, creating a hybrid nation not under the sway of European values. This was a bold move. Embracing the oriental was a liberating process for American women before and after the First World War, and Amy Lowell's Asian self-fashioning produced a brilliant body of hybrid work that is worth exploring. Her Chinese world is meant for the American masses, not Ezra Pound's elite readers. In her poem, Lowell creates a past in which the sea and the trade routes bring Asian arts to America, producing a hybrid flowering of the female voice. To deny Europe and to deny the European war was to redefine American culture according to ancient civilizations, specifically not invoking Eliot's Christian European vision.

It is a large claim to read "Lilacs" as the answer to Eliot and Whitman's European and New World self and nation narratives. But I want to claim Lowell's joyful celebration of ancient cultures of many colors in the making of an American civilization.

The Asian origin of the lilac Lowell lauds in the poem gestures, like Madame Butterfly, to a polite primitivism she shared with Pound and other modernist writers and painters in the West. For me, the imagism is connected to Amygism as well. I attribute to her public campaigns in Boston for the *reading* of poetry the pleasures of a set of illustrated children's books called *My Book House* given us by our working-class parents. The last volume was oversized and bound in purple, with Japanese haiku and watercolors of purple iris inside. We had to wash our hands before reading it. It wasn't really reading that the volume elicited, but a kind of rhythmic visual dreaming. Painting watercolors of iris at ten, practicing writing haiku at eleven, I had become a convert to culture, Amy Lowell's version of New England orientalism. The poetry, painting, and porcelain that Lowell introduced to Americans in her cultural project was the imagist secret Eliot and Pound wanted for their elite projects. Their vicious attacks on Lowell were caused by her determination to bring this culture to the masses.

By the time I held Amy Lowell's poems in my hands, I had already adopted her aesthetic. Lowell, like Oscar Wilde before her, campaigned for culture. My family, and others like us in the rising working classes, adored the rebellion against punctuality and cleanliness allowed by Wilde's silks and velvets and Lowell's suits and cigars. On the wall, my mother tacked a silk scarf featuring a horse with a flying mane evoked in a few Japanese brush strokes. She bought a lamp at the thrift shop and repainted the classical Chinese figures in red lacquer. The poetry of Lowell and Wilde, as well as their public lectures and the poetry they promoted, made a "strange meeting-house" for a working-class hunger for the beautiful. The lure of that Chinese/New England church was hard to resist. Both Lowell and Wilde gave us a way into culture that did not celebrate bourgeois values. Both writers were austere and sensual. To see and be like them was to reject the material and the middle-class, ready to "make . . . poetry out of a bit of moonlight / And a hundred or two sharp blossoms" (72). If I see in the patrician Lowell's great movement to bring (non-Christian) culture to the masses a contradictory message like the smell and taste of lilacs, she is a grand figure, an American intellectual opposed to the European Eliot and Pound.

Now that I inhabit a body like Amy Lowell's, it seems both meet and just to remember the flash and force of her presence on my own anorexic self in Boston in the 1950s.

Amy Lowell had an aura. She was stately, plump and full of authority. Oscar Wilde, my other hero, was stately, plump and full of wit. I wanted the wit and I wanted the authority. But then I didn't have the body for it. And, besides, I had to wear a uniform.

It says "Jane Connor" in round Catholic-schoolgirl letters inside the jacket of my first edition of Amy Lowell's *Complete Poetical Works*. That maidenly name, so seldom used since then, arouses no nostalgia. That Jane's neat signature in notebooks full of poems is never used in public. No, I have no pity for that ghost who slipped out of her name and lost it—and its Irishness—forever. In the family, there was a story told as a reply to the question "Isn't it supposed to be O'Connor?" The answer was that the *O* was thrown overboard as a life-preserver on the boat coming over. If losing the *O* helped the immigrants assimilate, losing the weight of all that Irish ballast might allow one to float free—to claim a poet's soul and a New England consciousness as far from the clogs and green satin ribbons, the lift onto Eamon De Valera's lap, the sound of John McCormack's aching tenor on the wind-up Victrola—as one could get.

Both the *O* and the *Connor* secretly migrated to New York while I lived my life elsewhere, to that New York where the only acceptable identity is ethnic. Both names mysteriously appeared in university listings fifty years later. Not too long ago, a colleague objected to my narrating a film on the grounds that I sounded "too ethnic." How devastated I was! I went home and listened to myself on the answering machine. Very ethnic indeed. A voice to match the girth, providing another false front to keep from being devoured. And all these years I thought I presented a solid New England front. I thought I was speaking in the voice of Amy Lowell and Eleanor Roosevelt. But I was really speaking in an unmistakably Irish immigrant English. What happened to that Boston/Harvard accent, faint as it was, that so enraged my mother when I first tried it out? Like Lowell's lilac, it remains somewhere underneath it all, perhaps, a fierce, false blue.

The only Irish hero I kept from those days was Wilde. I had no idea what he did to deserve prison, but he was the first great rebel and writer I wanted to imitate, and to be—body and soul. Bravery and wit were part of his charm, but it was his body I wanted. In the photographs, his face was fleshly and dissolute. The flesh of his hands and his portly figure somehow changed his sex from man to woman, back and forth, but settling somewhere in between.

If the fleshliness of Wilde's appearance shifted his gender into the female register—or, somewhere in between—how could the fleshliness of the elder Lowell shift her gender from female to male? Is this a result of all that dream reading in picture books as a child? What is it about excess flesh that marks the fat body as out of the bounds of gender, not to mention those of good taste, propriety and normality?

I was as much in love with the perverse bodies of Wilde and Lowell as I was with all the actresses who played in Boston in the fifties—a taste I shared with Lowell. But I never imagined until now what it was to live in and with such excess flesh, sending out such mixed signals, not least to myself. If it is true that flesh—not too solid flesh, but shifting flesh—allows for a move into the masculine, at this stage I should find it functioning as a badge of authority. But it announces vulnerability as well. Perhaps this is why my gallery of heroes includes paintings of the performance artist Leigh Bowery by Lucian Freud. I am drawn to the vulnerable beauty and power of so much massed masculine flesh, changed, changed utterly by excess into quite another gender.

Amy Lowell's body had this same queer magic. I don't think my father meant to send me this message. For it was he who gave me Lowell's book, and he meant to give me feminist role models. That this fact has escaped me for

half a century doesn't mean it isn't true. I have already written the narrative of
the bad father. The good father, or, at least the good-enough father, has just now
been dredged up on one of the *O*'s, salvaged from the wreck, young Mr. Connor,
half schoolmaster, preaching his wish for his daughter to find in that book the
words to speak to the Cabots, the Lowells, and a New England Protestant god,
to enter the strange meeting house of American culture. And he was half hod
carrier, working nights unloading ships and then, with union battles as his mes-
sage, taught history, coached basketball and took classes toward a Ph.D.

He chose my heroines, Lowell the poet and public intellectual, the aristo-
cratic voice of Eleanor Roosevelt on the radio he listened to so respectfully, the
voice that biographer Blanche Weisen Cook imitates so superbly. Women who
lacked beauty could have careers, my father hinted. I was very thin and scrag-
gly. The third in my father's trinity of role models for the aspiring poet-politician
who was going to forge the sword to fight for her sex from the smithy of her
Irish soul was Simone de Beauvoir. I confess that it is hard to believe that the
old curmudgeon not only gave me Amy Lowell, but also Beauvoir's *The Second
Sex*. He also wanted to let me know that the body's imperfect teeth, its mus-
taches and moles, did not matter. But the voice mattered. Best to sound like
Eleanor Roosevelt and think like Simone de Beauvoir.

So much for my rebellion. It was doubtless his wish, despite his refusal
to let me go, or give me any support, that I leave home and go to Radcliffe. He
had given me the weapons to make a war, a war of the women, in writing and
politics, that has since occupied my whole life. I don't remember discussing
Beauvoir with him. But surely I did. What I do remember is his reading aloud
from Lowell's "The Boston Athenaeum," and taking me to that hallowed place
for lectures:

> Thou dear and well-loved haunt of happy hours,
> How often in some distant gallery,
> Gained by a little painful spiral stair,
> Far from the halls and corridors where throng
> The crowd of casual readers, have I passed
> Long, peaceful hours seated on the floor
> Of some retired nook, all lined with books,
> Where reverie and quiet reign supreme!
> Above, below, on every side, high-shelved
> From careless grasp of casual interest,
> Stand books we can but dimly see, their charm
> Much greater than their titles are unread.[2]

It was an old-fashioned Boston bookshop, even then, in the fifties. The
cobblestones in the back alley of Boylston Street were not picturesque, but dirty.
The place had a faintly menacing smell of age and horses and straw. All old
bookshops challenge the bronchial tubes and make visits into feats of physical
endurance. But the back streets of Boston had a smell different from the smell

inside the shop of dust and moldy paper. I thought of the smell as some old New England air that was too rarefied for girls like me to breathe. It was air that was trapped in the alleys where Cabots and Lowells had spoken only to each other and God in those sepulchral whispers, muttering and coughs common to genteel Massachusetts speech. Their words were precious to them. This same air was circulating in old Unitarian churches and the buildings of Harvard College. The words in that air were solemn and weighty, severe and high-minded.

There was a rusty wrought-iron railing. A few steps down took you into a basement shop. A little bell on the door announced your entrance, but readers hardly looked up from their volumes at a book-crazy teenager. There one might browse for hours, and people did. There were books on shelves in alphabetical order and other books on tables and chairs, in piles on the floor, people standing and sitting in odd corners and in a treasured seat in the bow window.

In that shop I bought my first rare book. It was a secondhand copy of Lowell's *What's O'Clock* and I still have it. The quarto volume is bound in blue cloth with gray paper pasted on and a white label with black ink on the front. A bold ink splash blackens the cover. Brush strokes cross the back below three inky fingerprints. I was delighted by what seemed an almost Japanese signature of the reader prior to me. The marks, to me a tribute to Lowell's inky fingers, may have seemed a defacement to others. That is why I could afford to fancy myself a rare book collector at seventeen. Inside is penciled the date "November 5, 1955," and a bookplate reading "*Ex Libris*, Jane Connor." I'm mystified by the affectation of the bookplate.

No other books surviving from the time, neither *A Dome of Many Coloured Glass* (1919) in a similar edition, nor the precious 1955 *Complete Poetical Works of Amy Lowell: A Militant Crusader for the Cause of Modern Poetry* contain such a boast of ownership, though they were a major part of Miss Jane's "collection." "Jane Connor" is penciled in the corner of the front page of those volumes in a neat round convent-school hand. The name, unused for fifty years, now fills me with delight and panic, as if I am reading about someone I knew long ago in the newspaper and can choose whether or not to pursue a reunion or even finish reading the article about her, a strategy quite common to my practice of daily denials for making life tolerable. Some things one doesn't want to know. Other volumes from that time do not survive in my working library.

One remains, however. The crucial book is, of course, that other gift from my father, Beauvoir's *The Second Sex*—1953? Yes, 1953, and now in the library of the women's studies program at the City University of New York with all my feminist classics. Perhaps it, too, has a bookplate, marking the beginnings of a library given by a father to a feminist daughter. Did those books create the feminist? I am shocked at the need to acknowledge these gifts and their provenance. It is very hard to credit my father for these intellectual underpinnings, such character-forming ammunition for the battles ahead.

I am imagining Lowell's poems next to *The Second Sex* on my high school and college bookshelves. My narrative of parental opposition to my going to

Harvard on a scholarship must be altered. Leaving home and taking an exhausting room-and-board job got me through but gave me the distance to keep my working-class identity. Because of Amy Lowell and Simone de Beauvoir, I refused to assimilate. The picture must include the father who must have provided the earlier inkling that I could somehow read and think my way into that air at Harvard, while expressing disapproval when the scholarship was offered. Was he secretly proud? Of course he was.

Amy and Simone and Gordon Benjamin Connor. What a sight for a sore heart. Maybe we can all sit together in purgatory and smoke. While my father flirts with Beauvoir, perhaps I can ask Lowell what to do about acknowledging this striking instance of the old man's influence for the good. I'd be wearing the navy blue serge uniform of Mount Saint Joseph Academy, with its itchy white collar. Lowell would say how she got there just in the nick of time to save me from producing endless variations on "I fled him down the nights and down the days," and drowning in a lugubrious puddle of erotic religious fantasy à la Francis Thompson, the poet of choice in Catholic schools of the day. Imagine for yourself what Simone and Amy say to each other.

Amy's airs and Amy's words liberated me into a Boston-Harvard world of clarity and crispness of expression. Reciting Amy Lowell, I found a voice. Imitating her imagism, I filled notebooks with poems of tribute before moving on to Gerard Manley Hopkins. When Lowell was a girl, she too spent her first money on books. She chose a set of leather-bound Walter Scott and her gift money wasn't enough to pay for it. She asked for more and got it. Virginia Woolf spent all her dress money on books. I didn't have a dress allowance and already worked an eight-hour day all through high school. How do you learn to always ask for more? How do you teach others to ask for more? There is a moral here.

Amy Lowell was not the obvious choice, for me, as a model. Edna St. Vincent Millay was a working-class Irish girl from Camden, Maine. But we didn't know that. We knew she was a Vassar College girl, and she seemed far removed in class and spirit. If I had known then, as I do now, about Edna St. Vincent Millay's origins and her public and political poetry, she would have been my heroine. Amy's public image was stronger. Boston (and my father) remembered her public presence as a speaker and an intellectual. As a woman of ideas, Lowell could compete with Beauvoir, and with my father's other heroine, Eleanor Roosevelt. Three serious ladies; I mean, three serious women. While he held out these women as models, he joked mercilessly about their lack of good looks. I was anorexic and excessively thin, with no promise of beauty. But it was clear that my lack in this regard put me in very good company indeed.

Amy Lowell's American imagism for the people, as I call it, was a direct threat to the Eliot/Pound European modernist mode of the cult of genius. Lowell not only read poetry aloud in public, she proselytized for a whole new culture of poetry readers and writers of poetry. This indiscriminate cultural move infuriated the elitists Eliot and Pound, who were tireless publicists themselves, though not for poetry—for themselves as master poets. The problem with Lowell was that she imagined that the people as readers could become the people as writers. I was one of her faithful followers, trying to imitate the New England Modernism of poems like "Middle Age" (153):

Like black ice
Scrolled over with unintelligible patterns
by an ignorant skater
Is the dulled surface of my heart.[3]

It is odd to see Amy Lowell's "The Poem" (1925) in Genevieve Taggard's *May Days* anthology of poems from *The Masses*.[4] But not that odd. She sees the poem as a "twig / with a green bud at the end," that will flower if watered and fed. But if "you take my twig / and throw it in a closet with mousetraps and blunted tools, / It will shrivel and waste." What a democratic view of the art of poetry Lowell holds in her view of the twig, and its gardener generating lilacs up and down the land! But then, she also compared the poet's work to the carpenter's in the wonderful poem "Trades" (1919):

I want to be a carpenter,
To work all day long in clean wood,
Shaving it into little thin slivers
which screw up into curls behind my plane;
Pounding square, black nails into white boards,
with the claws of my hammer glistening like the tongue of a snake.
I want to shingle a house,
sitting on the ridge pole in a bright breeze.
I want to put the shingles on neatly,
Taking great care that each is directly between two others.
I want my hands to have the tang of wood:
Spruce, Cedar, Cypress.
I want to draw a line on a board with a flat pencil,
And then saw along that line,
with the sweet-smelling sawdust piling up in a yellow heap at my feet.
That is the life!
Heigh ho!
It is much easier than to write this poem.[5]

Amy Lowell could afford to play at being a working man. For men like my father, the physical work eventually took its toll, leaving his creativity like the "old twisted nail" of the uncultivated verse in "The Poem." The struggle from longshoreman to educator and public advocate for the blind was too hard on the working-class body and it dulled the working-class soul.

Amy Lowell's body and sou-ell were wracked by excess—not lack—and overwork. I think of our organs—Amy Lowell's stomach, my gall bladder, the breasts and uteri of so many feminists of my generation—as a vast and bloody offering to the gods of the workplace. Sometimes in my dream they are represented in painted tin, like Mexican church offerings that literally pray for miracles. The *milagros* tintinnabulate for a return to the women's bodies in a grand resurrection.

But I have not thought before of the trial of my father's working-class body and soul in the struggle out of his class, the loss of its poetry, the pity of it, what he did for me. Sacred heart of Jesus, pray for him.

If, at the time, I had thought of his sacrifice instead of my rebellion, then what? As it was, the cherished volume of Amy Lowell's poems was a great object of derision at Harvard and marked my origins in and rise from the masses Miss Lowell had educated to poetry. It saved me from assimilation into Harvard's values, the fate of most working-class scholarship students at elite institutions. Because they hated or derided Lowell at Harvard, I began to hate Harvard. No matter how much money and property she gave to Harvard, Lowell was not a "proper" poet. She was a woman, a public intellectual who promoted poetry, a believer that the masses could read and write. I am grateful to her, for her hold on my writer's ear was stronger than Harvard's war against excess.

Amy Lowell was not the working-class girl's saint. She was an excessive figure of power, and I needed a powerful talisman to pass through Harvard without losing my voice and class.

Lowell's narrative in "Lilacs" of a New England and national culture following the voyage of the lilacs from China to the New World in trade, is, of course, a cover for U.S. imperialism, opium wars, or the slave trade, perhaps. Her own family's money came from this trade and from the cotton mills, ubiquitous as lilac bushes all over New England. The exploitation of these workers, particularly the model workers, called the "Lowell Mill Girls," the last of the respectable white native working class, was the underwriter of all the lives of the Lowell poets, college presidents, astronomers and businessmen. The Lowell Mill Girls came from New England farms and they were exemplary workers, producing their own newspapers and journals, examples, perhaps, of Amy Lowell's blossoming twigs. But by the 1850s their numbers were replaced by Irish immigrants, who began to fight for the right to unionize. During World War I, Sevenels, the Lowell estate, was partially destroyed by arsonists who were reportedly protesting the Lowells' refusal to allow their factories to unionize in a resurgence of the struggle by new immigrants in the women's textile trades.

When Amy Lowell dreamed that the textile workers were rising up and marching again on her precious home, Sevenels, she had good reason to be afraid. Her wealth, every flower in her garden, bloomed because of hard labor in her family's cotton mills.

By rights I should have been a firebrand, too, rejecting Lowell and the New England capitalism she represented, ready to torch Sevenels in the name of social justice. But, like those early Lowell Mill Girls, I was seduced by poetry into the promise of culture. It was only at Harvard that my class identity became solidified. I thought how easily I could be dismissed from a world that vilified even its own benefactors. Amy Lowell and her work led me down the garden path to Harvard, but she also taught me the way out.

Now I can call upon the voice of another poet of the period, Lola Ridge (1873–1941). Brought up in Australia and New Zealand, Ridge was an immigrant Irish nationalist, anarchist, and feminist. *The Ghetto and Other Poems* (1918) was an imagist portrait of the struggles of immigrants. Ridge began writing in protest at the fate of the workers in New Zealand. She is famously remembered in Katherine Anne Porter's *The Never Ending Wrong* as a very thin figure stepping out to stop the police horses again and again at a protest meeting over the executions of Nicola Sacco and Bartolomeo Vanzetti. While Amy Lowell and Lola Ridge probably met during the ferment of little magazines when Ridge was briefly an editor of *Broom*, their politics were miles apart. Amy's brother Lawrence, Harvard president, headed a commission that denied Sacco and Vanzetti a retrial, earning Harvard the name Hangman's Hall among radicals.

Ridge was influenced by Lowell's poetry and doubtless helped by her. In her 1927 volume *Red Flag*, Ridge wrote a tribute to Lowell:

> Your words are frost on speargrass,
> Your words are glancing light
> On foils at play,
> Your words are Shapely . . . buoyant as balloons,
> they make brave sallies at the stars.
> When your words fall and grow cold
> little greedy hands
> Will gather them for necklets.[6]

The poem is a strange tribute. Lowell may have dreamed of an army of red flags marching on Sevenels, but the radical poet's tribute to her writing as both belligerent and elegant ("foils at play," "brave sallies," "Shapely") is also an assault. The speaker actually expects Lowell's overreaching words to fall from the sky and "grow cold." When Lola Ridge says that Amy Lowell's words are "shapely" and "buoyant" the reader imagines the praise for fat people on the dance floor—so light on their feet. Lowell's reputation did indeed grow cold. But the last lines are suggestive of an ambiguous relation to the poet's words and the poet's body: "Little greedy hands / Will gather them for necklets." The greedy hands remind us of photographs of Amy Lowell, with her fat little hands expressing the excessive in both body and soul. Since Ridge was excessively thin and a radical, "greedy" here also suggests left-wing rhetoric's prime villain, the "greedy capitalist." The word "necklet" is also ambiguous, with one reading imagining future readers gathering the words like flowers for a necklace, while in another reading the "necklets" can be the restraints worn by slaves and prisoners, as well as the hangman's noose that killed Sacco and Vanzetti, remembering Lowell's brother and Hangman's Hall. Then again, the greedy hands could be ours, gathering the poet's words for garlands to crown her. But necklets are not garlands to crown her. They suggest a splitting between head and body that Ridge imagines is maintained by the recovery of Lowell's verse.

$\mathbf{M}$y own hands are big and greedy. Like Lola Ridge, I am torn by loyalty to the poet as public intellectual, whose words were the impulse to my own sallies into the world of writing—and fear of losing my cherished class identity.

Lola Ridge would have preached her Irish firebrand revolutionary ideas to my father. He would be happier, I think, in Amy Lowell's genteel company. But then I have underestimated him for so long that I stop here, granting him a final scene in this drama. Amy is lecturing. Her glasses slip down her nose. She is explaining her version of the origin of American art in the China Trade voyage, the transplanting of Eastern culture, like lilacs, to be bred in New England. Ireland and all of Europe are left out of the narrative of "our" common past. So Dad is forced to support Lola in Irish royalty as both gather Amy's words for necklets. I am making a necklet of lilacs from Amy Lowell's words. It can protect the voice, and it can choke the voice. But certainly it is mine.

Notes

1. Amy Lowell, "Lilacs," in *What's O'Clock* (Boston: Houghton Mifflin, 1925), 74; hereafter, page numbers will be cited parenthetically in the text.
2. Amy Lowell, "The Boston Athenaeum," in *Complete Poetical Works* (Boston: Houghton Mifflin, 1953), 21.
3. Amy Lowell, "Middle Age," in *Complete Poetical Works*, 226.
4. Amy Lowell, "The Poem," in *May Days: An Anthology of Verse from the Masses-Liberator*, ed. Genevieve Taggard (New York: Boni and Liveright, 1925), 195.
5. Amy Lowell, "Trades," in *Pictures of the Floating World* (Boston: Houghton Mifflin, 1919), 171–172.
6. Lola Ridge, "Amy Lowell," in *Red Flag* (New York: Viking, 1927), 81. See also Nancy Berke, *Women Poets on the Left* (Gainesville: University Press of Florida, 2000).

NOTES ON CONTRIBUTORS

MELISSA BRADSHAW is an assistant professor of interdisciplinary humanities at Barat College of DePaul University. Coeditor of *Selected Poems of Amy Lowell,* she is currently completing a manuscript on Amy Lowell. Her research focuses on personality, publicity, and flamboyant excess in modernist literary culture.

ELIZABETH J. DONALDSON is an assistant professor of English and chair of the Interdisciplinary Studies Program at the New York Institute of Technology in Old Westbury, where she teaches American literature and medical humanities. Her current research focuses on mental illness and disability studies.

LILLIAN FADERMAN is the author/editor of several books on lesbian history and literature, including *Surpassing the Love of Men: Romantic Friendship and Love between Women from the Renaissance to the Present* (1981), *Scotch Verdict* (1983), *Odd Girls and Twilight Lovers: Lesbian Life in Twentieth-Century America* (1991), *Chloe Plus Olivia: Lesbian Literature from the Sixteenth Century to the Present* (1994), and *To Believe in Women: What Lesbians Have Done for America—A History* (1999), as well as a memoir, *Naked in the Promised Land* (2003).

MARGARET HOMANS is a professor of English and of women's and gender studies at Yale University. Her most recent book is *Royal Representations: Queen Victoria and British Culture, 1837–1876* (1998) and she has published widely on romantic and Victorian writers and on feminist theory. This is her second essay on Amy Lowell.

JAIME HOVEY is an assistant professor of English at the University of Illinois–Chicago. She has published essays on Daphne DuMaurier, Gertrude Stein, and Virginia Woolf, and is completing a manuscript on sexuality and modernist portraiture.

PAUL LAUTER is the Allan K. and Gwendolyn Miles Smith Professor of Literature at Trinity College (Connecticut). He has published widely on American literature, popular culture, and social activism and is the general editor of *The Heath Anthology of American Literature* (2002). His books include *Canons and Contexts* (1991), *The Conspiracy of the Young* (1970), and most recently, *From Walden Pond to Jurassic Park: The Cultural Work of American Studies* (2001). He has written several essays on Amy Lowell.

JANE MARCUS, Distinguished Professor of English at the City University of New York Graduate Center and the City College of New York, is the author of *Art and Anger: Reading Like a Woman* (1988), *Virginia Woolf and the Languages of Patriarchy* (1987), and *The Young Rebecca West: Writings of Rebecca West, 1911–17* (1982), and the editor of several volumes of criticism on Virginia Woolf. Her newest books, *Hearts of Darkness: White Women, White Race* (2003) and *Black Books, White Looks* (2004), on Nancy Cunard, are published by Rutgers University Press.

JAYNE E. MAREK is an associate professor of English at Franklin College, She teaches creative writing, modern literature, and film studies, and her research includes topics in women's studies, critical theory, film, and poetry, and her first book, *Women Editing Modernism: "Little" Magazines and Literary History* (1995), examined women's work in small magazine publishing early in the twentieth century. Her current projects include a novel set in the 1930s and a critical study of women editors of the Harlem Renaissance. She is also a dramaturg and playwright who has written a one-act comedy-drama about the friendship between Katherine Mansfield and Virginia Woolf.

ADRIENNE MUNICH is a professor of women's studies and English at the State University of New York-Stony Brook. Author of books and articles about Victorian culture and Queen Victoria and coeditor of critical essay collections, she also coedits the journal *Victorian Literature and Culture*.

JEAN RADFORD, formerly of Goldsmiths College, University of London, is a freelance writer/researcher. She is editor of *The Progress of Romance* and author of books on Norman Mailer and Dorothy Richardson and numerous articles on women and modernism.

BONNIE KIME SCOTT is a professor of women's studies at San Diego State University. Her feminist studies of modernism include *Joyce and Feminism* (1984), *The Gender of Modernism* (1990), *Refiguring Modernism* (2 vols., 1995), and *Selected Letters of Rebecca West* (2000). She is currently editing the volume *The Gender Complex of Modernism* and writing a book on Virginia Woolf's uses of nature.

ANDREW THACKER is a lecturer in English at the University of Ulster at Jordanstown, Northern Ireland. His main research interests are in modernism and Michel Foucault. He is the coeditor of *The Impact of Michel Foucault on the Humanities and Social Sciences* (1997) and author of a number of articles on imagist poetry, E. M. Forster, James Joyce, and modernist little magazines. He has recently finished a book titled *Moving through Modernity: Space and Geography in Modernist Writing* (2002).

MARI YOSHIHARA is an associate professor of American studies at the University of Hawaii at Manoa. Her areas of specialization include U.S. cultural history, literary and cultural studies, women's/gender studies, and U.S.-Asian relations. She is the author of *Embracing the East: White Women and American Orientalism* (2002). She is also an amateur pianist, currently working on a new research project on Asians and Asian Americans in the world of classical music.

GENERAL INDEX

Aldington, Richard, xv, xxii, 142–143, 146, 152n. 33, 155, 156–158, 160–163, 173

Allen, Gay Wilson, 3

Anderson, Margaret, 12, 138–141, 171, 172; *My Thirty Years' War,* 141

Ayscough, Florence, xxii, 139, 150n. 12, 151n. 16; (and Lowell) *Fir–Flower Tablets,* 121–125

Bakhtin, Mikhail, 105–106, 108, 116

Barnes, Djuna, 1; *Nightwood,* 81

Blake, William: *America,* 114; "Songs of Experience," 21

Bogan, Louise, 1

Browning, Elizabeth Barrett, xviii, 9, 11, 17–19, 21, 31–34, 43, 49–50; *Aurora Leigh,* 18; *Casa Guidi Windows,* 18; "Cry of the Children," 18; "The Runaway Slave at Pilgrim's Point," 18; *Sonnets from the Portuguese,* 17

Browning, Robert, xix, 9, 10, 17, 19, 21, 22, 23nn. 1, 5, 32, 115

Bryher (pseud. Annie Winifred Ellerman), xix, xxii, 14, 43–55, 57n. 28, 118, 116, 138, 141; *Amy Lowell: A Critical Appreciation,* 46, 50; *Arrow Music,* 50, 55; *Beowulf,* 55; *The Coin of Carthage,* 55; *Development,* xix, 44, 48; *The Fourteenth of October,* 55; *Gate to the Sea,* 55; *The Heart to Artemis,* 44, 54–55; *The January Tale,*

55; "Miskos," 50; *Raun,* 55; *Two Selves,* 44, 48–49; *West,* 44, 49–50, 51, 54

Coleridge, Samuel Taylor, 9, 23n. 1, 88; "Frost at Midnight," 22; "Kubla Khan," 87–88

Dickinson, Emily, xviii, 9, 11, 20–21, 28, 31–34, 43

Doolittle, Hilda. *See* H.D. (pseud.)

Duse, Eleonora, 13, 45–47, 138, 177

Eliot, T. S., xiv, xxii, 29, 160, 172; and class, 193–194; comparison to Lowell, 1, 2, 3–4, 187–189, 193; "Hysteria," 108; *The Waste Land,* 94, 187

Ellerman, Annie Winifred. *See* Bryher (pseud.)

Ellis, Havelock, 54

Farr, Florence, 106–107; *The Music of Speech,* 106

Fletcher, John Gould, 107–108, 120–121, 142–143, 156–160, 162–163; *Breakers and Granite,* 107; *Irradiations,* 156–157; "London Excursion," 112

Flint, F. S., 156–159, 160; "Easter," 161; "Imagisme," 159

Ford, Madox Ford (Hueffer), xiv, 171; "On Heaven," 156–157

Freud, Sigmund, 45, 49–50, 54–55; fetishism, xx, 84–87; *Leonardo da Vinci and a Memory of His Childhood,* 82; sublimation, xx, 21, 81–89

Frost, Robert, xv, 18, 25n. 33, 47, 145, 156; "Birches," 15

Fuller, Margaret, 28

gender, xv, xxii, 28, 29, 51, 55, 120–134, 136; ambiguous, 78–79, 86, 190; boundaries of, xviii, xxiii, 4–7, 138, 179; performance of, 8n. 16, 125–129; roles, xvi, 81

Hall, Radclyffe: *The Well of Loneliness,* 81

H.D. (pseud. Hilda Doolittle), xix, xxii, 2, 11, 13–14, 29, 30–31, 45, 47–48, 50, 54, 55, 81, 137, 141–143, 146, 151n. 33; and imagism. 154–155, 156, 158, 160, 16, 162, 163; *Sea Garden,* 44; *Tribute to Freud,* 54

Henderson, Alice Corbin, 11; (and Monroe) *The New Poetry: An Anthology,* 11, 165

Hulme, T. E., xiv, 142–143, 154

Hunt, Leigh, 9

Hurston, Zora Neale, 2

imagism, xvii, xxi, 21, 44, 46, 47, 53–54, 84, 104–116, 136; and anthologies, xi, xxii–xxiii, 108–114; and art, 90–101; definition of, 3, 52, 161; Lowell's feud with Pound over, xiii–xiv, xxii, 2, 3–4, 14, 19, 27–28, 139–140, 141–143, 151n. 28, 154–156, 158, 172–174; origins of, xiii–xiv, 20, 136–149, 154–156, 158. *See also Some Imagist Poets* (Works index)

Joyce, James, xxi, 109, 141; *Ulysses,* 115–116

Keats, John, xi, xx–xxi, 3, 9, 38, 53, 62, 68–69, 80, 90–101, 139; *Endymion,* 91–92; "The Eve of St. Agnes," 90–98; *Hugh Selwyn Mauberly,* 106; "La Belle Dame sans Merci," 94–96; "On First Looking into Chapman's Homer," 91

Larsen, Nella, 1

Lawrence, D. H., xvi, xxii, 27, 54, 137, 141, 156, 163, 171; and imagism, 143–149; *New Poems,* 144; *The Rainbow,* 63, 147; *Touch and Go,* 144; *Women in Love,* 144

lesbianism, xviii, 5–6, 8n. 16, 14–16, 25n. 28, 28, 34, 42n. 36, 63–64, 141, 179, 188; and bodies, xxiii, 167–185; and community, 5; and chivalry, 77–89; and desire, xx, 27, 38–40, 50–53; and eroticism, 66–75; and literary tradition, 38. *See also* sexuality

Li T'ai-Po, 122, 127; "Cha'ang Kan," 123–125

Lowell, Amy: "Amygism," xxii, 14, 53; body of, xxiii, 3, 4, 138, 167–183, 186, 190, 194; childhood of, 2, 191; letters of, 136–149; and class, xiv, xix, xxii, 186–197; education of, xiv–xv, 10–11; and New Poetry, xiv, xxii–xxiii, 46–47, 49, 139, 154–163; and orientalism, xxi–xxii, 120–134, 187–189; and Sevenels, 2, 3, 11, 35, 62, 63, 69, 70, 146, 168, 154–175, 176, 186, 195–196; and sisterhood, 9–23, 23n. 4, 33, 138; and translations, xxii, 120–125. *See also* imagism; lesbianism; sexuality; Works index

Lowell, Bessie, 138

Lowell, James Russell: *A Fable for Critics,* 28

Lowell, Lawrence, 196–197

Lowell, Lotta, 12, 24n. 13

Lowell, Percival, xxi, 176–177; *Soul of the Far East and Occult Japan,* 121

Martin, Violet. *See* Ross, Martin (pseud.)

Meynell, Alice, 11, 24n. 9

Millay, Edna St. Vincent, 1, 11, 14, 171, 193; "Evening in Lesbos," 14; "Sappho Crosses the Dark River into Hades," 14

Milton, John, 93–94

modernism, xviii, xx, xxii, 18, 43, 44–46,

77, 90, 109, 113, 120–121, 136–149;
aesthetics of, xviii, xxi, 104–108;
early, xiv, xv; high, xv, xxii, 3; new
studies of, 136–149
Monroe, Harriet, xiii, xvi, xvii, xxii, xxiv,
11, 46–47, 139–140, 141–142, 144,
150n. 15, 161; (and Henderson) *The
New Poetry: An Anthology,* 11, 165;
Poets and Their Art, 140; *A Poet's
Life,* 140
Moore, Marianne, 2, 160
Moraes, Francisco: *Palmerin of England,*
94–98

Nung Chu, 122

Poe, Edgar Allan, 9, 23n. 1
poetry, forms of: dramatic monologue,
xv, 22, 115; narrative, xv, xvi; lyric,
xvi, xv, xx, 14–16, 27–40, 40n. 2, 52–
53, 64–66; polyphonic prose, xxi, 47,
84, 104–116, 129–133, 161, 162; vers
libre, xii, xiii, 107, 108, 116, 140
post-colonial studies, xviii; and
imperialist attitudes, xxi–xxii
Pound, Ezra, xxii, xxiii, 1, 3, 9, 29, 35,
53, 110–111, 115, 146; and class,
188–189, 193–194; and polyphonic
prose, 104, 106–108; relationship
with Lowell, xiii–xiv, xxii, 2, 3–4, 14,
19, 27–28, 139–140, 141–143, 151n.
28, 154–156, 158, 171–172, 173; and
translations, 121, 123–125, 136; and
vorticism, 14, 155, 156
WORKS: *Cantos,* 108; "Canto II," 19;
"Canto LXXVII," 171; *Catholic
Anthology,* 108; *Des Imagistes,*
xiii, xxii, 142, 155, 158, 159, 161;
"A Few Don'ts by an Imagiste,"
107, 155, 159; "In the Station of a
Metro," xii; *Ripostes,* 154; "The
River-Merchant's Wife," 123

Rich, Adrienne: "Twenty-one Poems," xx
Ridge, Lola, 196–197
Robinson, Edwin Arlington, 18
Ross, Martin (pseud. Violet Martin), 35–
40; (and Somerville) *Irish Memories,*

36; *The Real Charlotte,* 36; *Some
Experiences of an Irish R.M.,* 35
Rossetti, Christina, 11, 13
Russell, Ada Dwyer, xx, 3, 51, 52, 59–
75, 138–139

Sappho, xviii, xx, 5, 9, 11, 12–16, 24n.
19, 31–33, 43, 53, influence of, 77–
81, 87, 106, 188
sexuality, xviii, xx, xxiii, 5, 11–12, 18,
27–40, 54, 60, 63–66, 89n. 9, 138,
178–179; and desire, xx, 16, 28–30,
77–89; and eroticism, 7, 14, 33–34,
47, 87; and homophobia, xx, xxiii.
See also lesbianism
Shelly, Percy Bysshe, 52–53, 90, 92–93,
99; *Adonais,* 92
Somerville, E. Œ. (pseud. Edith
Somerville), 35–40; (and Ross) *Irish
Memories,* 36; *The Real Charlotte,* 36;
Some Experiences of an Irish R.M.,
35
Spenser, Edmund, 95–96; *The Faerie
Queen,* 95
Stein, Gertrude, 2, 62, 63, 67, 187; *Four
Saints in Three Acts,* 187; *Tender
Buttons,* 108, 109
Stevens, Wallace, 18, 160
Strachey, Lytton, 44

Teasdale, Sara, 11, 13, 14, 18, 30–31, 32;
"Sappho," 13

Untermeyer, Louis, xxii, 140, 165, 180–
181
Untermeyer, Jean, 29, 160, 181–182

Victoria, queen of England, 17–19

Wheatley, Phillis, 11, 23nn.7, 8
Whitman, Walt, 186–188
Wilde, Oscar, 127, 189–190
Williams, William Carlos, 171
Wood, Clement, xvi, xx, 2, 65, 174
Woolf, Virginia, 22, 43, 186; "Modern
Fiction," 112; *Orlando,* 81

Yeats, William Butler, 106–107; "Sailing
to Byzantium," 115

INDEX OF LOWELL'S WORKS

"Afternoon Rain in State Street," 113, 114

"Apology," 60, 62, 80

"Appuldurcombe Park," 65, 66

"April," 69

"Aquarium, An," 113

"Artist," 72

"Astigmatism," 142

"As Toward One's Self," 52

"Aubade," 16, 68

Ballads for Sale, 40, 62, 66, 67, 72

"Basket, The," xvi, 84, 85, 107

"Bather, A," 39–40

"Blockhead," 61

"Blue Scarf, The," 86–87

"Bombardment," 144

"Boston Athenaeum, The," 191

"Bronze Horses, The," 105, 114–115

"Bullion," 72

"Bungler, A," 61

"By Messenger," 127

Can Grande's Castle, 47, 105, 107, 114–116, 125, 129

"Captured Goddess, The," 78

"Clear, with Light, Variable Winds," 88

"Cremona Violin, The," 66

Critical Fable, A, xvii, xix, 3, 13, 14, 28–32

"Daimio's Oiran," 127

"Decade, A," 63, 69, 74

Dome of Many Colored Glass, A, 90, 99, 156

"Eleonora Duse," 45–46

"Fairytale, A," 59

Fir–Flower Tablets (and Ayscough), 121–125, 133

"Free Fantasia on Japanese Themes," 127–129

"Frimaire," 75

"Garden Party by Moonlight, The," 69

"Great Adventure of Max Breuck," 83

"Grievance," 67

"Grotesque," 74

"Guns as Keys: And the Great Gate Swings," xxii, 47, 114, 116, 129–133

"Hedge Island," 114

"Hippocrene," 67

"In a Castle," 84, 85–86, 107

"In a Garden," xiii, 68, 88, 142

"In Excelsis," 71

"Interlude," 41n. 23, 69

John Keats, 90, 97

"July Midnight," 72

"La Vie de Boheme," xvii

Legends, xxi

"Letter, The," 16, 52, 70

"Lilacs," 186–189, 195
"London Thoroughfare. 2 A.M., A," 108
"Lover, A," 127

"Madonna of the Evening Flower," 69, 70, 72
"Malmaison," 47, 141
"Manifesto," 3
Men, Women, and Ghosts, xv, 47, 108, 111, 112
"Midday and Afternoon," 109–110
"Middle Age," 194

"Nerves," 53, 74
"Nights and Sleep," 111
"Nuance," xii
"Number 3 on the Docket," xvi

"On a Certain Critic," 68, 99–100
"On Christmas Eve," 62–63, 67
"On–Looker, The," 6–7, 50–51
"On Reading a Line Underscored by Keats," 98–100
"Opera House, An," 113
"Overgrown Pasture, The," xvi, 25n. 33

"Paradox," 67
"Patience," 59–60
"Patterns," xv, 6, 66, 70–71
"Pickthorne Manor," xvi, 66
Pictures of the Floating World, xx, 5, 6, 16, 50, 66, 68, 69, 125–129, 133
"Planes of Personality: Two Speak Together," 50
"Poem, The," 194
"Poetry, Imagination, Education (essay)," 48
"Preparation," 69, 74
"Prime," 71

"Rainy Night, A," 68, 72
"Red Slippers," 113–114
"Road to Yoshiwara," 127

"Sea–Blue and Blood–Red," 114–116
Selected Poems of Amy Lowell, The (ed. Munich and Bradshaw), xv

"Shadow, The," 83–84
"Shower, A," 72
"Sisters, The," xviii, xix, 9–22, 31–34, 48–50, 54
Six French Poets, 44, 47, 146, 165
Some Imagist Poets, xiii, xvi, 143, 148, 154–163
"Song for a Viola D'Amore," xx
"Sprig of Rosemary, A," 52, 70, 74
"Spring Day," 105, 108–113, 168–169, 182
"Strain," 53, 74
"Stupidity," 61
"Suggested by the Cover of a Volume of Keats's Poems," 99
"Summer Rain," 72
Sword Blades and Poppy Seed, xx, 59–60, 66, 67, 78–81, 82–89, 108, 140, 144, 156, 162

"Taxi, The," 61, 81
Tendencies in Modern American Poetry, 31, 44, 47, 52, 165
"Thompson's Lunch Room—Grand Central Station," 113
"Thorn Piece," 62, 67, 72
"To a Gentleman Who Wanted to See the First Drafts of My Poems in the Interests of Psychological Research into the Workings of the Creative Mind," 65
"To John Keats," 98–99, 100
"To Two Unknown Ladies," xix, 27, 34–40
"Towns in Colour," 105, 111–114, 116
"Trades," 194
"Two Speak Together," xx, 5, 16

"Up in Michigan," 67

"Venus Transiens," 5, 16, 70
"Vernal Equinox," 51–52, 70, 141
"Vespers," xii, 71–72
"Vicarious," 126–127
"View of Teignmouth in Devonshire," 99–100

"Weather–Cock Points South, The," 52, 72–73

What's O'Clock, xii, 10, 12, 14, 31, 66, 72

"Wheat–in–the–Ear," 72

"Wheel of the Sun, The," 53, 70

"Which, Being Interpreted, Is as May Be, Or Otherwise," 66